IMAGES
of America

GREENFIELD

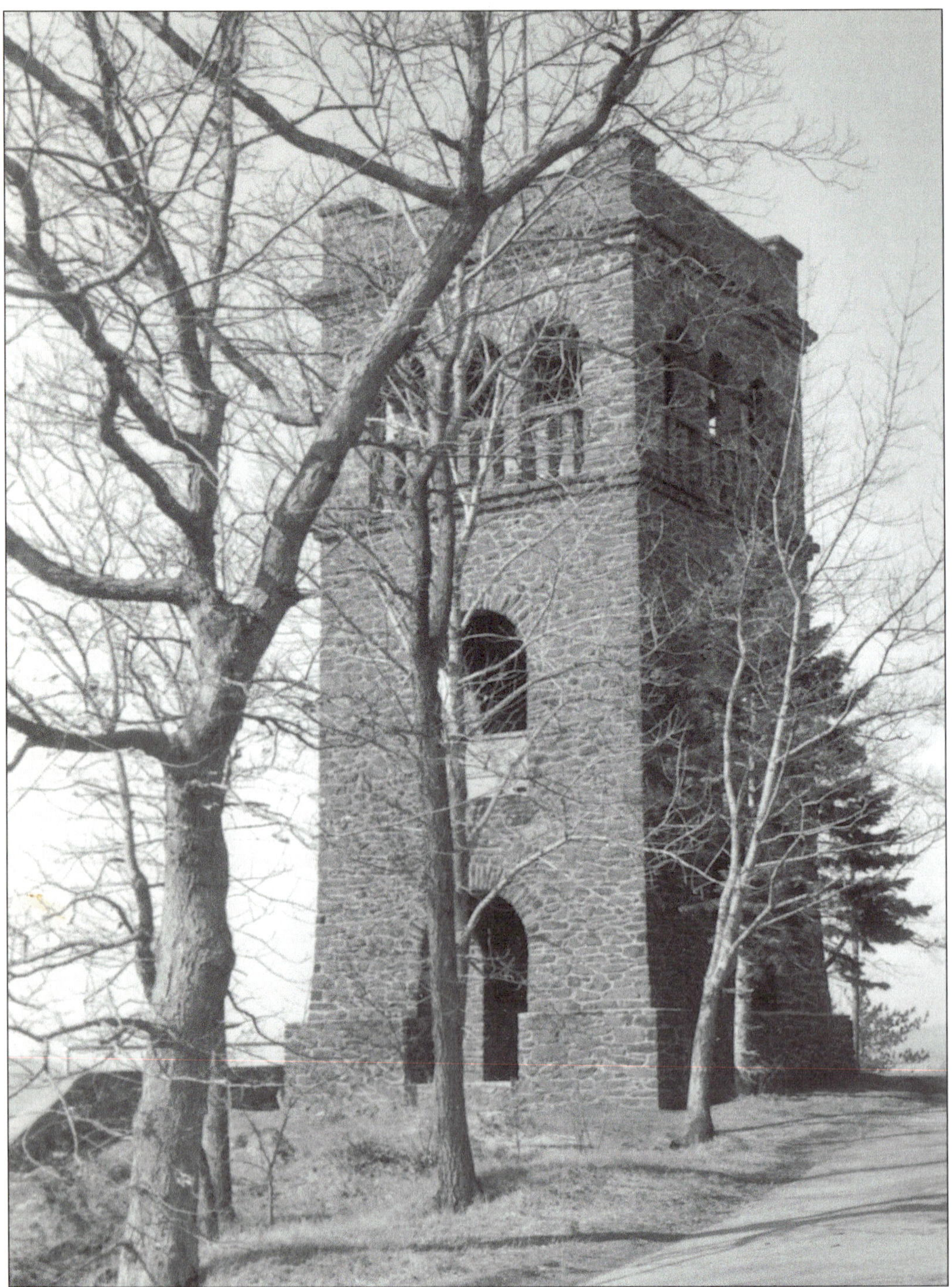

Poet's Seat Tower is a well-known symbol of Greenfield, located on Rocky Mountain—a stone's throw from a natural "armchair" in the rock face called the Poet's Seat. The present tower was designed by Jerome Ripley Allen and constructed by Peter Barber in 1912. It replaced an earlier wooden tower placed there *c.* 1870 by the town's Rural Club. It was originally built without railings, and the current ones were installed in 1976.

IMAGES
of America

GREENFIELD

Peter S. Miller and William C. Garrison

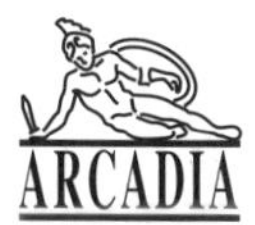

ISBN 0-7385-0335-5

Published by Arcadia Publishing,
an imprint of Tempus Publishing, Inc.
2 Cumberland Street
Charleston, SC 29401

Printed in Great Britain.

Library of Congress Catalog Card Number: Applied for.

For all general information contact Arcadia Publishing at:
Telephone 843-853-2070
Fax 843-853-0044
E-Mail arcadia@charleston.net

For customer service and orders:
Toll-Free 1-888-313-BOOK

Visit us on the internet at http://www.arcadiaimages.com

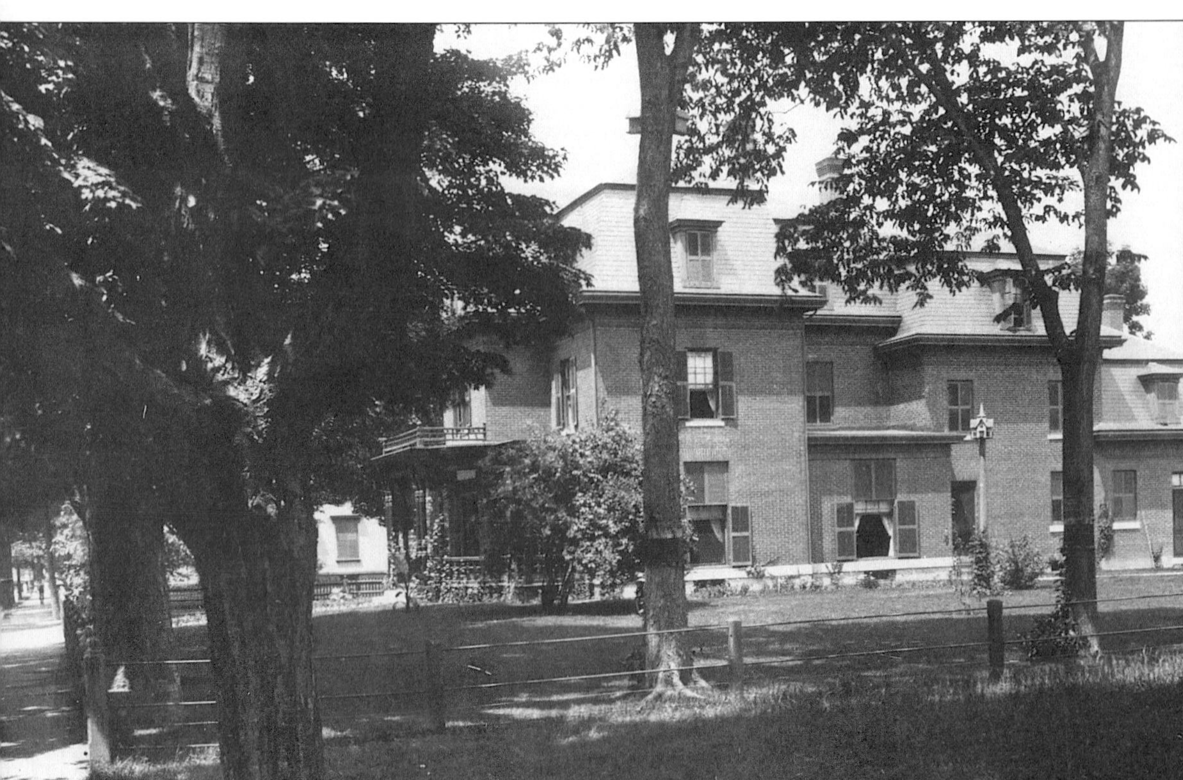

The Wait-Devlin House, currently the home of the Historical Society of Greenfield, was built in 1851 by Charles P. Child on the corner of Church and Union Streets. The mansard roof was added later. In 1914, the society had a choice between two houses to serve as its museum: the Coleman-Hollister House (the present McCarthy Funeral Home) or this one.

CONTENTS

Acknowledgments		6
Introduction		7
1.	Downtown	9
2.	Community Life	37
3.	Homes and Citizens	69
4.	Trains to Automobiles	83
5.	Going to Work	105
6.	And a Few More	121

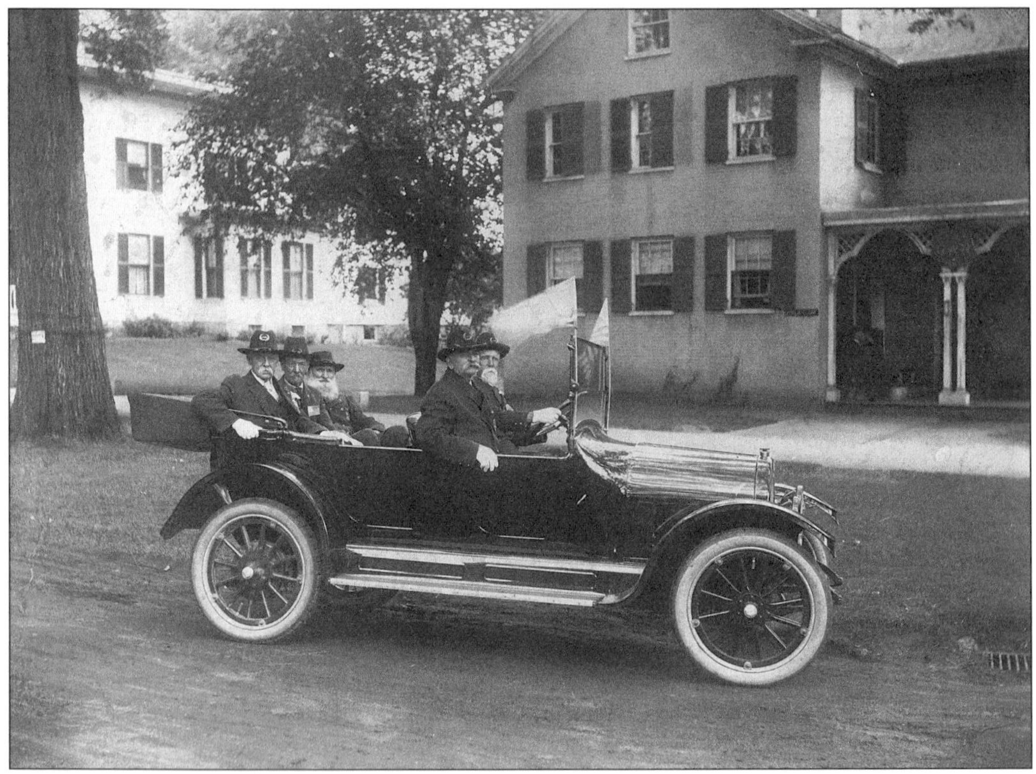

Grand Army of the Republic members pose in a car in the late 1920s in front of their post headquarters on Main Street, where the present county courthouse is located. The GAR was organized by veterans of the Civil War.

ACKNOWLEDGMENTS

The authors wish to express their sincere appreciation to Jane Adamoyurka, Sarah Hollister, Peter Miller, and *The Recorder* for sharing not only their photographs but also their knowledge of Greenfield history. We are grateful to Al Burrows and Greenfield Industries Inc. for sharing a wealth of photographs depicting the industrial history of the town. This book was written on behalf of the Historical Society of Greenfield, and the bulk of the photographs are from the museum's collection. It would be impossible to list all the people who donated photographs over the past 90 years, but they, too, have our thanks. We offer many thanks to Tim Blagg for sharing his time, editing skills, and knowledge of local history.

This book is dedicated to all the Greenfield photographers of the past 150 years. We are honored to share with you a small part of their vision.

INTRODUCTION

Greenfield has always been at a crossroads.

Before Europeans even dreamed of attempting to sail across the great ocean to their west, Native Americans passed through this area, paddling north and south on the great river that some tribes called *Quinnehtuck* or "long, tidal river" and others *Gownitigue* or "long river," which we now call the Connecticut.

They visited the area for thousands of years, hunting its game animals, fishing its streams, gathering nuts and native plants in its forests. They used the many streams of the area like today's Americans use highways. Their light dugouts or canoes could travel faster and easier than a person could on foot.

They also used footpaths—many of which followed trails originally made and used by animals—to move east and west, from New York state to the Atlantic at what is now Boston or Cape Cod. Much of what we now know as the Mohawk Trail—Route 2—is in fact laid out on the old Native American route.

Later, canals were built around waterfalls on the river to allow barges and boats to move, and roads were cut along the routes of old trails. Greenfield was important to both means of travel. When the railroads came, they, too, followed the Native American paths up and down the valleys and two major routes crossed in the middle of the town.

One snaked its way up the Connecticut River and then into Vermont. The other came out west from Boston, passed through Greenfield, and eventually dove into a great tunnel through the mountains near North Adams to arrive at Troy, New York. In the days before automobiles became common, an intricate and complete system of electric railways ran around the region, allowing people—for the first time—to easily work in one town while living in another. These trolleys also permitted weekend day trips for recreation.

In the 1960s, the interstate highway system was built, tying the country together with smooth webs of concrete. Interstate 91, running north and south, replaced earlier highways and met an improved Route 2, running east and west, in Greenfield.

This history of being where traffic meets has been important to Greenfield for several reasons. First, it brought business to town as visitors flowed in from the surrounding area. Second, it permitted manufacturing concerns to easily move raw materials in and finished products out.

Convenient transportation also allowed the town's residents a choice. They could stay and live a full and peaceful life, or they could take any one of the four major routes out of town and try their luck somewhere else. That is as true today as it was when the first Native Americans arrived.

This easy access to good transportation also allowed wave after wave of immigrants to arrive, each in turn being regarded with some suspicion by its predecessors and each in turn submerging itself in the common culture and taking its place in the professional and moneyed classes.

Perhaps because of this tradition of immigration, which, after all, goes all the way back to the Native Americans who found their way east after the glaciers retreated some 100,000 years ago, Greenfield was usually a tolerant place. Although each generation had its prejudices, each also managed to continue to get along with the newest immigrants without serious trouble.

Another contributing factor was factory life, with its emphasis on talent and ingenuity. Workers who came up with a better way to machine tools or cutlery, or to mass-produce baby carriages were rewarded, regardless of their ethnic background. All workers shared in the profits of better processes—that was the hallmark of the "American method of manufacturing," which was invented in the Connecticut Valley between 1820 and 1860.

Factories were split into small groups, each led by a foreman hired by the company that owned the place. They paid him, he paid the workers, and all shared in some way if the profits were increased. It was an effective motivating tool, and it allowed anyone who was willing to work hard and think hard about the job to prosper.

Many did.

All of this social mobility and profit taking led to a town that blossomed when the economy was good, and that in turn led to surges of building. Designation as the county seat also helped concentrate governmental services in town. Homes, shops, commercial blocks, and manufacturing facilities sprang up, ran, were closed, and replaced with bigger and better versions. The history of the town is written in its buildings and homes, and this photographic glance at the last 150 years in Greenfield is intended to allow readers to follow that record while seated comfortably in their favorite armchair.

Please enjoy the tour.

—Tim Blagg

One

DOWNTOWN

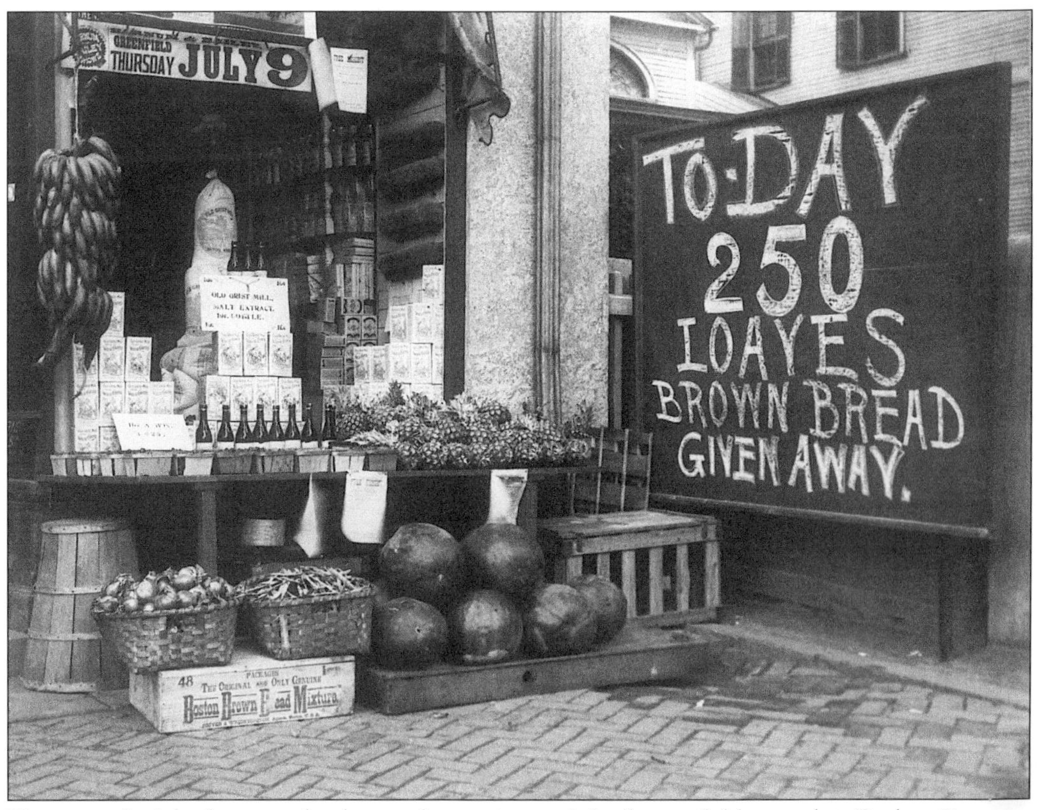

This wonderful photograph shows the variety of foods available at the Cutler Grocery, located at the eastern end of the Mansion House Block. It was started by Nahum S. Cutler in 1904 after his shoe factory, Cutler, Lyons, and Field, failed. The west wing of the Leavitt-Hovey House, now the public library, is visible at the right. In 1910, Greenfield had 19 grocers, 8 meat markets, and 7 fruit stores.

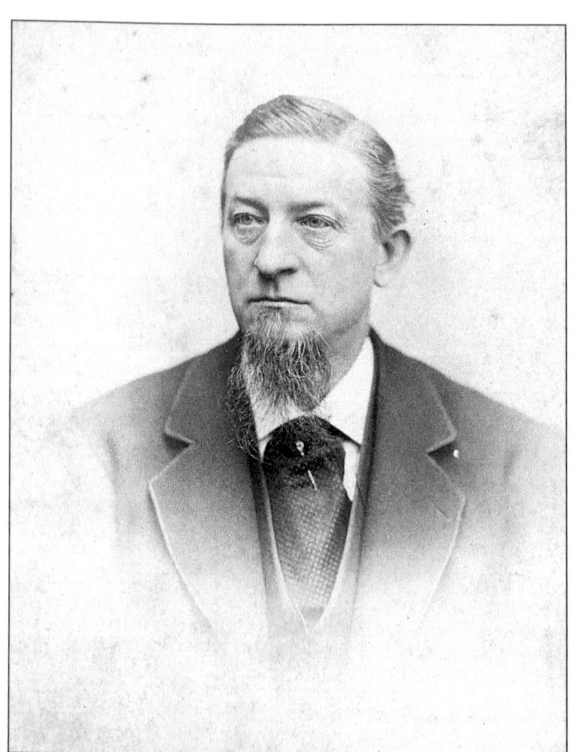

This is a self-portrait of Benjamin Franklin Popkins (1822–1905). Popkins was the first professional photographer to open a permanent studio in Greenfield, beginning in 1847. He traveled extensively but always came back to Greenfield. Because of this traveling, he had studios in four different spots in town, including the building on the northwest corner of Main and Federal Streets. He was the first local photographer to move away from daguerreotypes—printing on metal—into printing on paper.

This self-portrait of photographer Pelham Bradford shows him standing in front of a sign by his shop at Federal and Main Streets. His sign advertising ambrotypes—an early form of printing—is visible over Stewart's store. Willard's old tavern building is in the background.

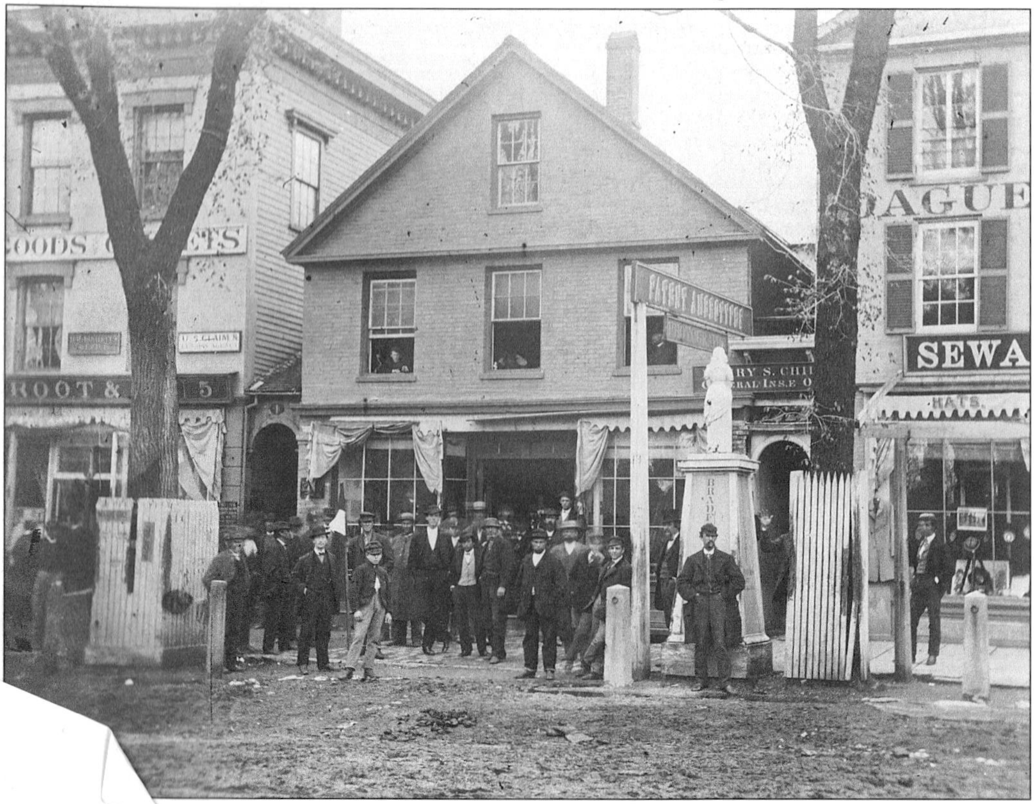

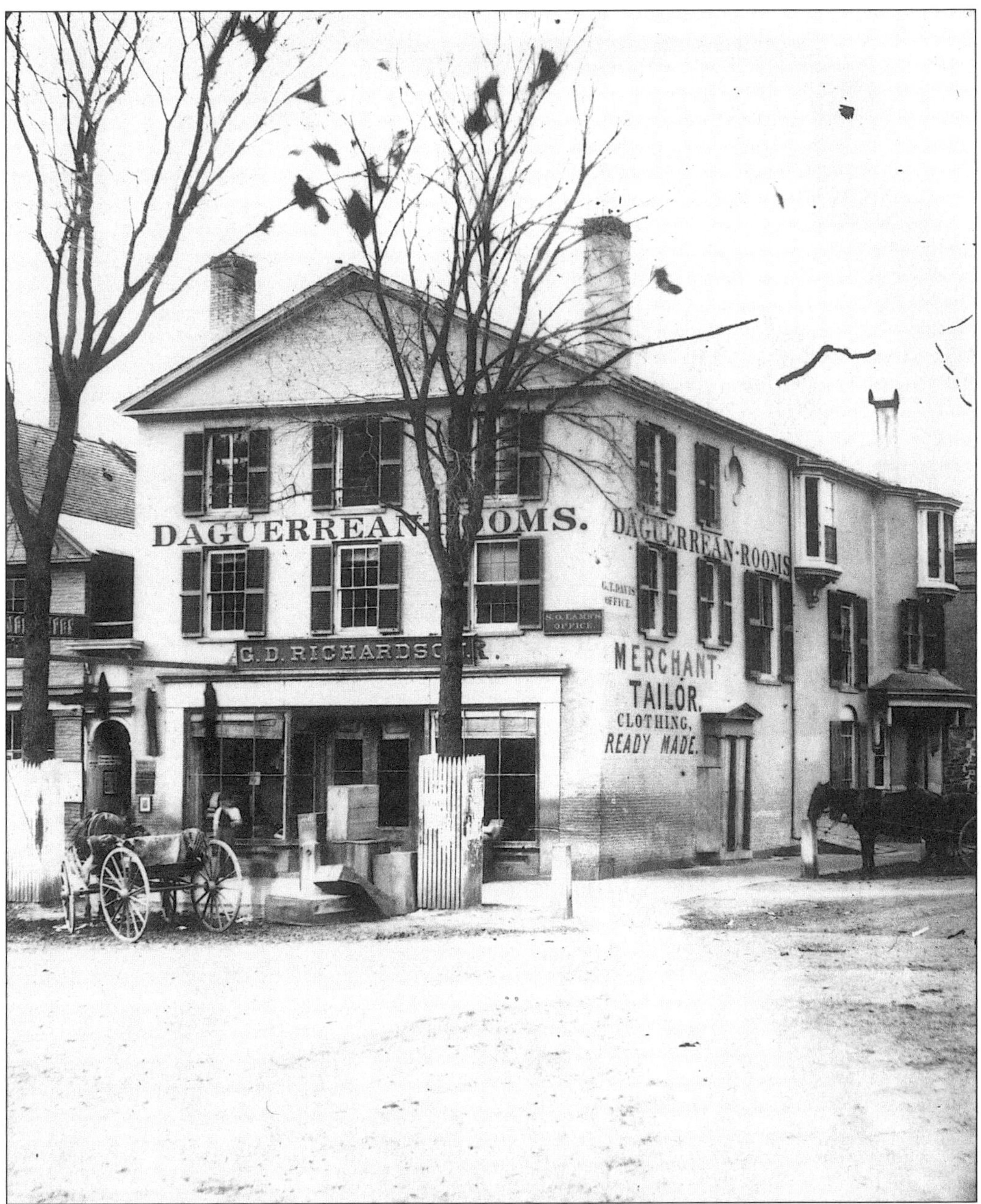

Shown here is the Corner Store Block at the corner of Federal and Main Streets. The building housed the photograph studios of Willis Knowlton, Erskine C. Ely, Pelham Bradford, and later, Benjamin Popkins. This photograph was taken *c.* 1869 by Bradford. The building was taken down in 1911 and replaced by the Franklin Savings Institution. Daguerreotypes were the first commercially viable photographs and were popular in the 1840s and early 1850s.

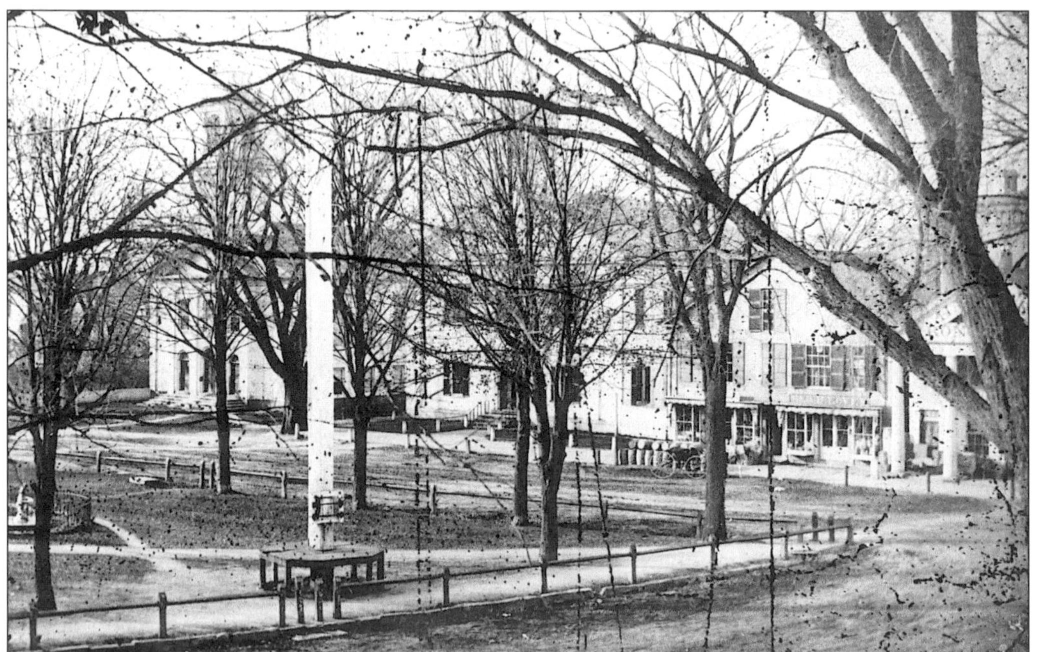

This 1868 view of the west side of Court Square shows the Hollister House, the original brick Second Congregational Church, and the second Franklin County Courthouse. This courthouse was altered three times to fit changing tastes in architecture. First a wooden Greek Revival and then a brick Gothic Revival, it is now the Colonial Revival town hall. The next two wooden buildings were moved in 1876 to form a single building that is still standing at the corner of Chapman and Main Streets.

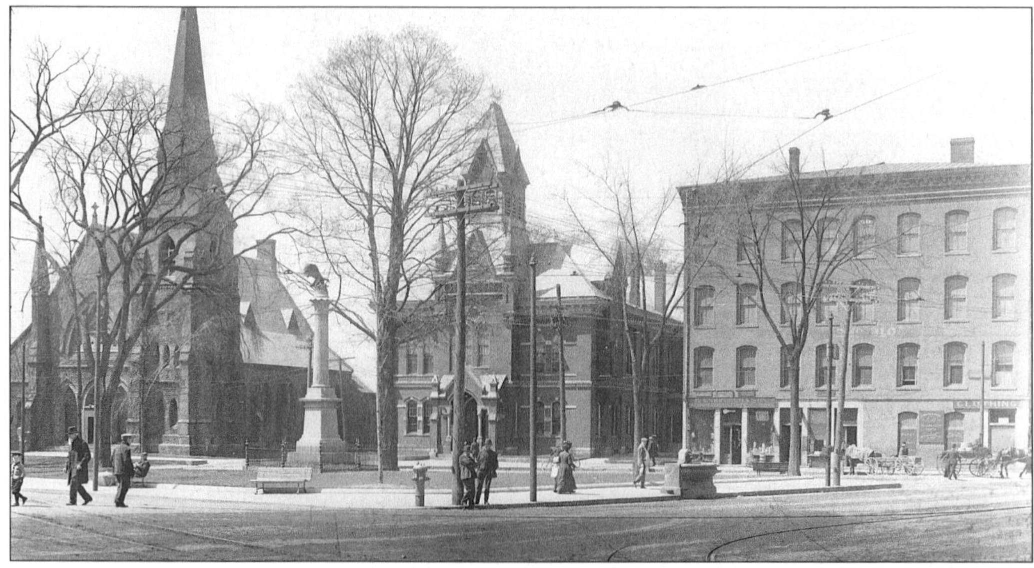

This Court Square scene *c.* 1900 shows the Second Congregational Church, the second Franklin County Courthouse, and the George Arms Block. Note the trolley tracks and the brick paving on Main Street. The horse trough was installed on the common in 1903 to commemorate the 150th anniversary of the town. It is now installed in Shattuck Park on Federal Street.

This portrait is of the Reverend John F. Moors (1819–1895), minister of the Unitarian church in Greenfield from 1860 to 1884. Moors was regimental chaplain for the 52nd Massachusetts, a Franklin County regiment that fought in Louisiana. Later, he was one of the founders of the Prospect Hill School for Girls, which later became Stoneleigh-Burnham School.

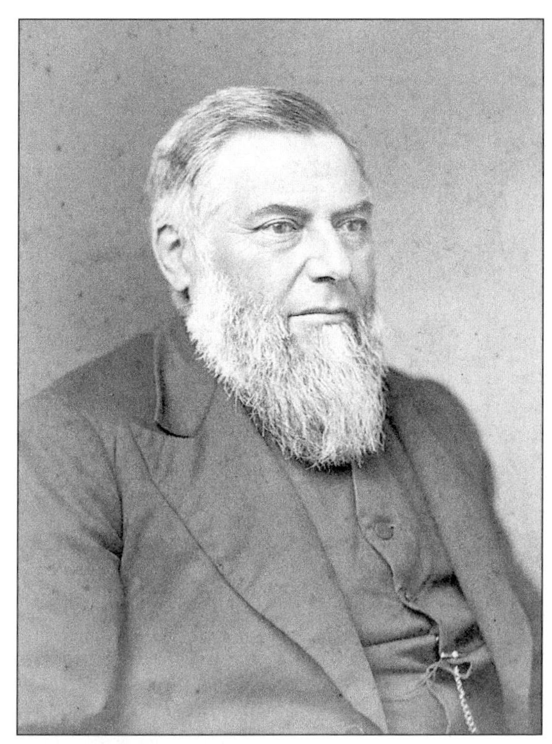

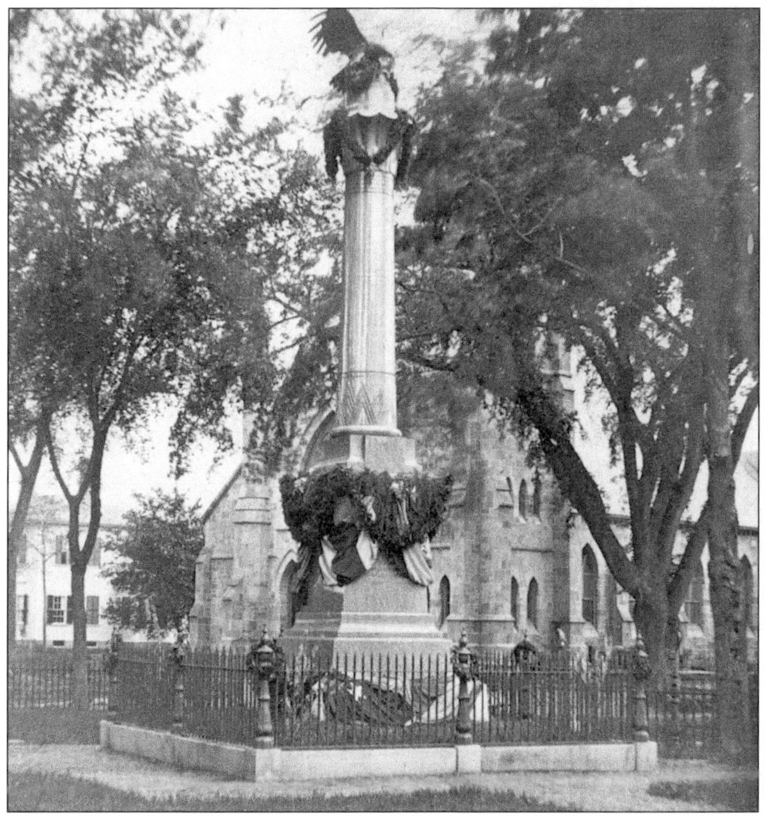

This photograph shows the Soldiers Monument on the common, not long after it was dedicated on October 6, 1870, to honor the 50 Greenfield men who died in the Civil War. The eagle destroying two copperhead snakes symbolizes the national government suppressing the rebellion. It was designed by George Keller and built by J.G. Batterson of Hartford. Greenfield poet Frederick Goddard Tuckerman read a specially composed poem at its dedication.

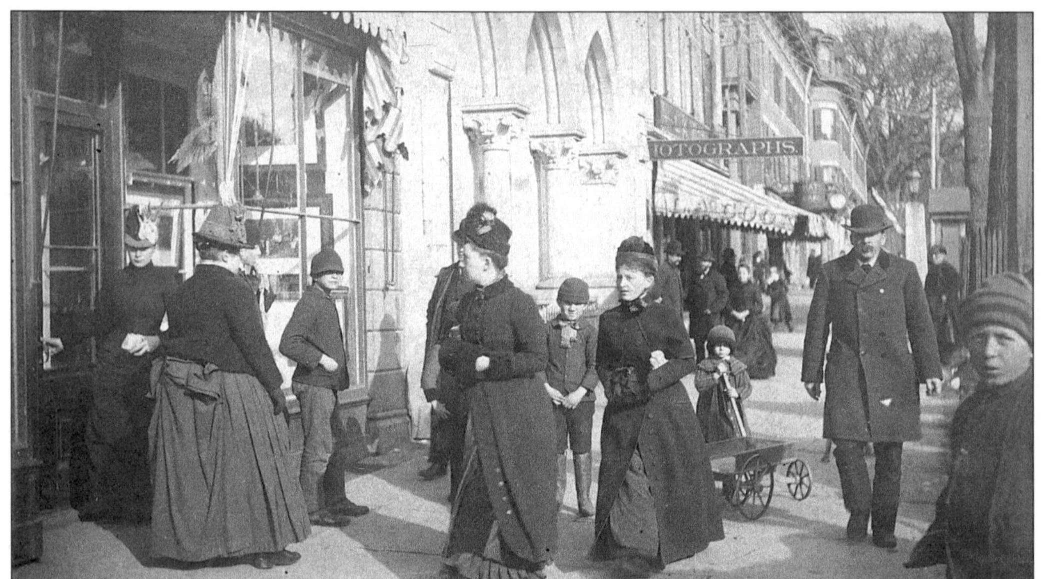

This Main Street scene is in front of the Sanborn and the Franklin County Trust Company Blocks. Note the sign for the Benjamin F. Popkins Photography Studio, located in the corner building. In the background is the Mansion House. This photograph dates from *c.* 1890.

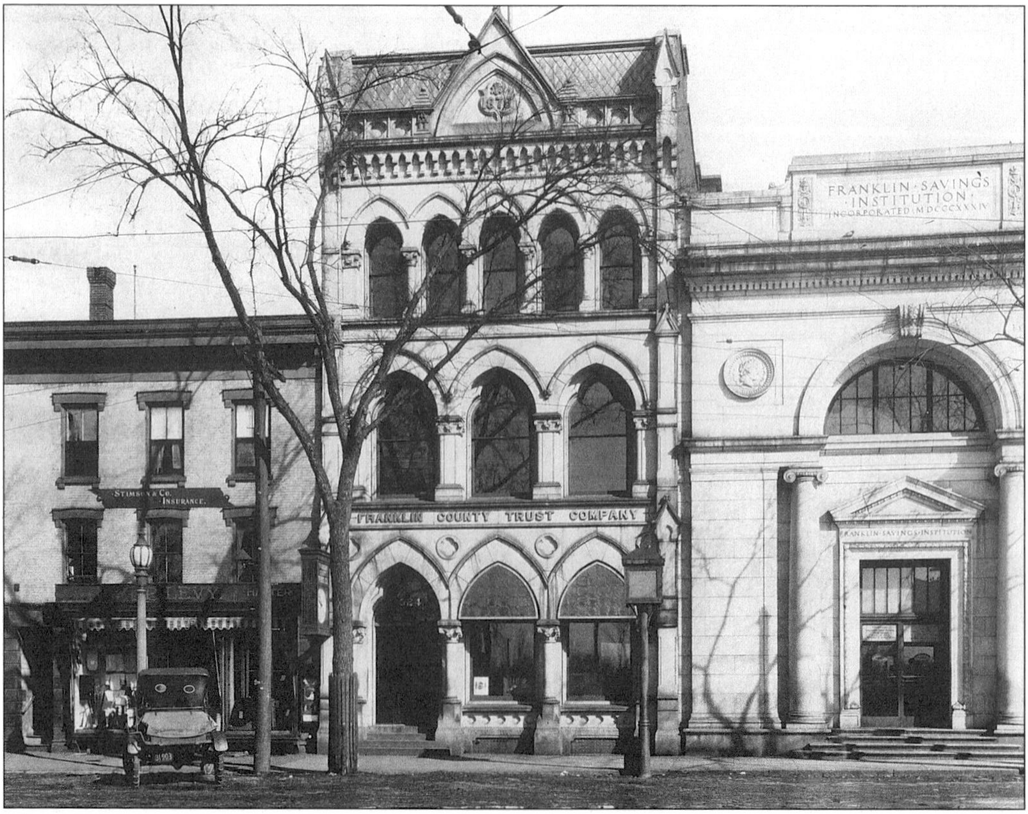

The Gothic Revival Franklin County Trust Company Block was built in 1870. In the 1970s, the facade was replaced and the Sanborn Block, to the left, was razed.

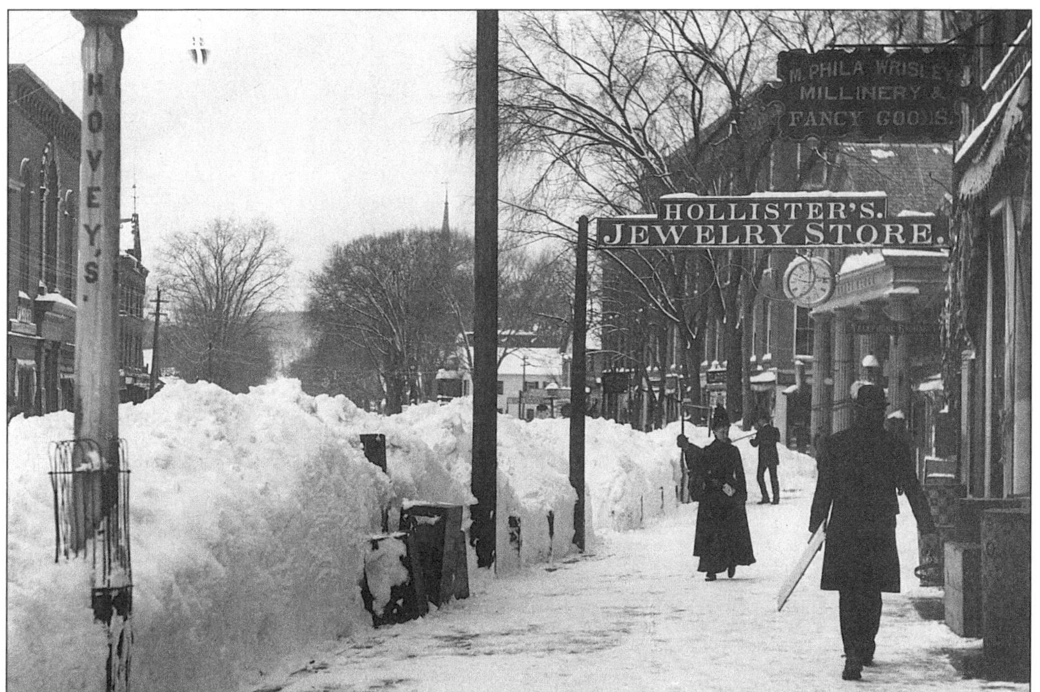

This winter scene on Main Street is in front of Hovey's Drugstore (now Baker Office Supplies) and dates from *c.* 1890. Hovey lived in the present library building, and Hollister lived in the present McCarthy Funeral Home. Note the columns of the Colonnade Block, the cupola of the American House Block (above the sign for Wrisley's Millinery), the overhead wires, and the Baptist church steeple.

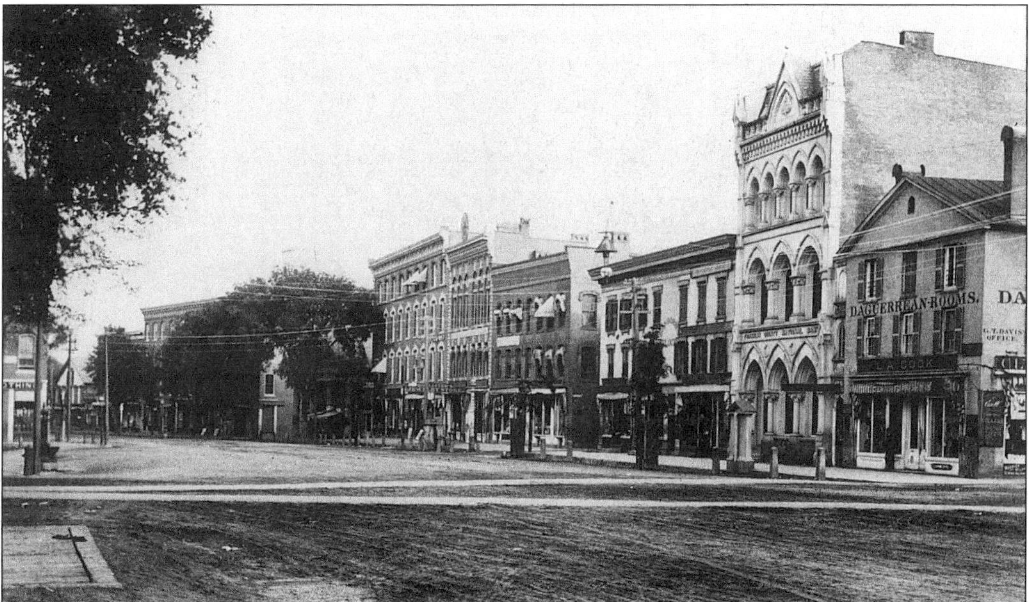

This view of Main Street remained unchanged from 1876 to *c.* 1910. Note the old town clock on the Hollister Block. This photograph, taken *c.* 1880, shows the northern blocks just west of Federal Street.

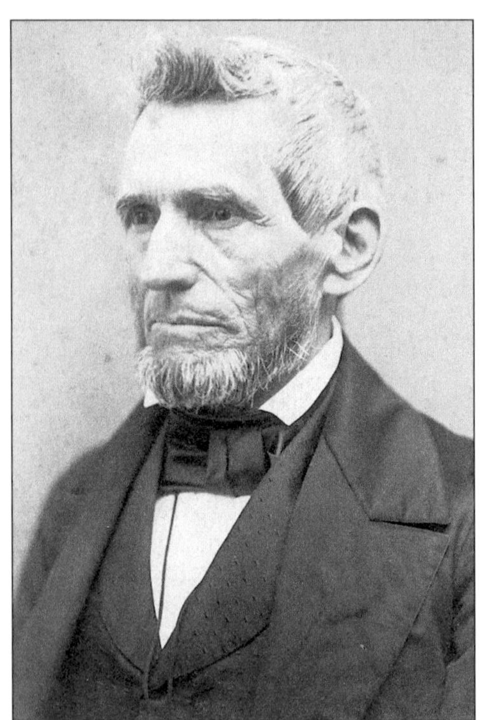

Judge Franklin Ripley (1789–1860) was the son of Jerome and Sarah Franklin Ripley. Judge Ripley was raised in the Colonnade Block. After serving on Gen. Isaac Maltby's staff during the War of 1812, Ripley worked as a lawyer and businessman in Greenfield. He was an officer in two of the local banks and became Franklin County judge of probate.

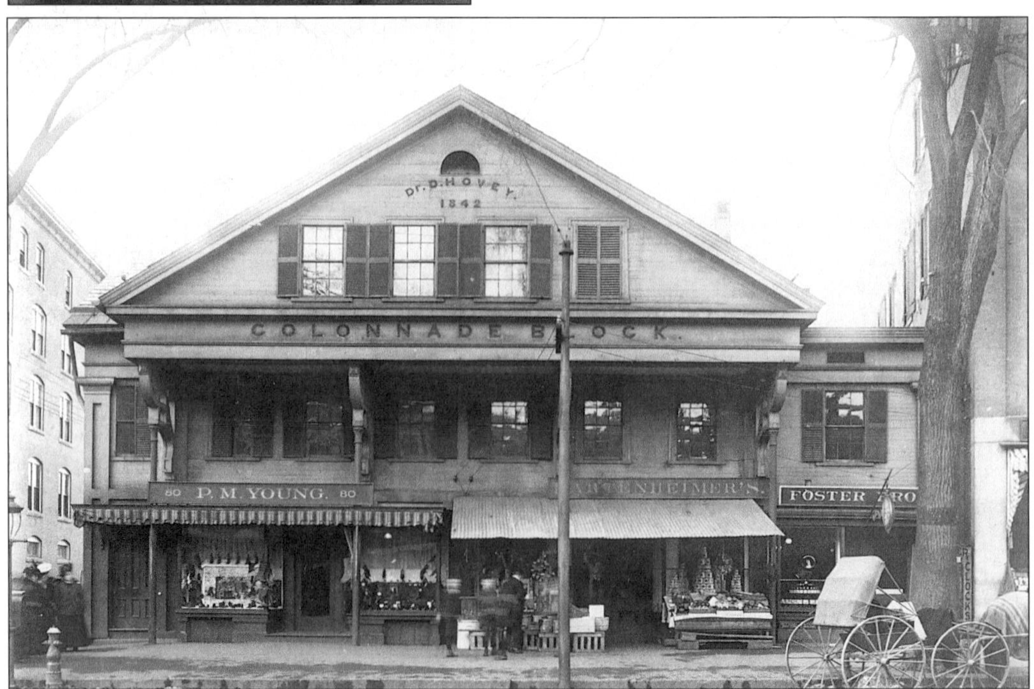

The Colonnade Block, built in the 1790s, was located at Davis and Main Streets and was the store and home of Jerome Ripley. In 1842, Dr. Daniel Hovey changed it into a Greek Revival-style building, complete with front columns. The Colonnade Block was torn down in 1975 to make way for the Heritage Bank building, now the downtown branch of Greenfield Community College. This photograph dates from *c.* 1890.

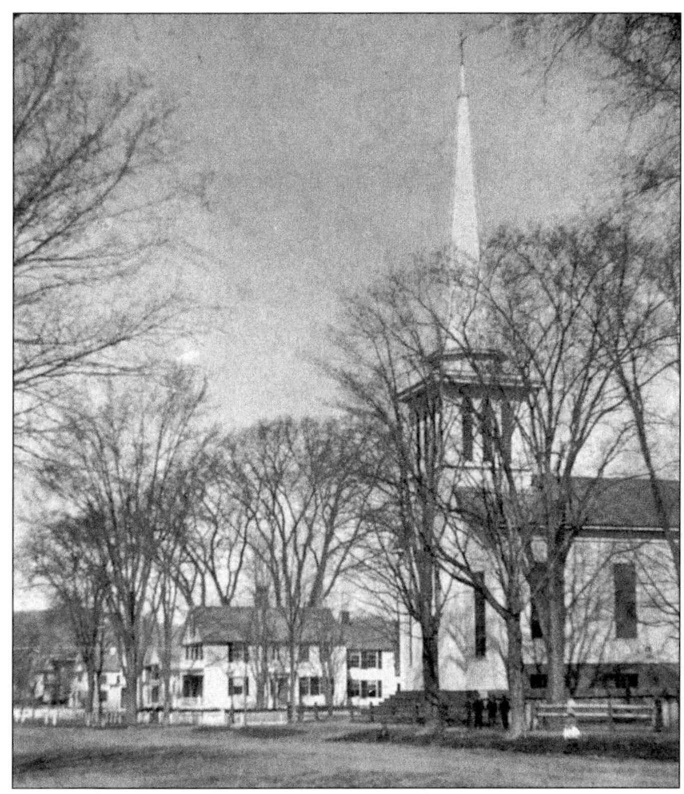

The Baptist church stood at Wells and Main Streets from 1865 to 1913, when, ironically, it became the Bijou Theater. Later, the building was expanded into a commercial and apartment building, the Benson Block. After a fire in 1939, it was rebuilt in its present four-story appearance.

This shows the south side of Main Street, looking west from the upper floors of the new Pond Block *c.* 1874. Washington Hall is to the left and the new brick-front Botsford Block is in the middle. The gap between two white buildings is the location of the railroad arch—the point at which the tracks run under Main Street.

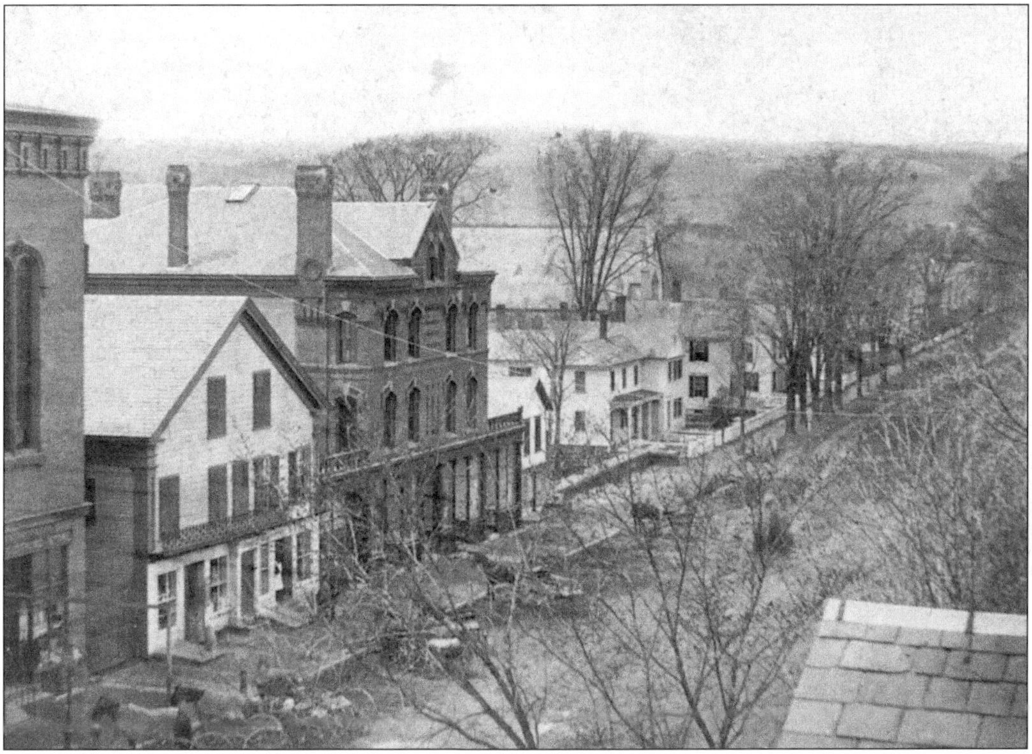

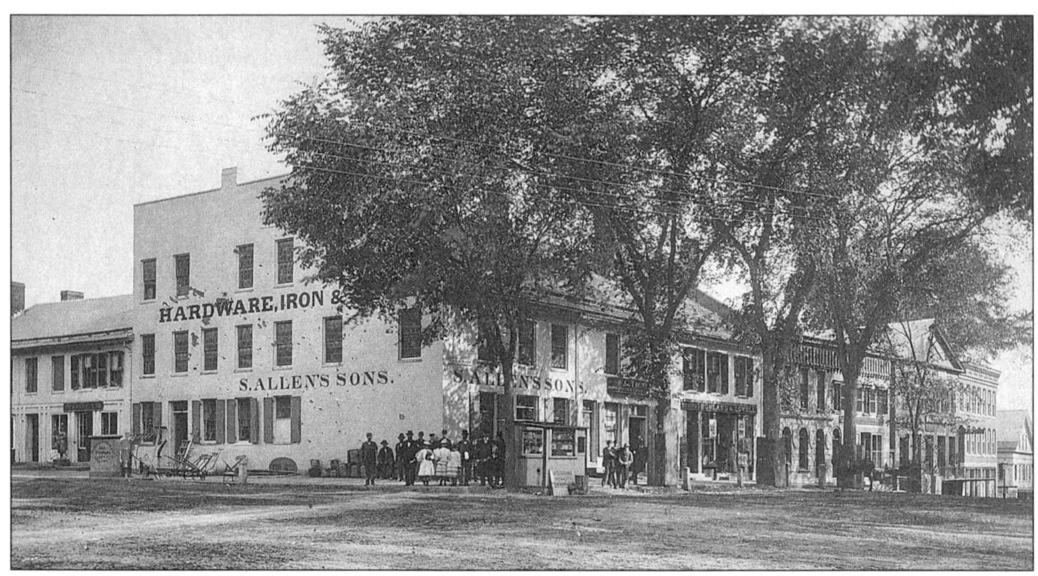

This view of Bank Row was taken *c.* 1880. It shows the second version of the S. Allen Block, built in 1827 by Charlotte Willard. This building at the corner of Main Street and Bank Row had a complicated history. It was referred to as the Willard Building–S. Allen & Sons Block because during construction, storefronts were sold off separately; one was retained by Allen, one sold to Elijah Gould, and one kept by Charlotte Willard.

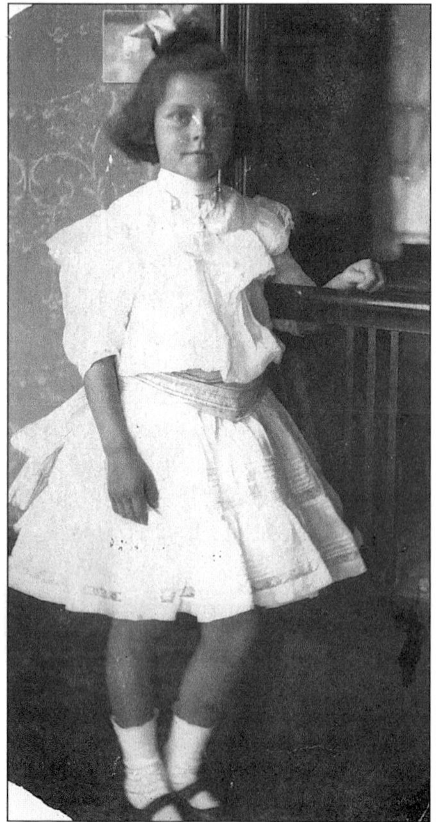

Pictured here is Margaret Allen, daughter of Franklin and Nettie Allen. She was born in 1897 and married William Howe in 1921. Franklin Allen was the proprietor of S. Allen's Sons Hardware Store. This photograph dates from *c.* 1907.

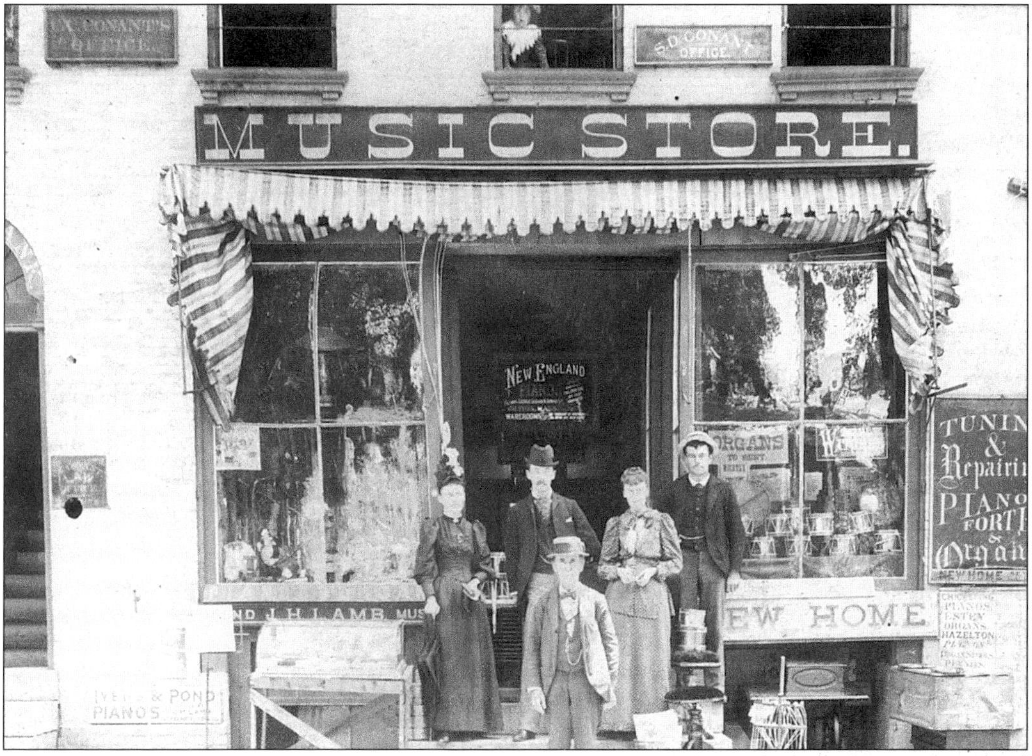

J.H. Lamb's Music Store was located in the S. Allen Block on Bank Row. The staff, plus a girl in the upstairs window, posed for this picture on June 16, 1893.

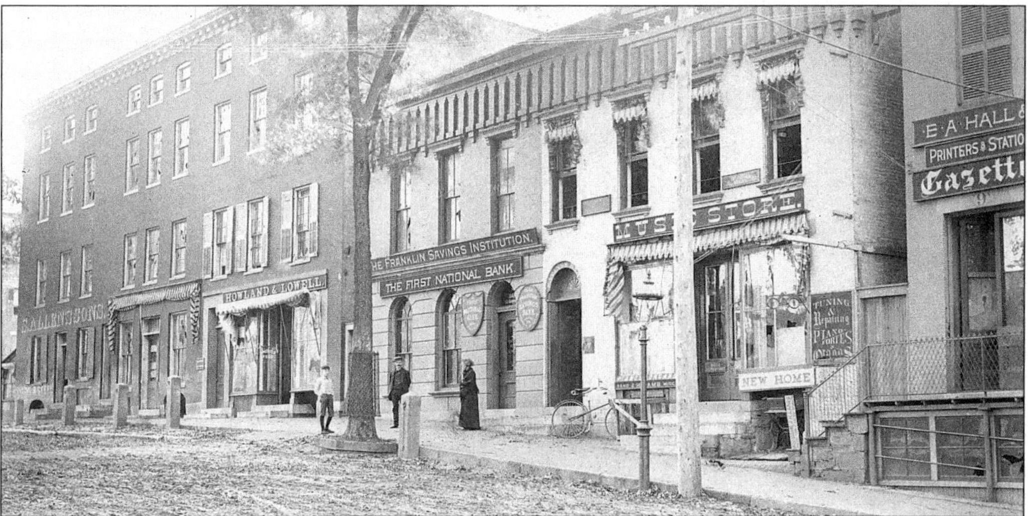

This photograph shows the banks of Bank Row. The First National Bank was downstairs and the Franklin Savings Institution upstairs. Next door to the banks was J.H. Lamb's Music Store. To the left of the bank is Howland & Lowell druggists (later Fiske and Strecker). These buildings were torn down to build an art deco-style bank in 1929. Also note E.A. Hall, who printed the *Courier & Gazette* newspaper and the sign for New Home, a brand of sewing machine made in the town of Orange. The broken windows probably prompted this photograph, which was taken *c.* 1890.

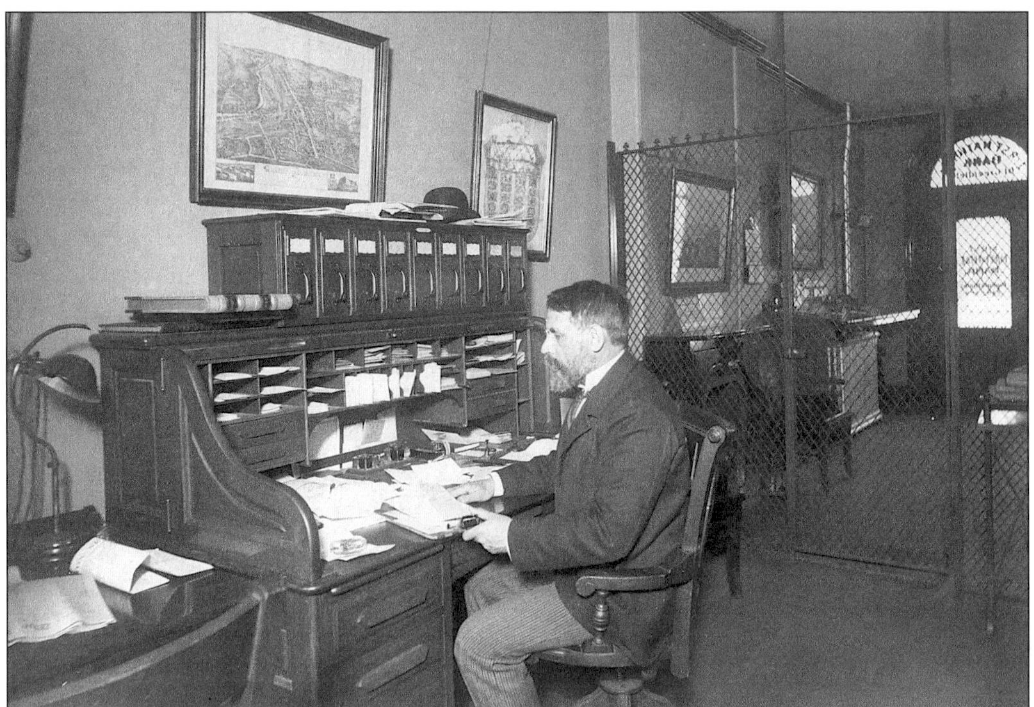

Pictured here is an officer in the First National Bank on Bank Row in the 1890s. Above the desk is a copy of the 1877 bird's-eye-view map of Greenfield. To the right of that is a frame containing old currency. This old currency is still on display in the Fleet Bank branch on Federal Street.

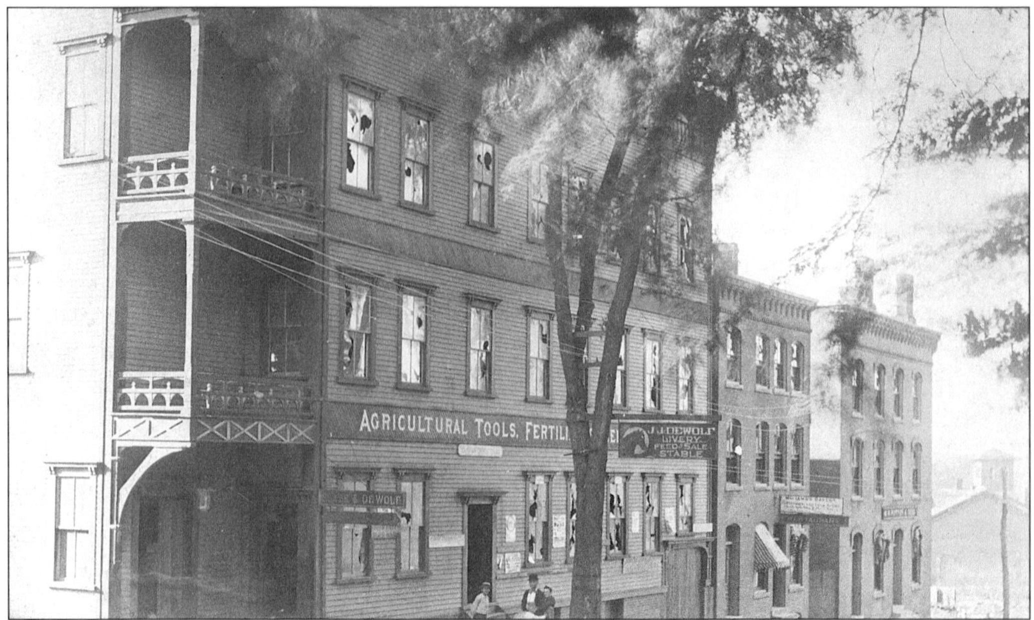

The Slate and DeWolf firm sold hardware and agricultural tools from this store on Bank Row. The photograph was taken *c.* 1890. Note all the broken windows, perhaps the result of a hailstorm.

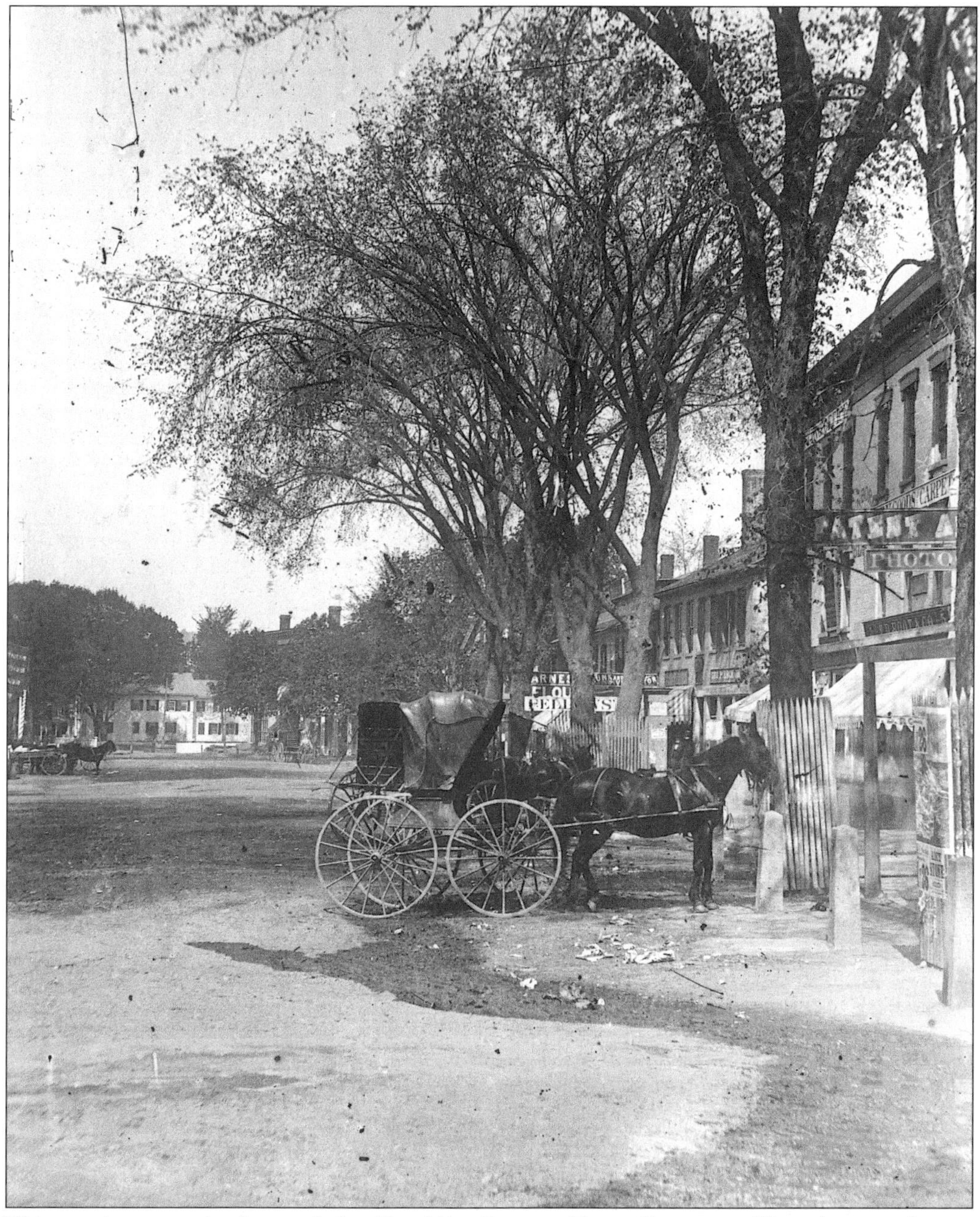

This carriage was in front of the Franklin County Trust Company. The photograph was probably taken by Pelham Bradford *c.* 1869. The first lower building is the Bird-Hovey Block. The next is the Hollister Block, which burned in 1873. The Hovey Block was rebuilt and expanded at about the same time.

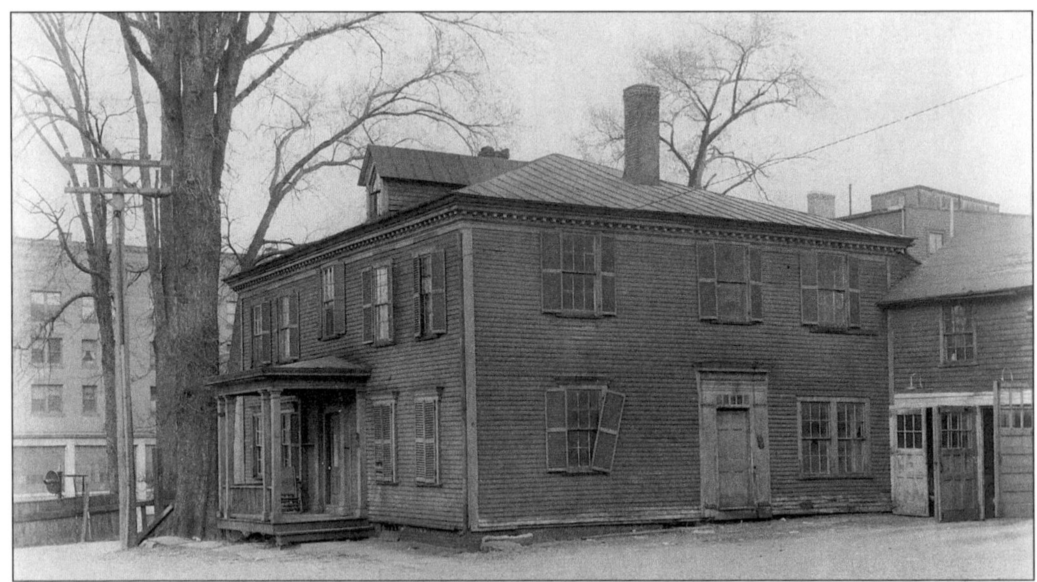

This is the Reverend Roger Newton house as it stood at the northwest end of Newton Court in April 1934. Newton was the second minister in town, presiding over services at the meetinghouse at Trap Plain (now Four Corners). His house stood from 1793 to 1848 at the present site of the town hall, which was originally the second Franklin County Courthouse. Newton's home was moved to make room for the new courthouse.

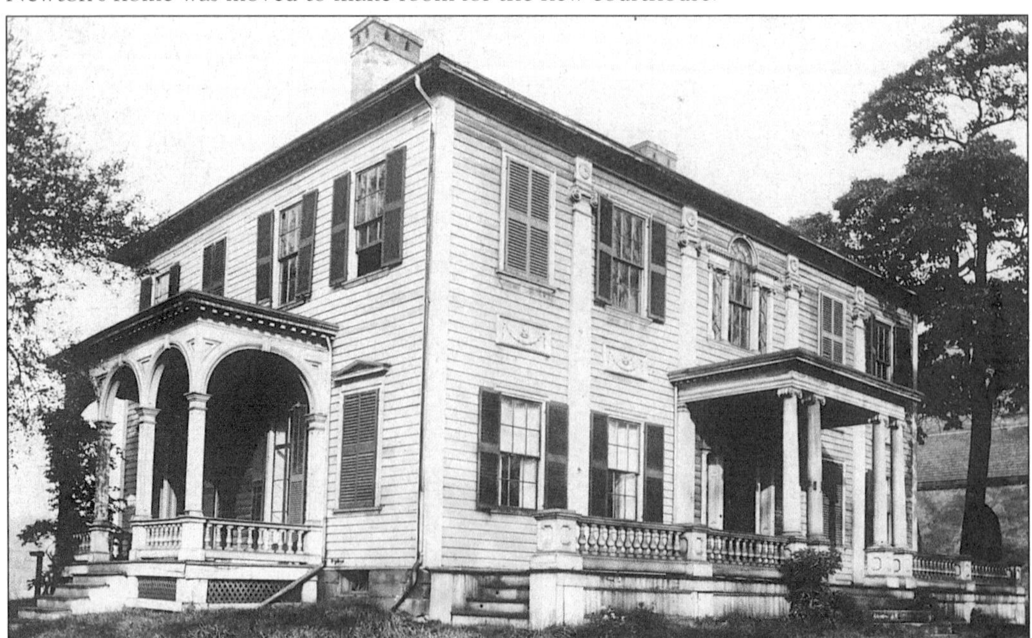

The Coleman-Hollister House was designed and built by Asher Benjamin in 1796–97 for lawyer and newspaper proprietor William Coleman. Coleman later founded the *New York Post* with Alexander Hamilton and was its editor for many years. Due to severe financial problems, he lost the property and never lived in the house. Over the years it has served as the High School for Young Ladies and as the home of the Hollister family from 1864 to 1914. This view of the high-style Federal building dates from *c.* 1910. Today it is the McCarthy Funeral Home.

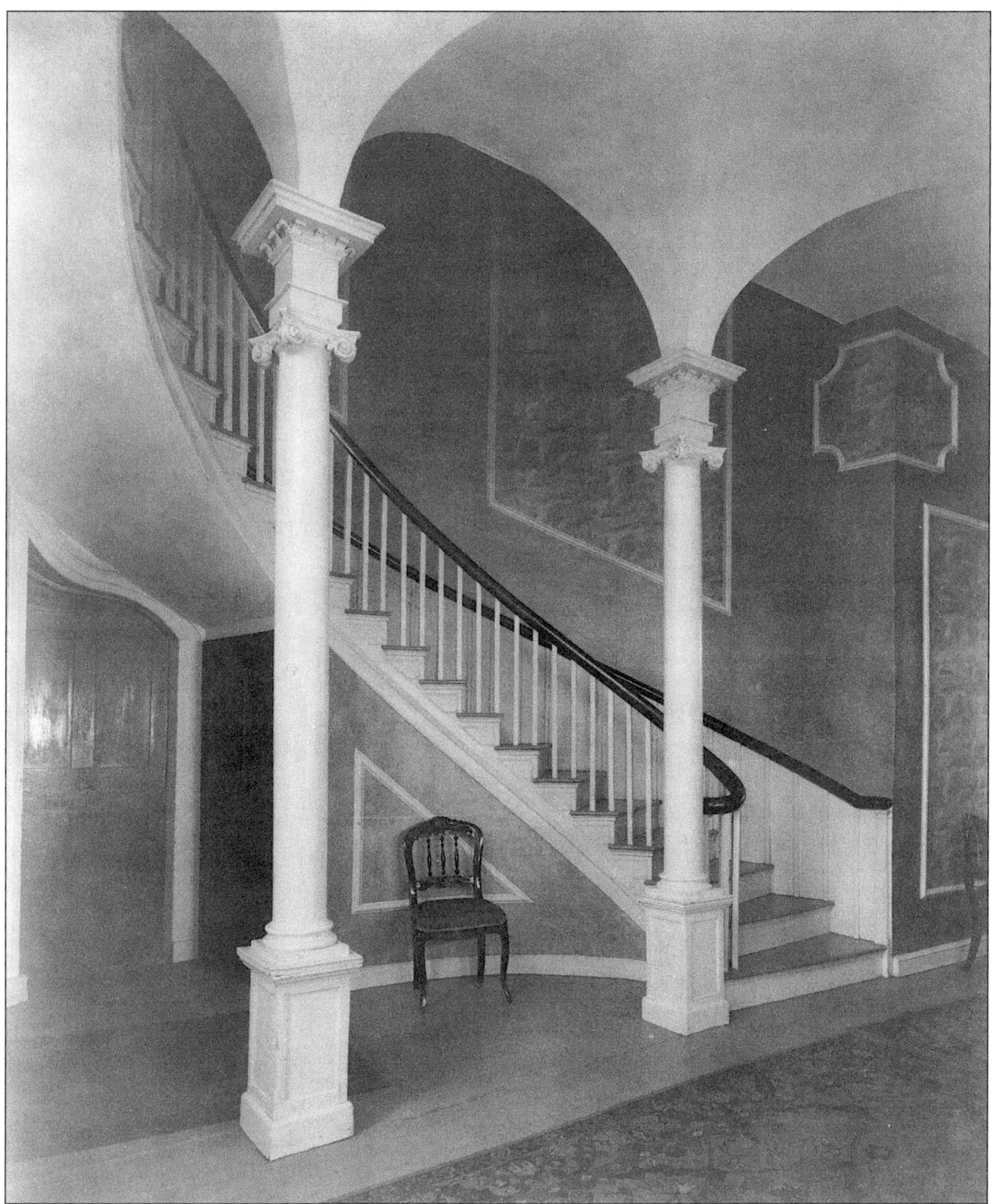

This freestanding spiral staircase in the Coleman-Hollister House was designed by Asher Benjamin, the first American architect who published his designs in the United States in a book printed in Greenfield in 1797. Now the McCarthy Funeral Home, this building retains many of its original design features. The column at the left is removable to create more room for dancing and other functions. The doorway leads into the Octagon Room.

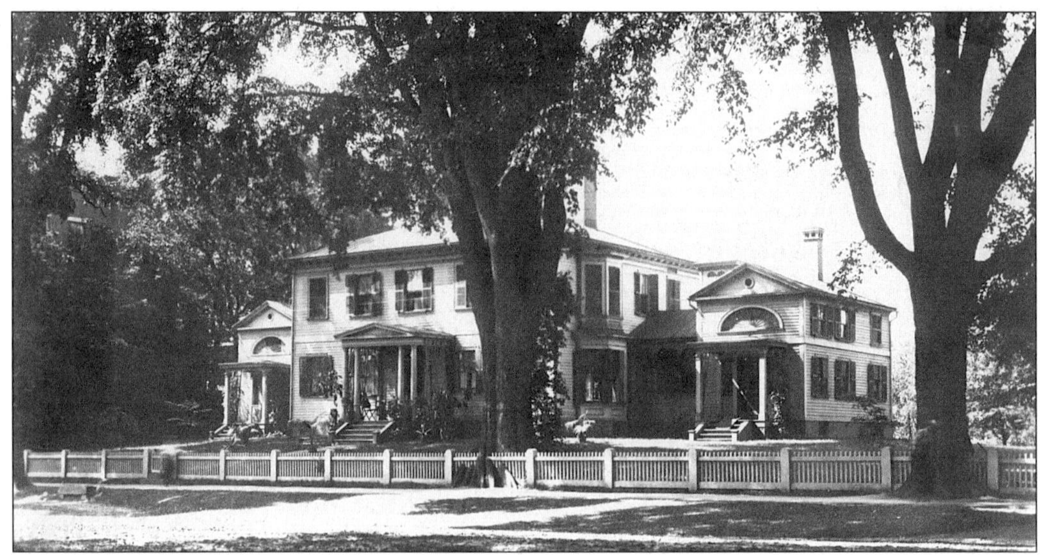

This is a *c.* 1900 view of the Hovey family home, now the public library. The house was designed and built in 1797 for lawyer Jonathan Leavitt by builder-architect Asher Benjamin. Leavitt had his law office in the left wing and the dining room in the right wing. The place was known as the "Social Villa" because of all the social events hosted in the rear gardens. During the Hovey ownership, pioneering woman doctor Phylinda Dole had her office in the left wing.

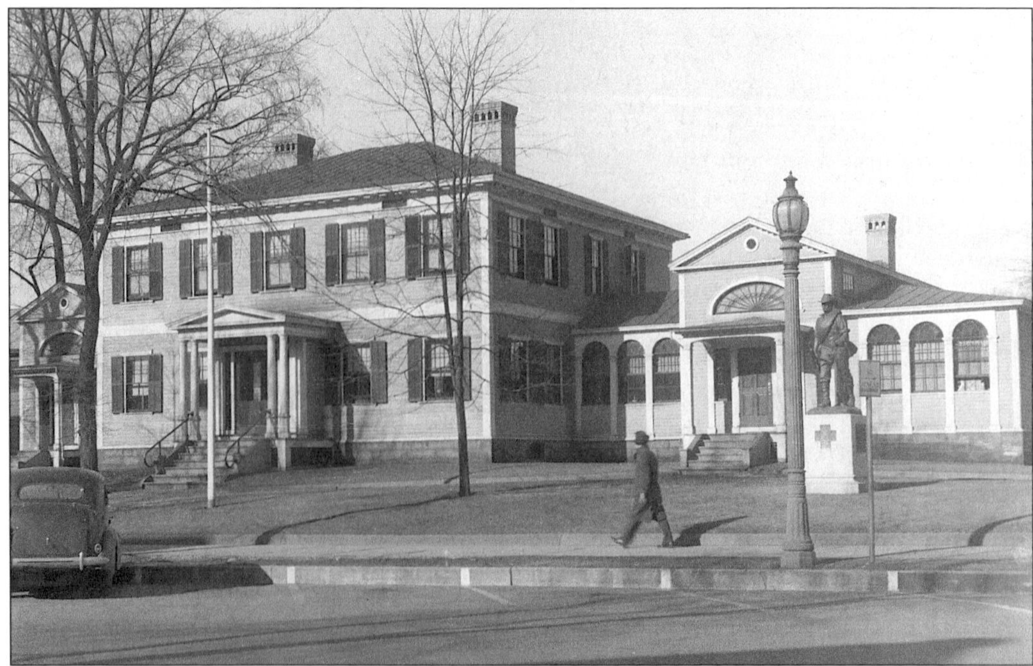

This photograph shows the Greenfield Public Library in 1938. In 1909, the town purchased the Leavitt-Hovey House, rebuilt the wings, gutted the interior, and built an addition to contain the stacks. In 1977, all of the outside woodwork and the windows were replaced with the exception of the porticos. In 1997, citizens voted to renovate this beloved building once again instead of moving the library to a more modern space. There is very little left of the original structure, but it does retain its graceful exterior design.

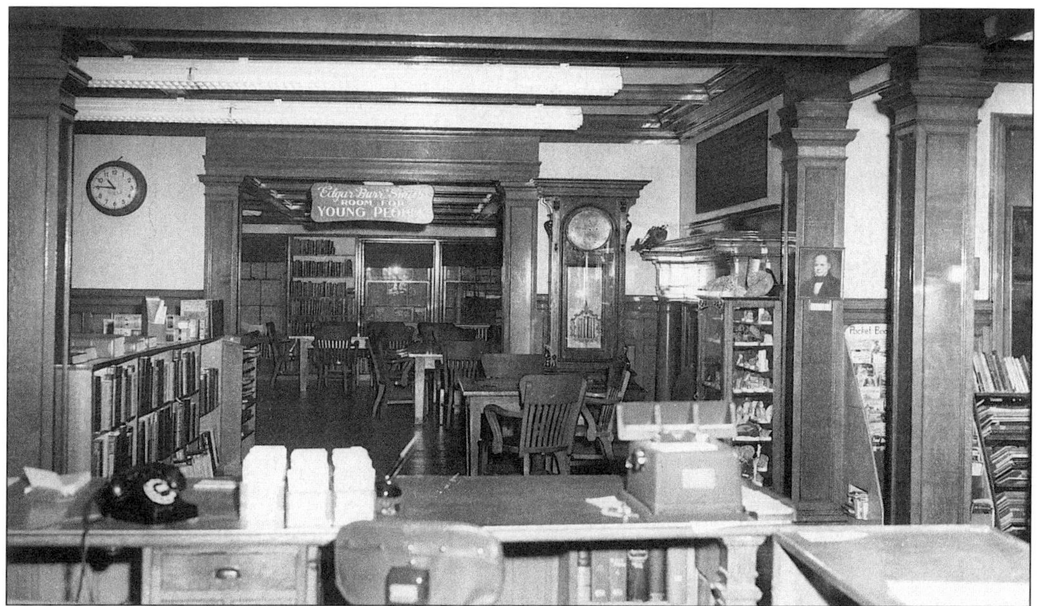

This view shows the interior of Greenfield Public Library in the 1950s. The photograph was taken from the librarians' desk looking toward the Edgar Burr Smith Room for Young People. It shows some of the original layout and details from when the building was originally turned into a library by the town in 1909.

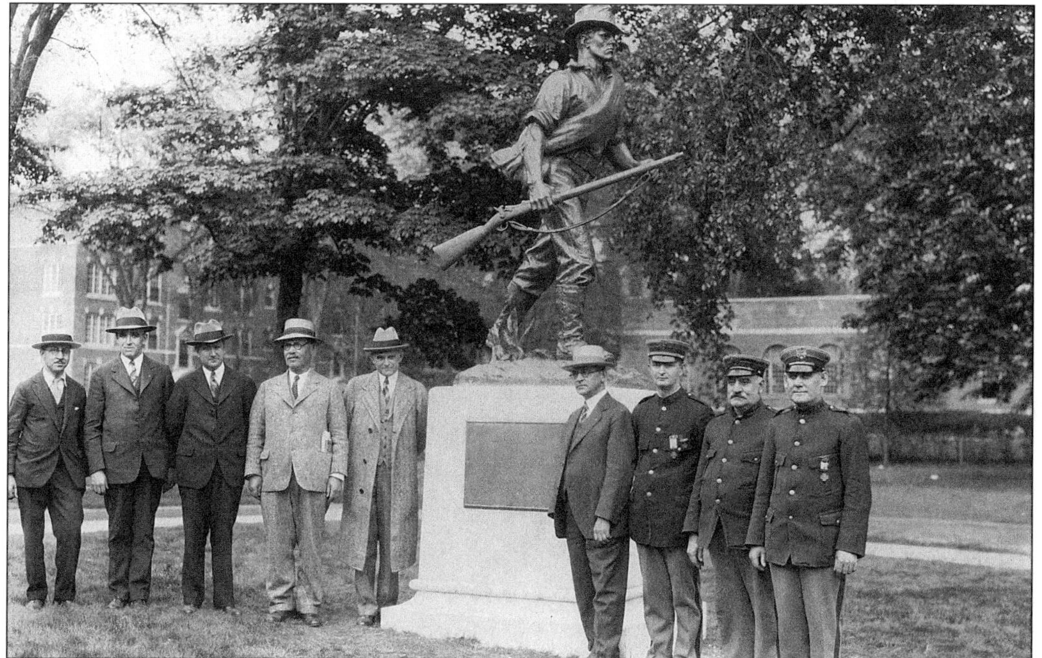

The Spanish-American War Monument, located in front of the Greenfield Public Library, was dedicated on June 9, 1928. Gen. Frederick Pierce, who commanded Greenfield's Company L during the war, is fourth from left. John W. Haigis, politician, banker, and founder of WHAI radio, is fifth from left. Seventh from left is George Bliss, a veteran of that war, and Bill Gorey is second from left.

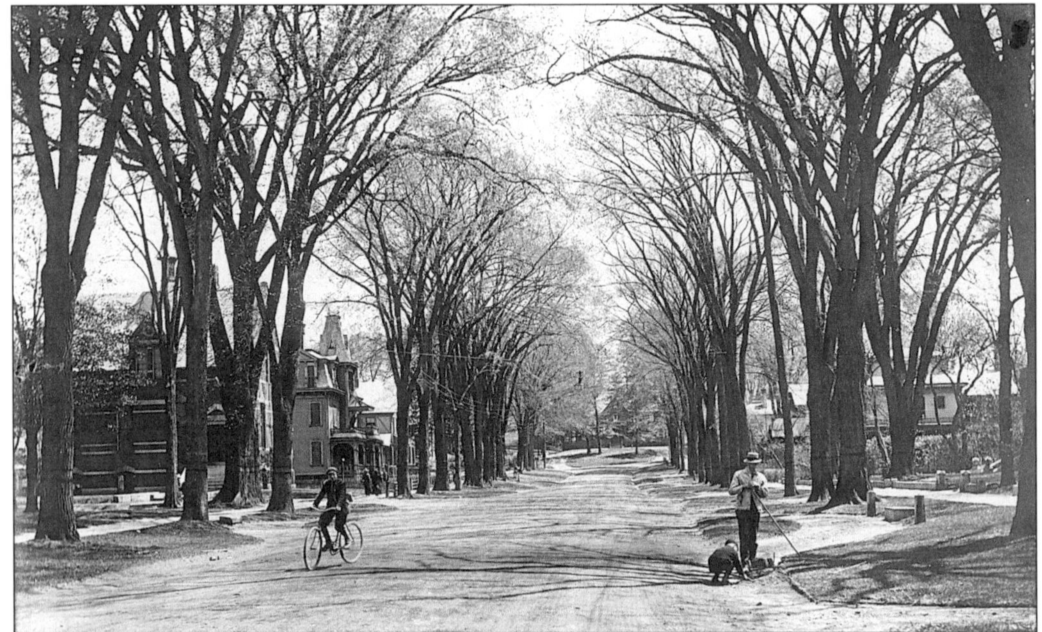

This is the east end of Main Street, *c.* 1900, with the intersection with Franklin Street near the boy on the bicycle. The houses remain, but none remain single-family residences. The elm trees were all lost in the late 1950s to Dutch elm disease. The brick building on the left was built in 1878 as a private lending library by Gov. William B. Washburn. It is now the home of the Franklin County Arts Council.

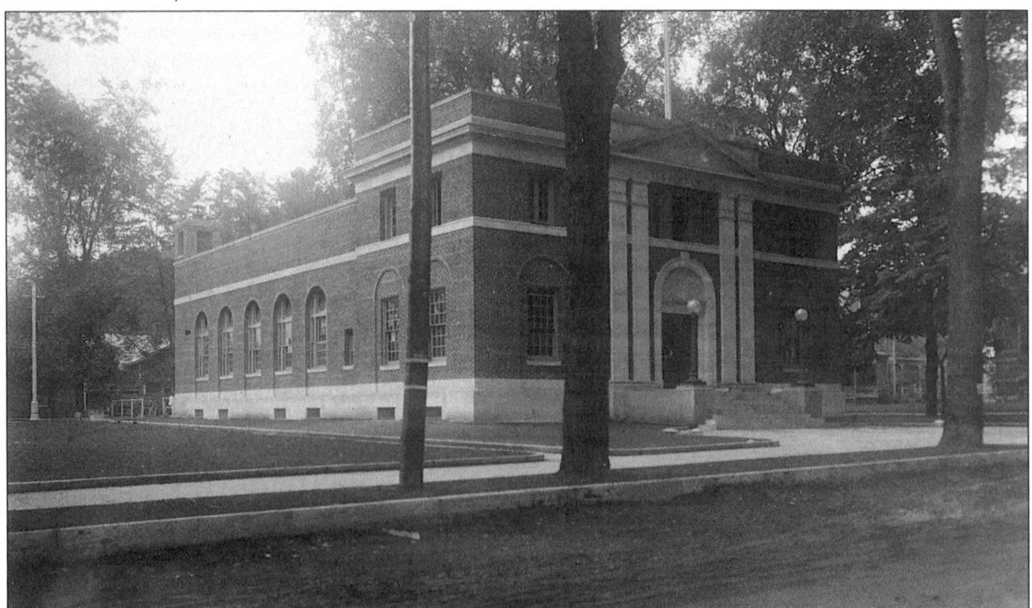

The Greenfield Post Office was originally constructed in 1915-16, replacing the W.E. Wood House. Before occupying this building, the post office rented space in various commercial buildings, including the Masonic Block. The first post office began operating in Greenfield in 1792. Thomas Dickman, a printer who was the town's first newspaper editor, was the first postmaster.

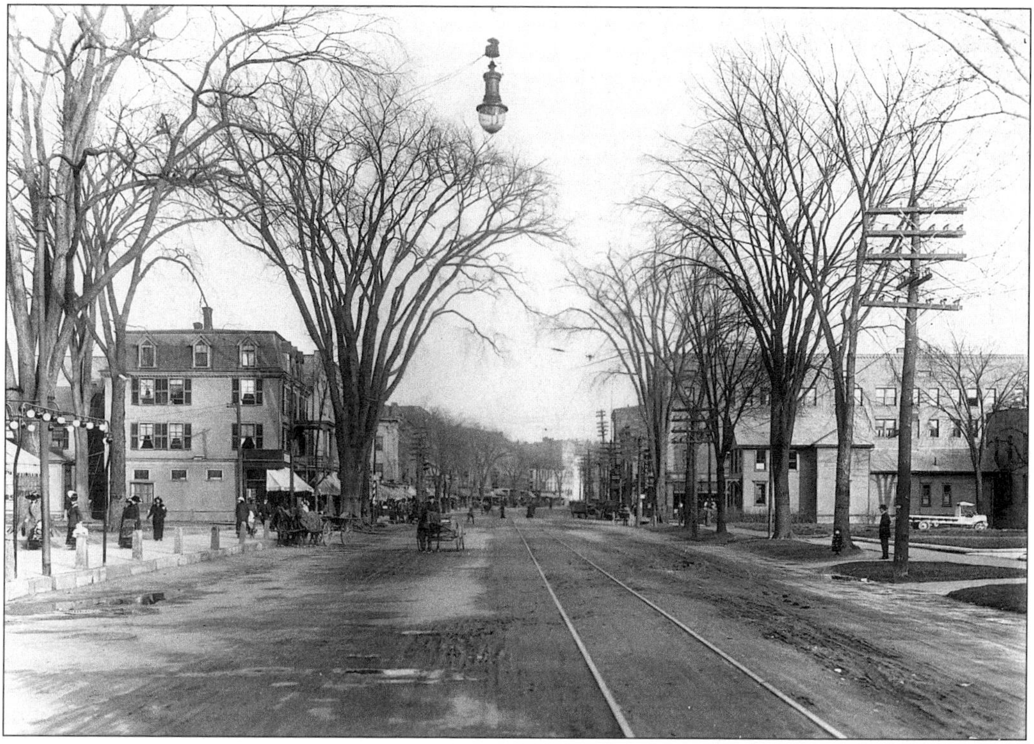

This photograph shows the middle section of Main Street from the old Main Street School (later a J.C. Penney store), looking east. The first house on left was the Elm House, later moved back and replaced by the Henri Cohn Block (now the World Eye Bookstore). Note the trolley tracks and the elm trees in this *c.* 1910 photograph.

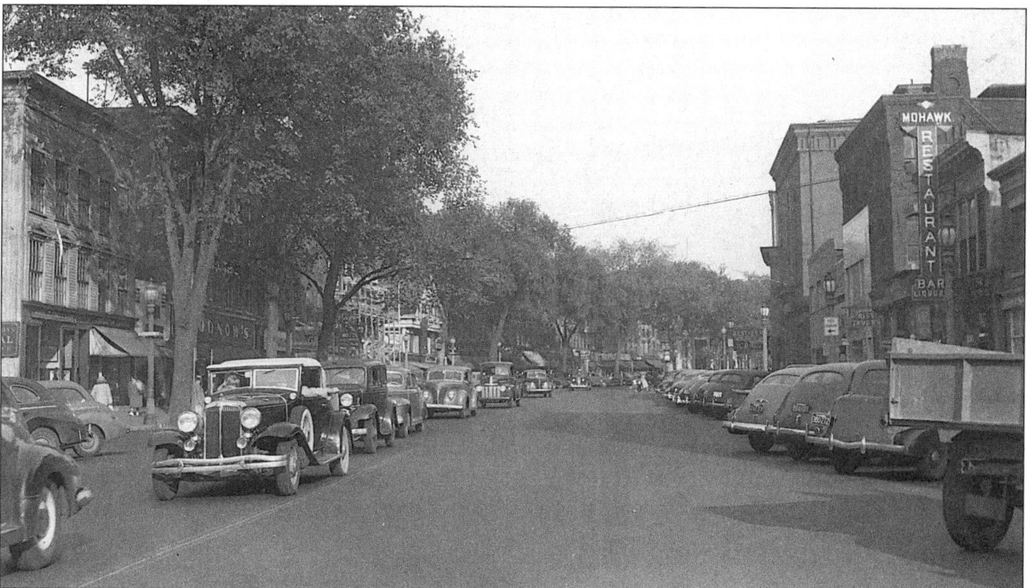

This photograph was taken *c.* 1947, looking east on Main Street near the intersection of Chapman Street. A mixture of restaurants, shops, and hotels made for a busy place in the years immediately following World War II.

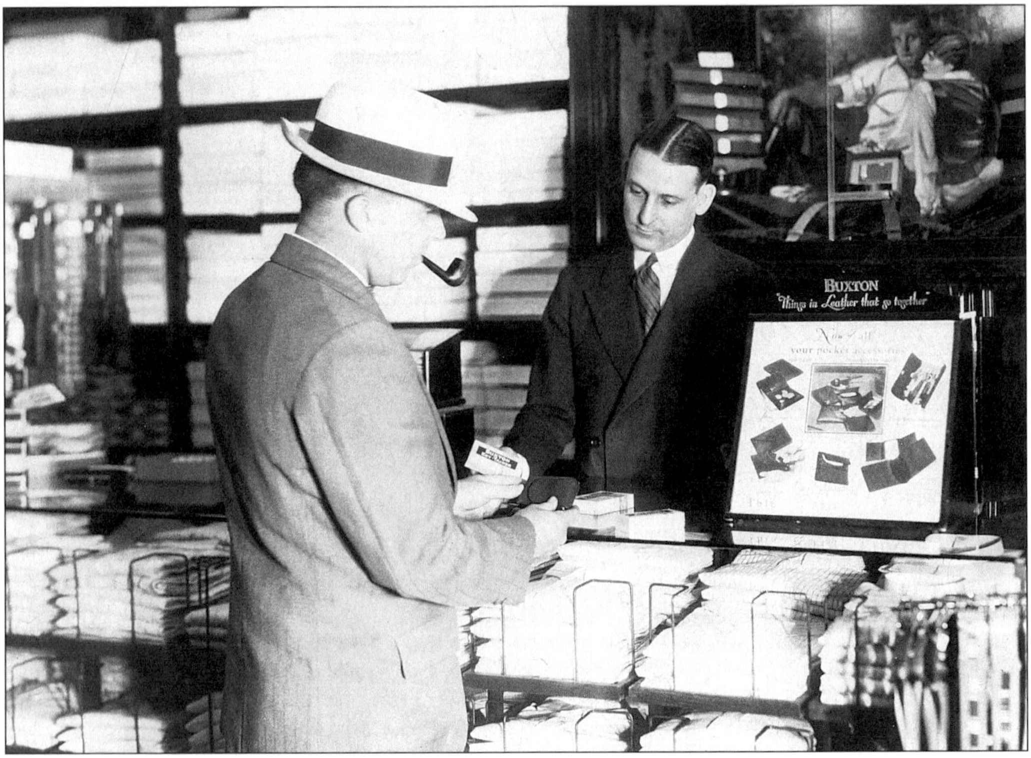

Forest Dimond, a longtime employee of H.G. Carson (later Michelman & Carson's Clothing Store), helps a customer in August 1926. The store was located at 242 Main Street.

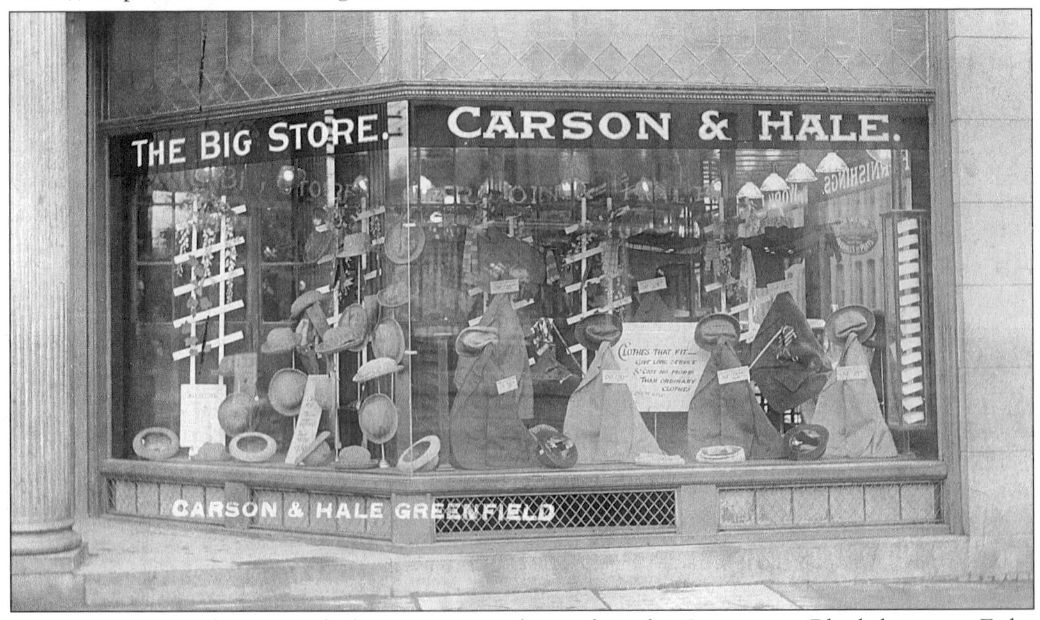

The Carson & Hale men's clothing store was located in the Davenport Block between Fiske Avenue and Miles Street. It was later purchased by Barney J. Michelman and became Michelman & Carson Company. The label across the bottom of this 1910 print probably means that the negative was also used for an advertising postcard.

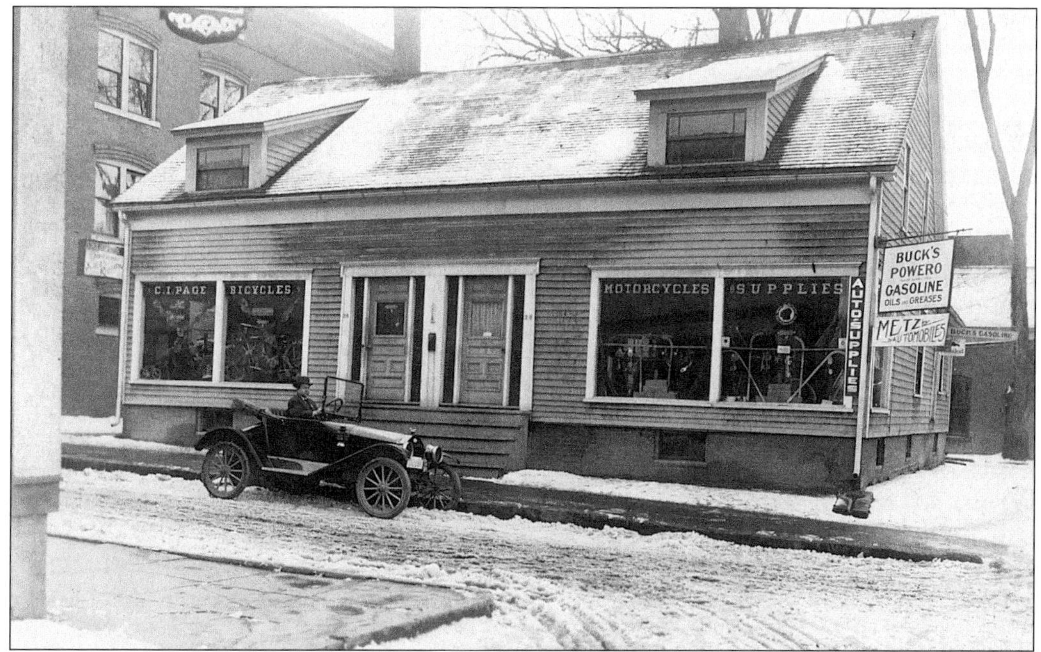

This photograph shows C.I. Page's Bicycle and Motorcycle Shop at the corner of School and Ames Streets. Charles Page was only in business selling bicycles and recharging batteries from *c.* 1917 to 1919. Metz Automobiles were manufactured in Waltham from 1909 to 1922. The site is now a parking lot for the Loyal Order of Moose building.

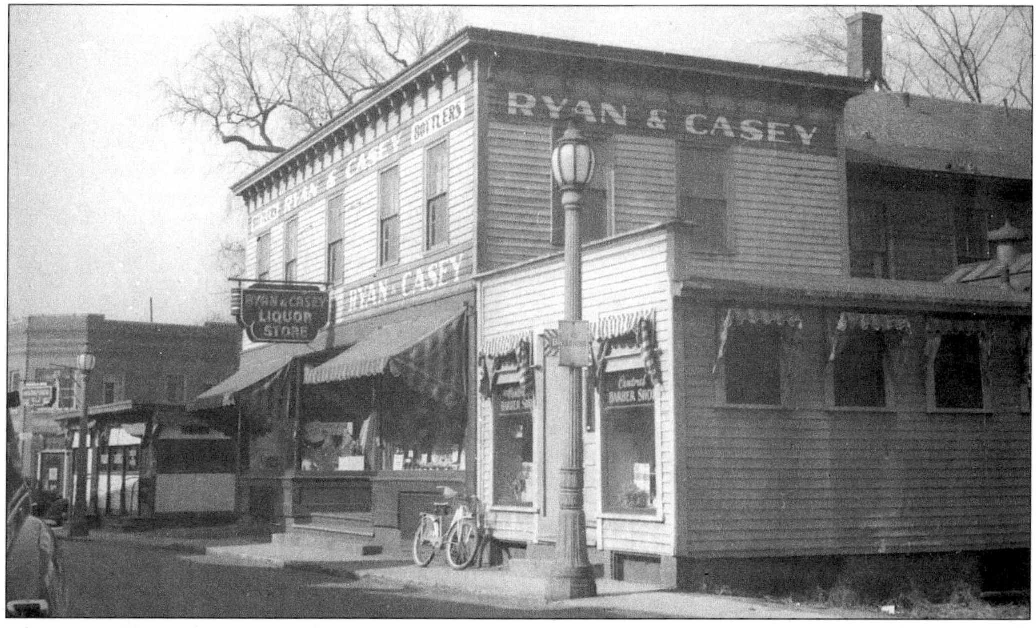

This *c.* 1940 view shows Ames Street before its buildings were razed for parking lots. From left to right are Frank's Lunch, Ryan & Casey Liquor Store (still in business elsewhere in town), and the Central Barber Shop (Harold Carrier, barber). In 1999, the town of Greenfield installed some new streetlights, similar to the one seen in the foreground, as part of a "streetscape" program.

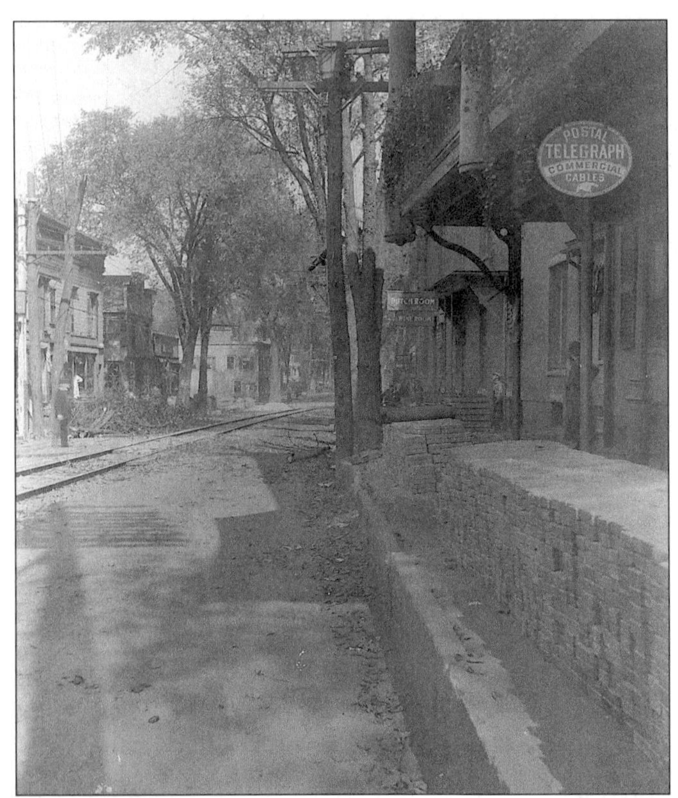

Here are before and after shots of the paving of the southern end of Federal Street, *c.* 1900. Note the workers on the sidewalk in the "before" photograph. The level of the street was raised dramatically, meaning the trolley tracks had to taken up then re-laid. In some towns, the cost of this type of change put trolley companies out of business.

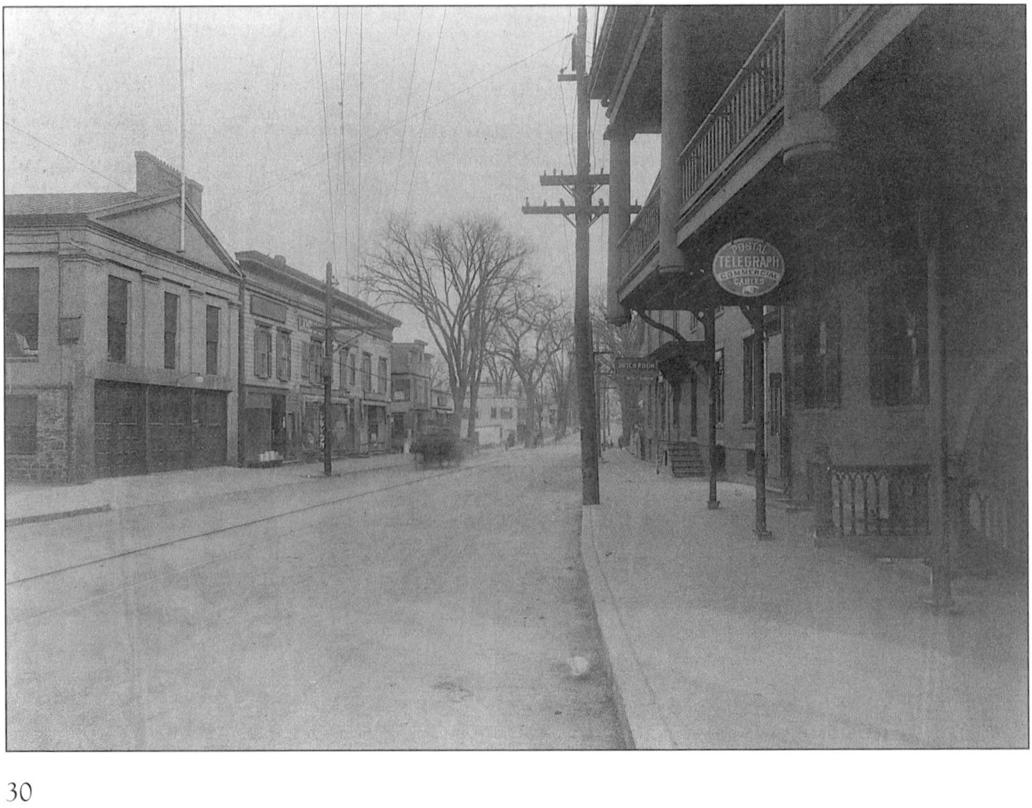

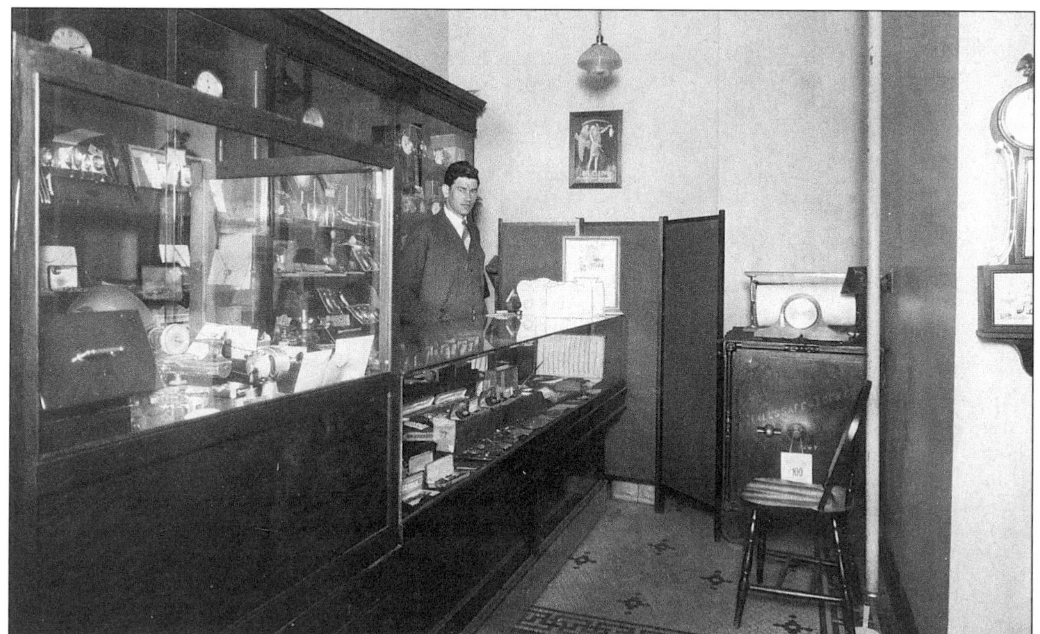

James E. Cleary, in business for more than 52 years, stands at the counter of his jewelry store on Main Street. On a whim, he carefully inset two gold rings in the sidewalk in front of his store. The rings are still there.

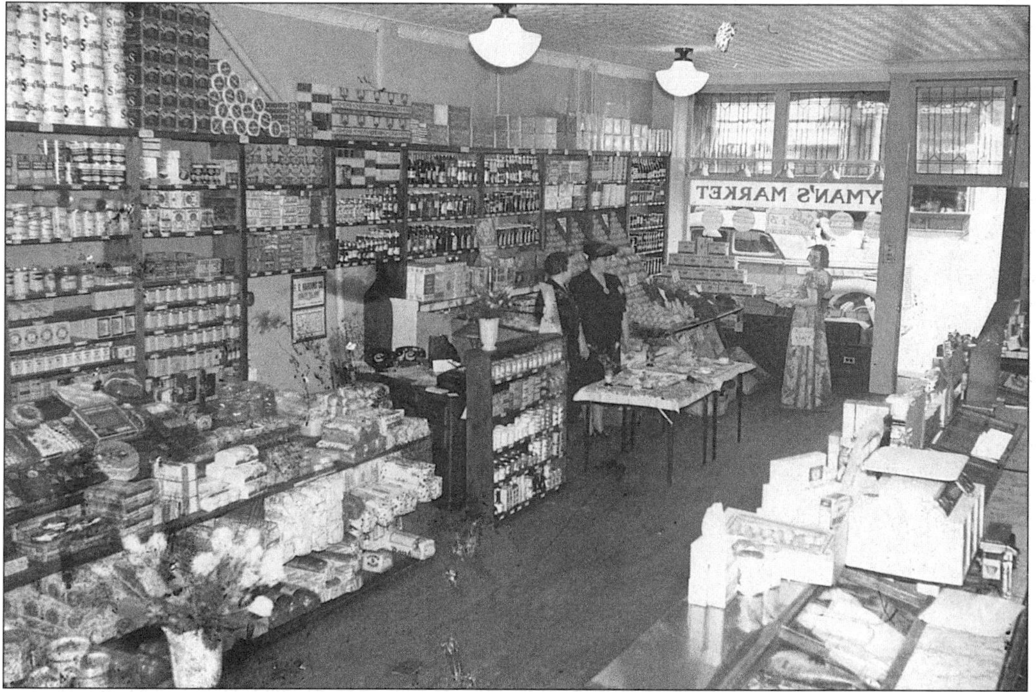

This photograph was taken as a merchandise promotion at Lyman's Market on Federal Street, c. 1940. Pearl Tanner, wearing a hat, helps Eva Baker Lyman serve snacks. What appears to be a girl in the front of the store is a poster advertising Kraft cheese. Note that all goods are behind the counter to be retrieved by a clerk. Self-service was not yet a common method of retailing.

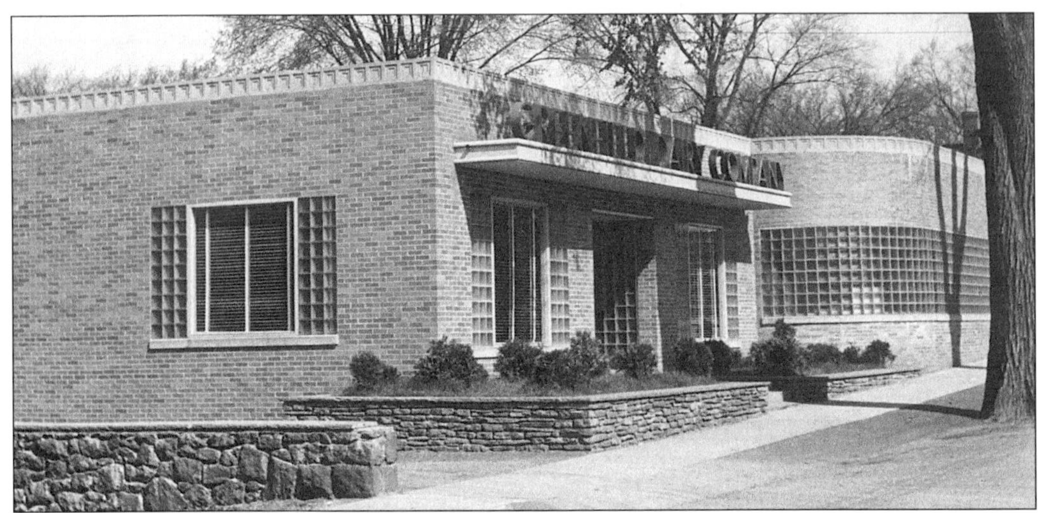

The Greenfield Dairy Company on School Street provided home delivery of milk, manufactured Snow's Ice Cream, and contained a restaurant. The company gradually dropped parts of its business, and today it only makes ice cream for wholesale. The building was designed by architect James Britton of Greenfield. Note the glass block walls in this 1946 photograph.

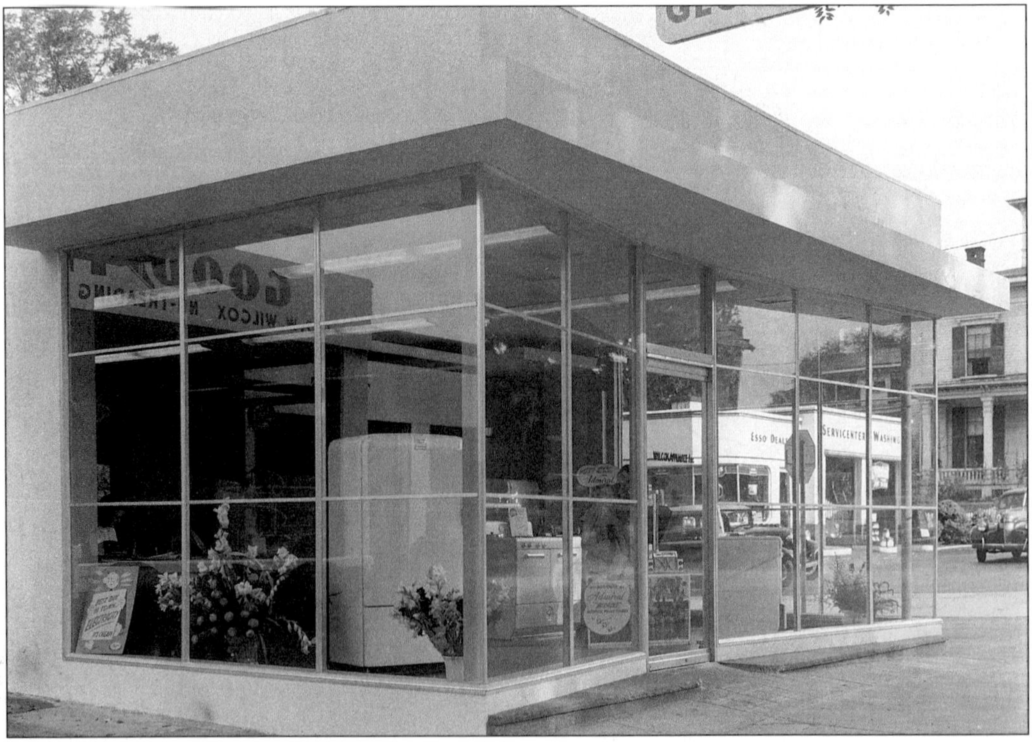

This building at the corner of Pleasant and Federal Streets was designed by James Britton. Built in the 1940s, it had Denny's Sandwich Shop as an early occupant . At the time of this late 1940s photograph, George W. Wilcox had several businesses on this site, including the appliance shop seen here, a service station for the Buick automobile dealership, and a tire repair shop. Behind the Esso Servicenter is the Baptist church parish house, formerly the home of Theodore Leonard.

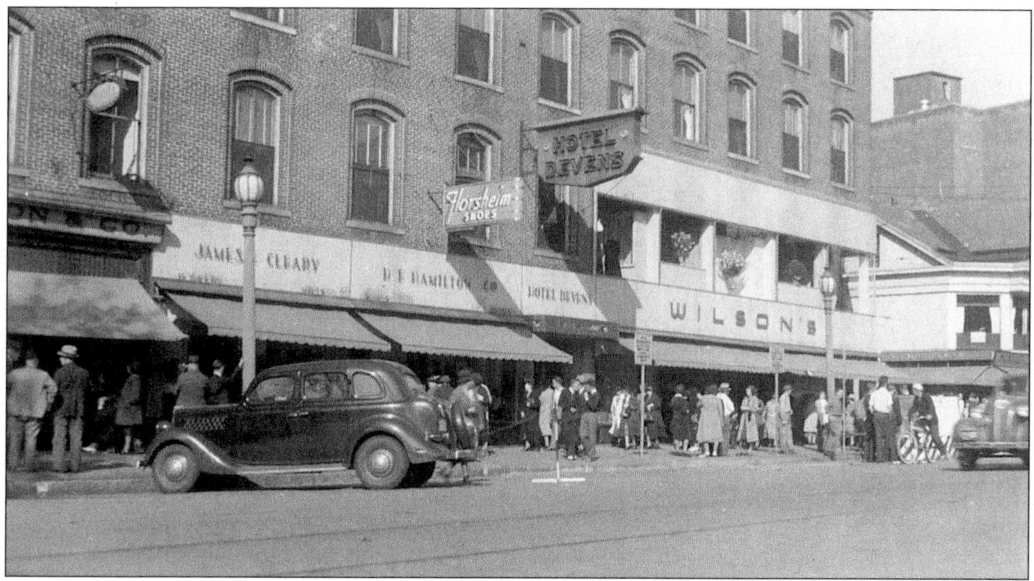

This 1947 photograph shows two veteran shops that are still in business: Cleary's Jewelry and Wilson's Department Store. The Hotel Devens and the Hamilton shoe store no longer exist.

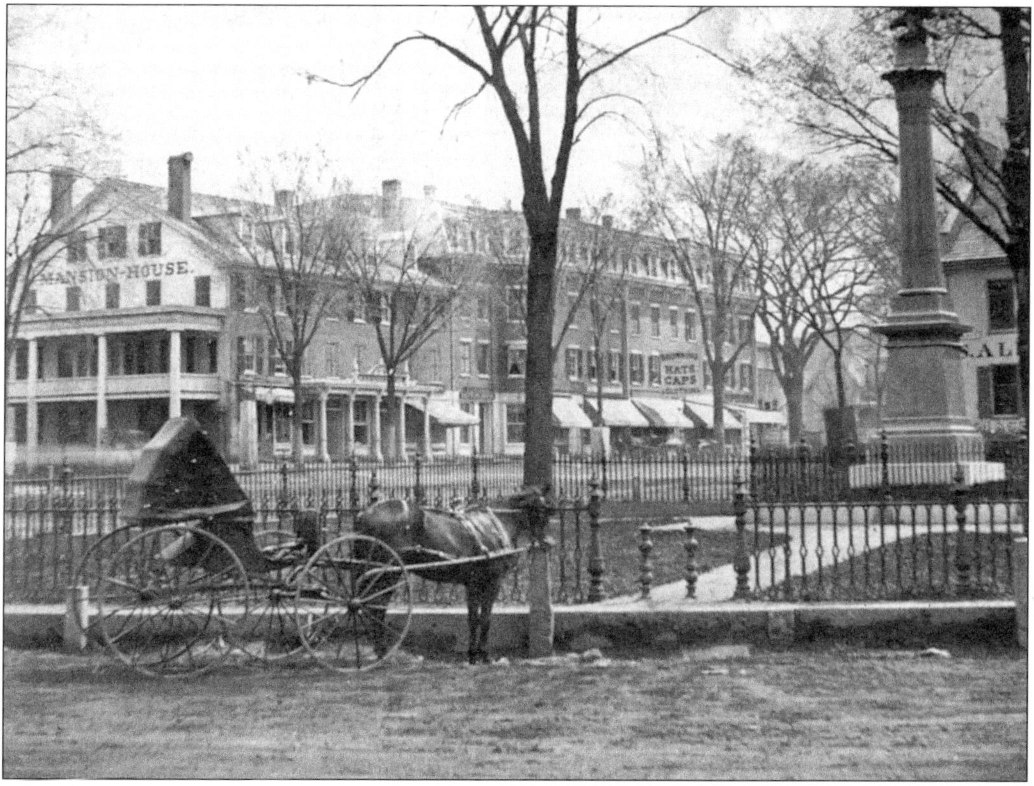

This photograph was taken looking northeast across the town common *c.* 1872. Note the older and newer sections of the Mansion House and the elaborate fencing around the common.

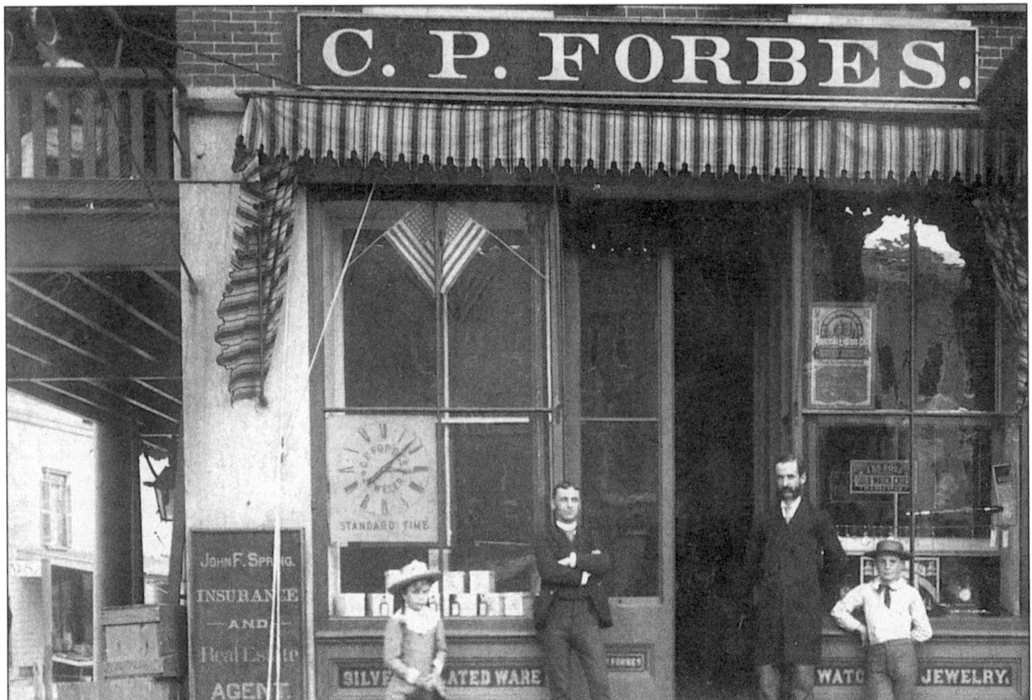

This *c.* 1880 photograph shows, from left to right, an unidentified girl, Fred L. Gaines, Charles P. Forbes, and Theodore C. Forbes. The C.P. Forbes Store was located in the Mansion House from *c.* 1865 to 1959. During the 1890s, Theodore C. Forbes added cameras and photographic supplies to the business. Today, Willett "Bill" Forbes owns and operates the camera and framing business in a shop farther west on Main Street. His children, the fifth generation in the business, sometimes work in the shop.

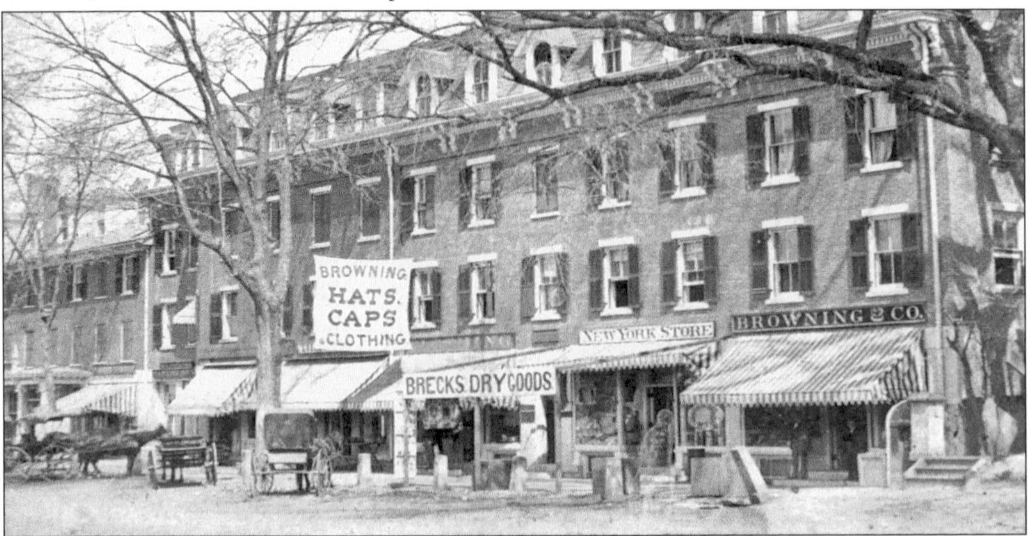

This 1873 stereograph shows the eastern end of the Mansion House, which was completely finished before the top section of the west end was built. Unlike many motels along the interstate highways today, small-town hotels were a mixture of retail shops, offices, restaurants, and guest rooms.

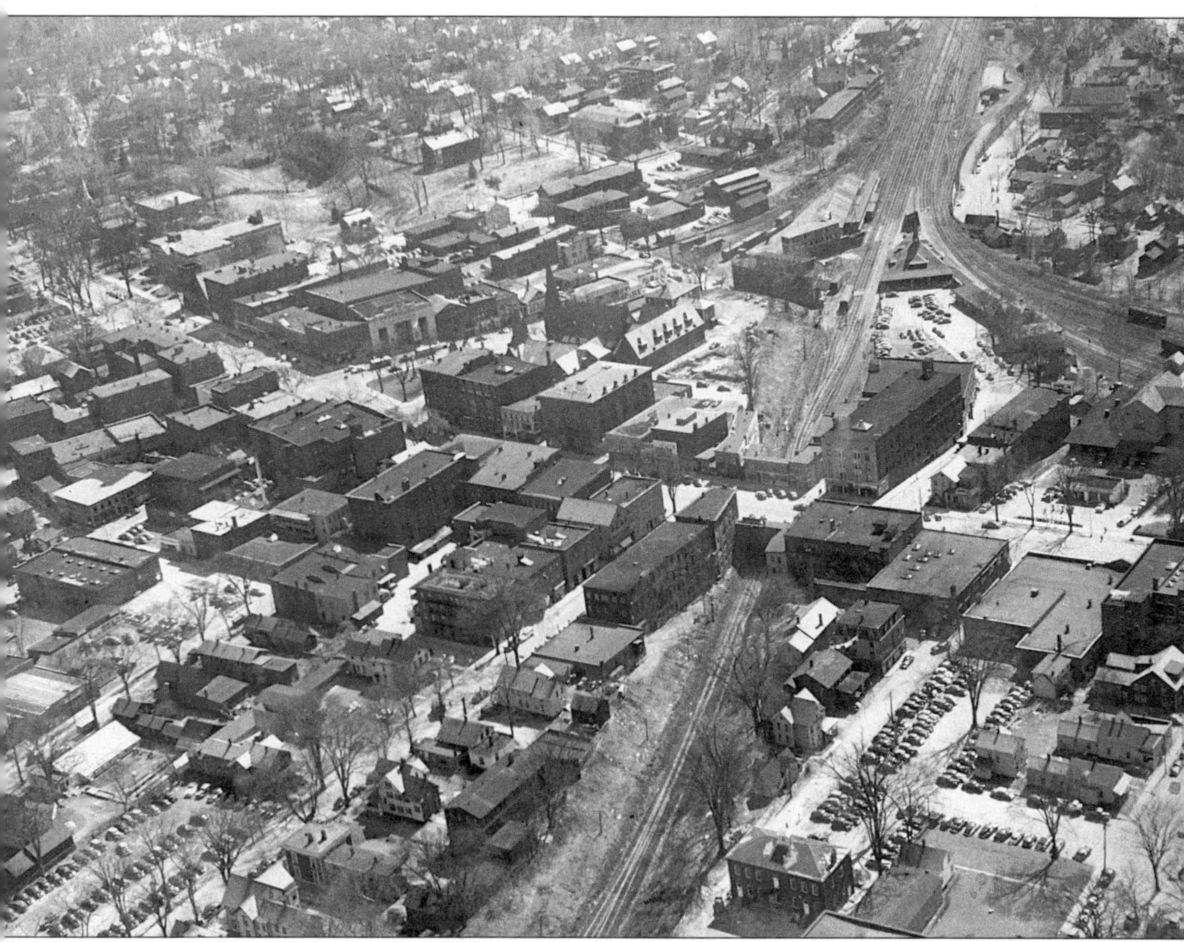

This aerial view of downtown in the late 1930s shows the main line tracks of the Boston & Maine Railroad running north and south. It also shows the railroad's western route (upper right), the rail yard of the Franklin Lumber Company, and the railroad station. Note how buildings on Main Street are built above the tunnel.

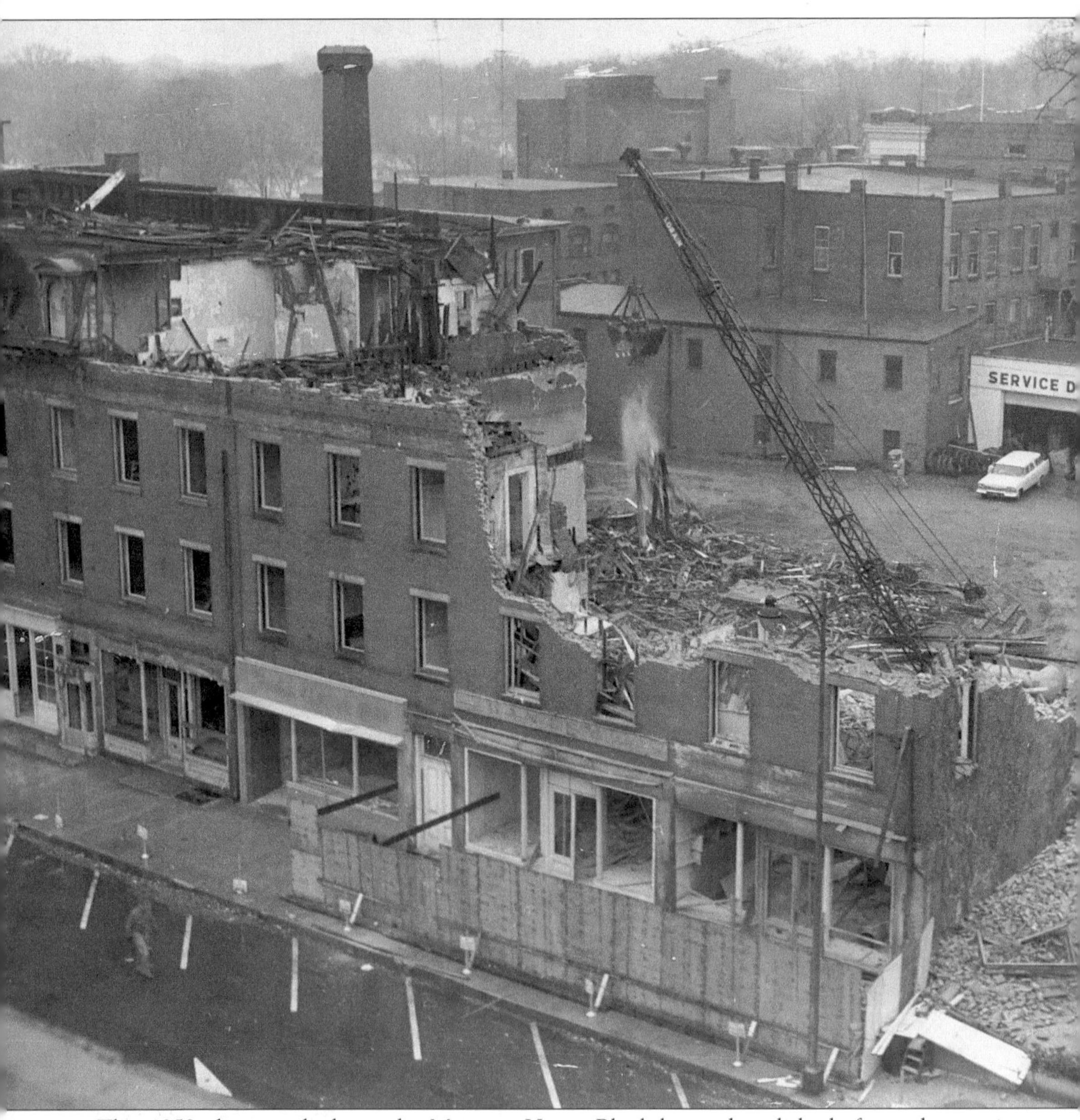

This 1959 photograph shows the Mansion House Block being demolished after a devastating fire on January 9, 1959. Parts of the block had stood on this site between Federal Street and the present Greenfield Public Library since the early 1800s. At its peak, the block contained a hotel on the top three floors and at least six street-level businesses. Until this fire, the commercial heart of Greenfield was located at the Federal and Main Street intersection. After the fire, the focus drifted west on Main Street. With the exception of one structure, the Levy Building at the corner of Federal and Ames Streets, all buildings in this photograph have been torn down. In the 1990s, there was renewed interest in the downtown area, with new shops opening.

Two

COMMUNITY LIFE

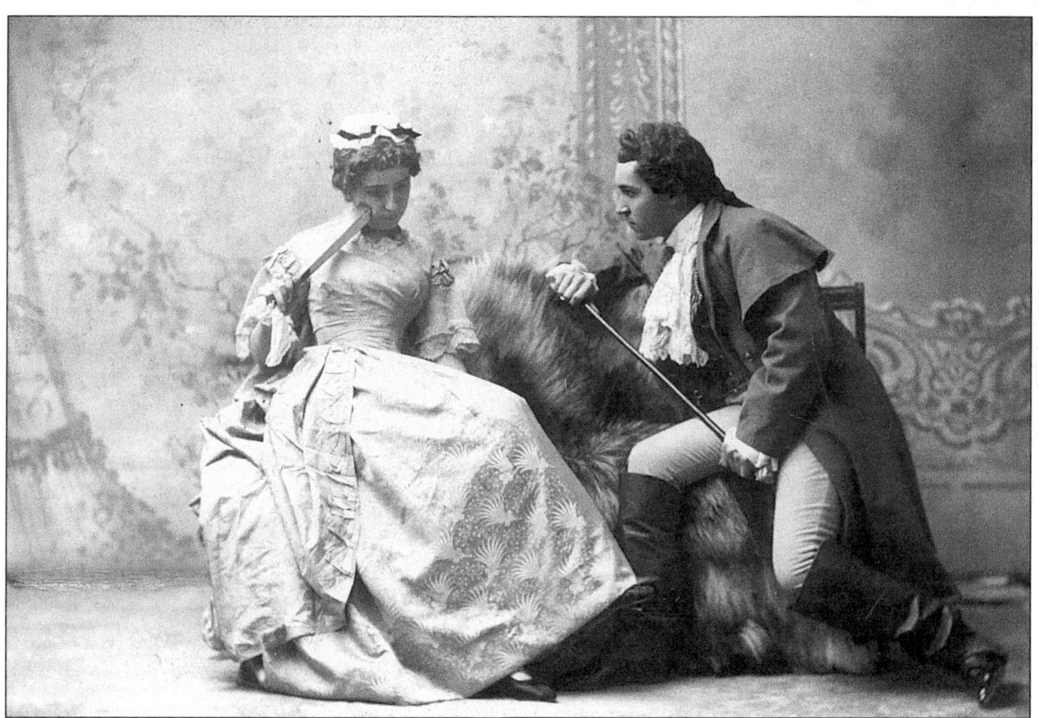

The Greenfield Comedy Club produced *She Stoops to Conquer* for the 1895–96 season at Washington Hall. Annie E. Potter and Albert L. Hall were two of the stars.

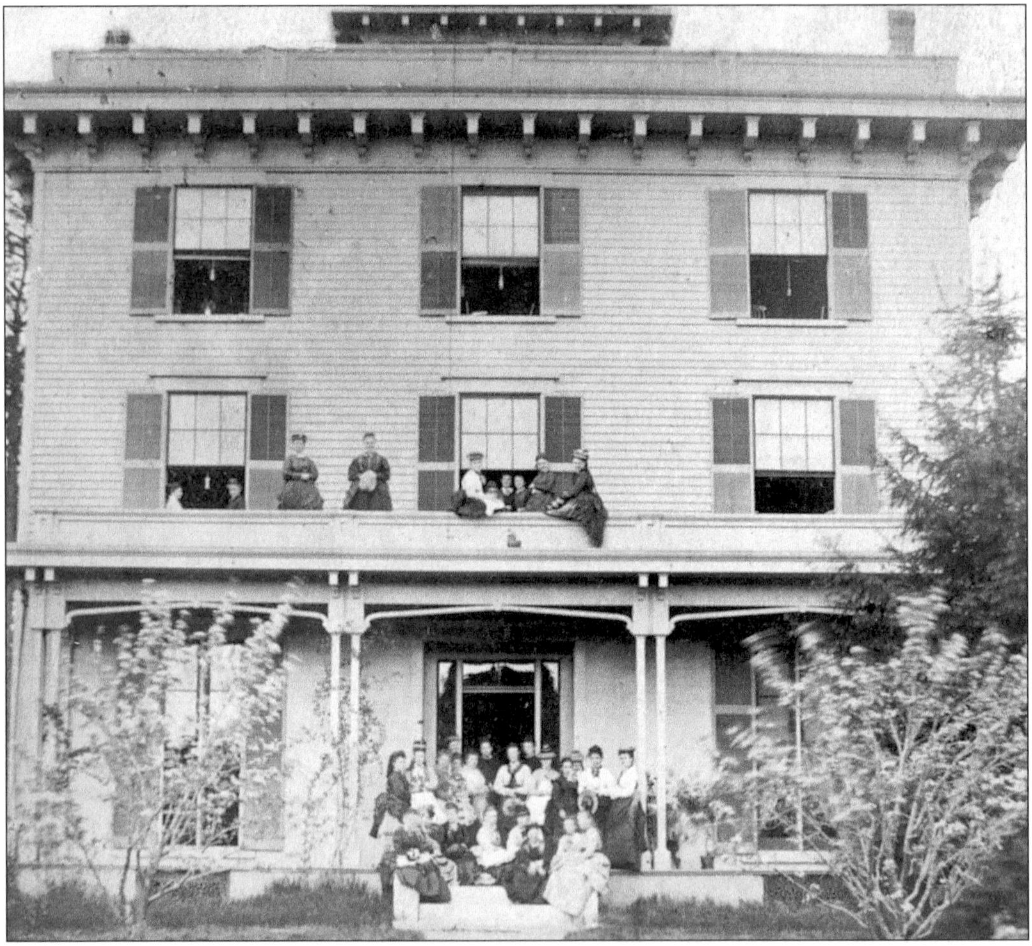

Here is Prospect Hill School for Girls on what is now Armory Street. Formerly the home of D.H. Carpenter, the building was converted to a school in 1868. It was well equipped with classrooms, a library, a chemistry lab, and a "room for light gymnastics." The school offered a full range of subjects, including Greek, Latin, music, studio art, civil government, and moral science. This photograph dates from the 1880s. This building still survives; Stoneleigh Burnham School is a descendent of Prospect Hill.

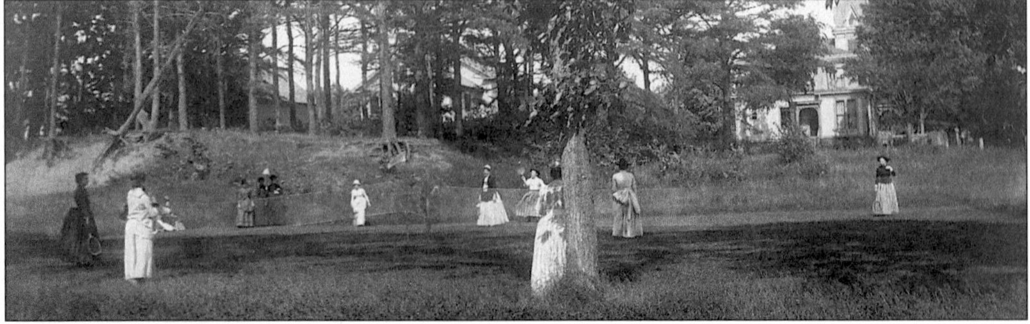

This photograph shows students of the Prospect Hill School for Girls playing tennis sometime in the 1880s. Note the girls' formal attire. In the background is the Solon Wiley House, which still stands, at 60 Congress Street.

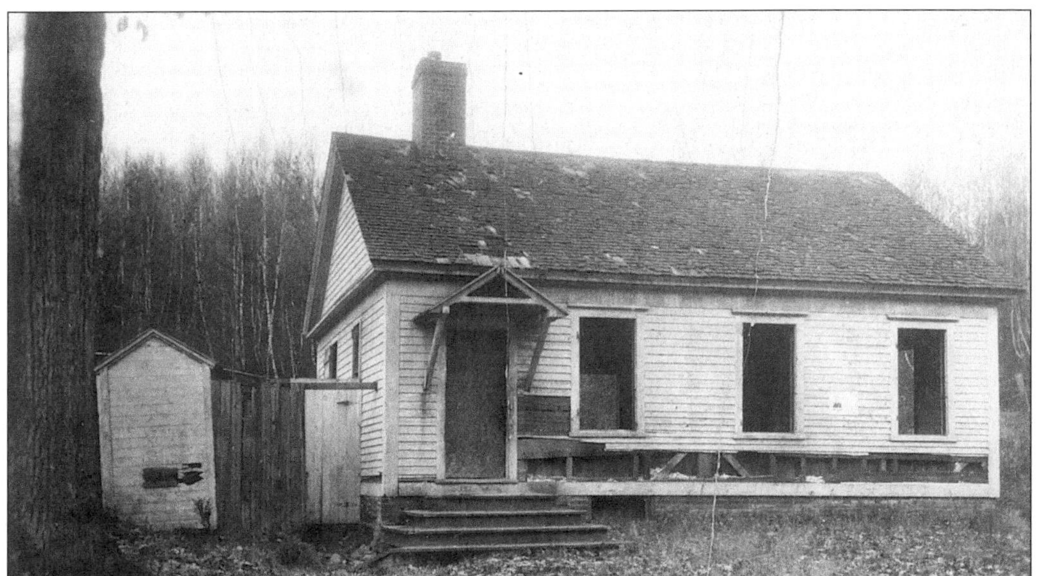

The Factory Hollow District Schoolhouse, in use from 1837 to 1922, was located on the north side of Gill Road, east of Lampblack Road. The building was damaged by fire, as seen in this 1926 photograph. Note the attached privy to the left. The school was located on the side of the present French King Highway (Route 2A). Joel Merriam donated the land for the school and after the building was demolished, the land reverted to his heirs.

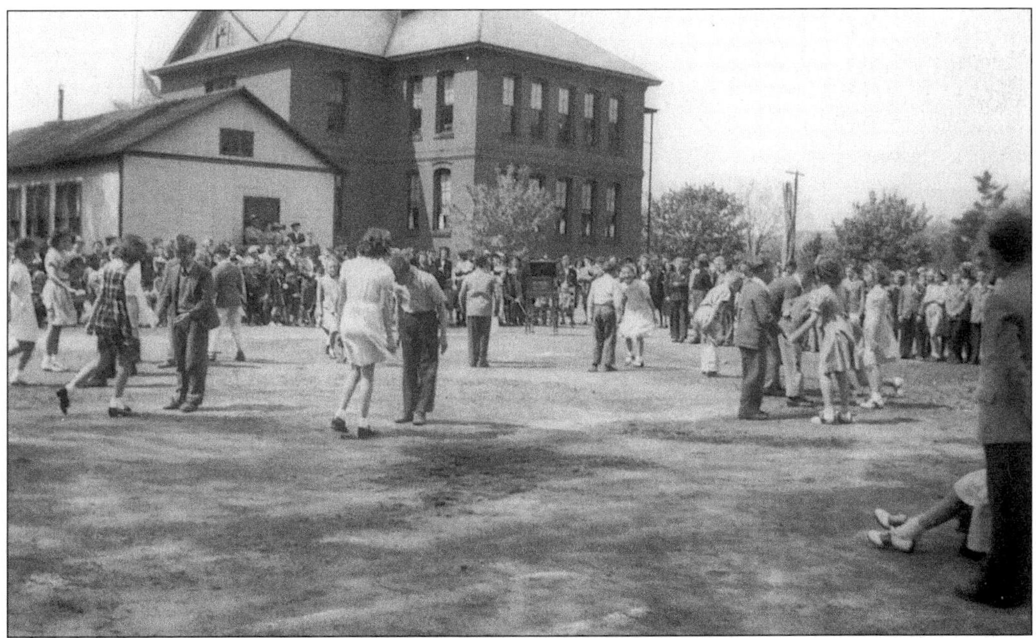

Celebrating May Day are these fourth graders at the old Four Corners School on Bernardston Road, currently the location of the Burger King restaurant. This photograph was taken in 1945. The wooden building on the left housed the kindergarten classroom.

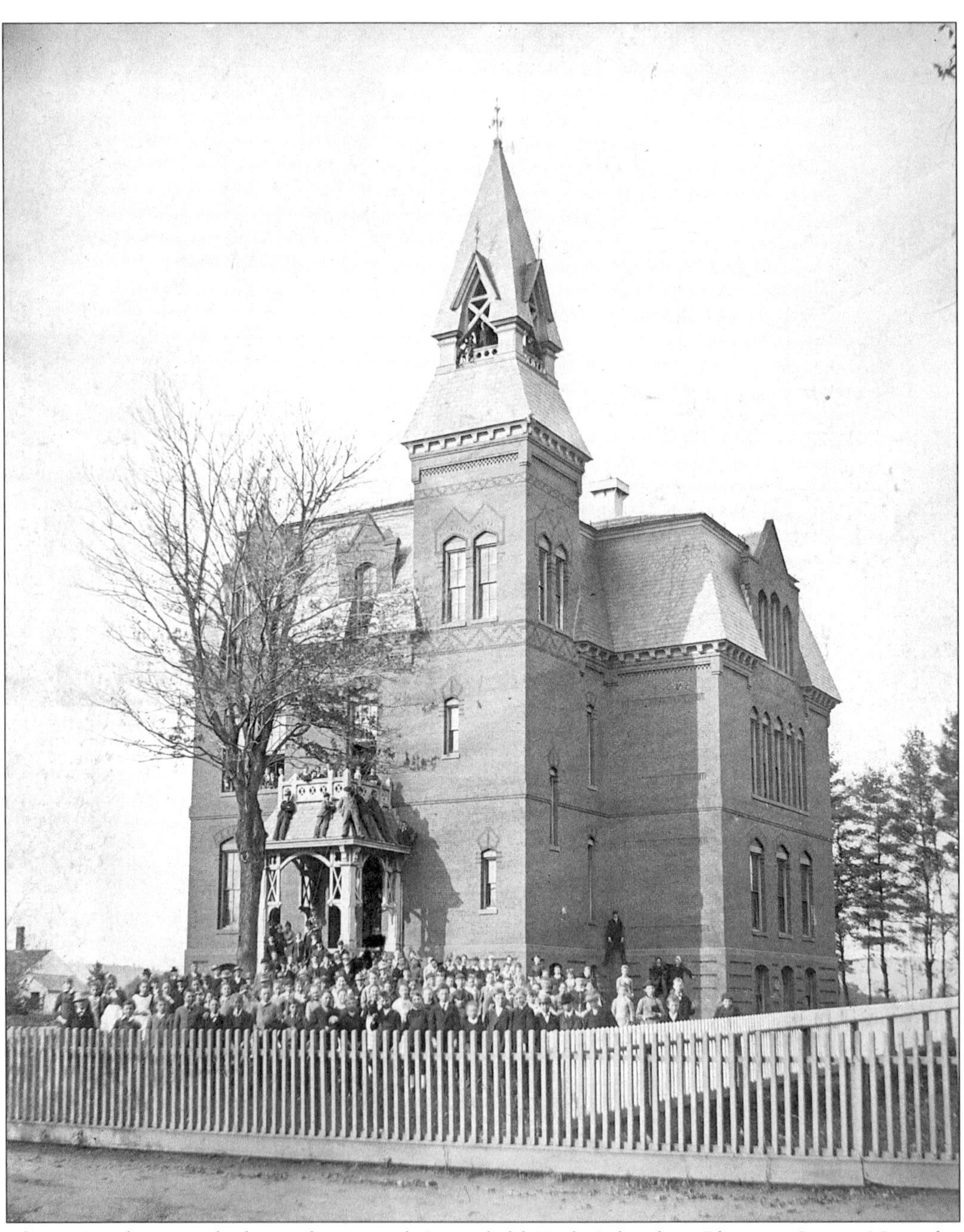

This 1873 photograph shows the second Greenfield High School on Pleasant Street. Note the children in the tower and on the front porch roof. Eventually, the Davis Street School and the School Street schools were added to this large lot. By the early 1950s, the town was using the third floor as a gymnasium and the rest of the building was used for nonschool purposes. Of the schools in this complex, only the Davis Street School remains today.

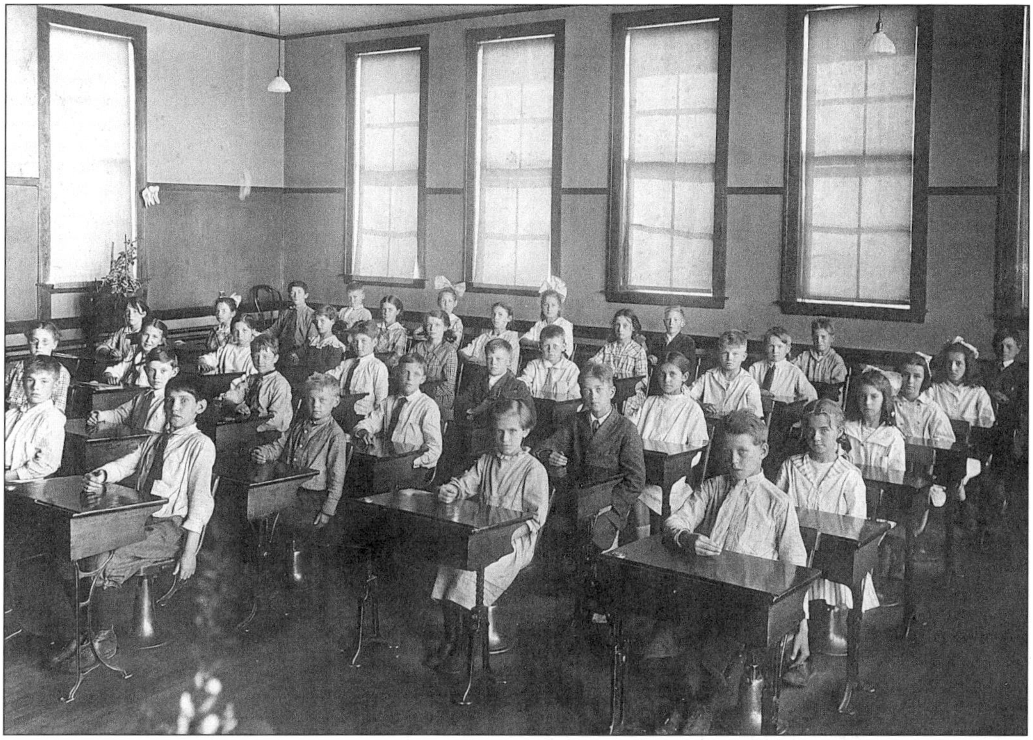

This photograph of an unidentified class of elementary school students was taken *c.* 1910. Note the lack of decoration in the room, the straight lines of desks, and the large bows worn by the girls in the back row.

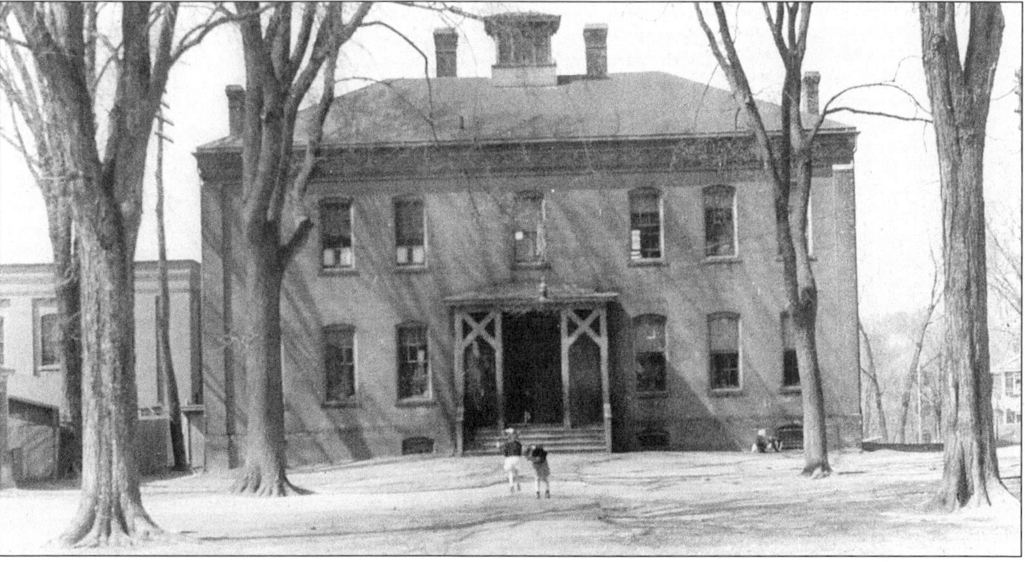

This *c.* 1890 photograph shows the Main Street Elementary School on a large lot that extended along Wells Street to Main Street. To the left is the Goodell-Pratt tool company administration building. When the school was sold, the Main Street section was sold off for commercial building lots. The much earlier Fellenberg Academy grounds were here or slightly to the east. The building now houses American Legion Post 81.

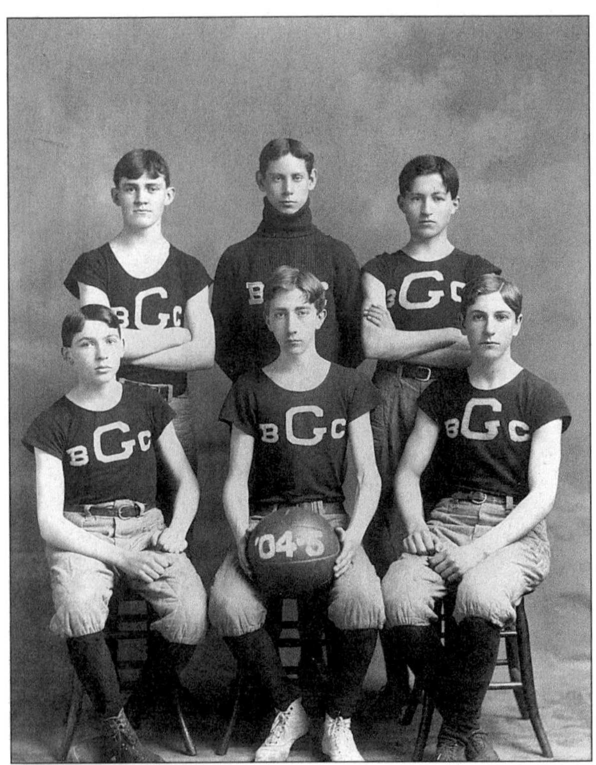

Members of the Greenfield Boy's Club basketball team of 1904–05 pose for this photograph. They are, from left to right, as follows: (front row) James Harrington, Charles McCarthy, and ? Murphy; (back row) George M. Sauter, James Sullivan, and James Burke.

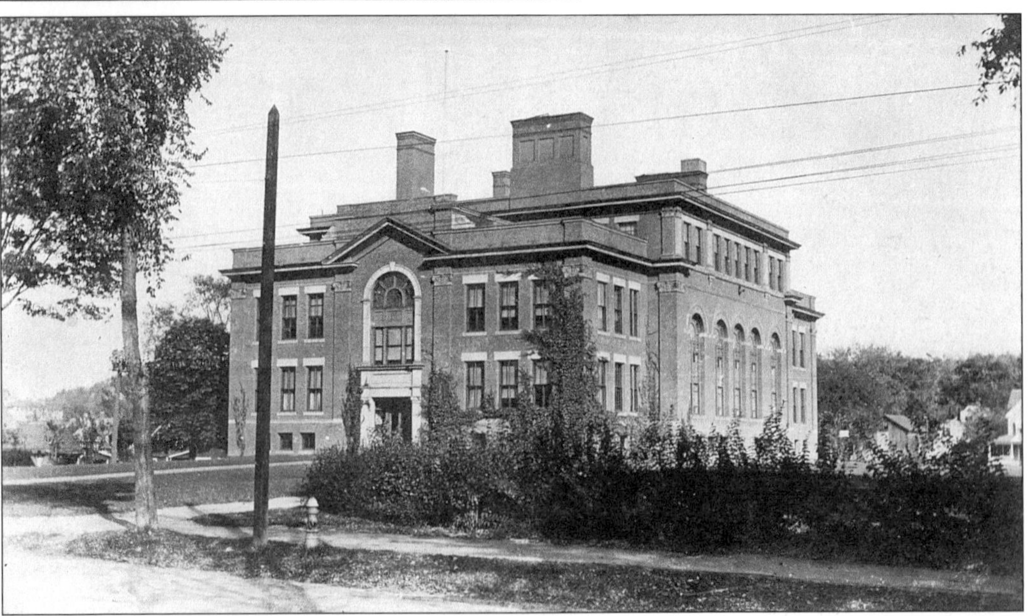

This school building on Federal Street, shown *c.* 1930, has a complicated history. Built in 1895 as the third Greenfield High School, it burned in 1904. Soon rebuilt and enlarged, it served as the Greenfield Junior High School from 1924 to 1958 and an elementary school from 1958 to 1962. From 1962 to 1974, it was the original home of Greenfield Community College. In 1974, it reverted to an elementary school, called Federal Street North. In 1990, it was joined by a new wing to Federal Street South Elementary School.

This senior class photograph of Herman Walker (1907–1985) was taken in 1925. Walker was a busy boy with a gift of gab, according to his yearbook notes. His fellow students said he "could talk a Ford into becoming a member of the Rolls-Royce class." Walker operated funeral homes in the towns of Warren and West Brookfield. His son, David Walker, owns Walker Funeral Home on High Street.

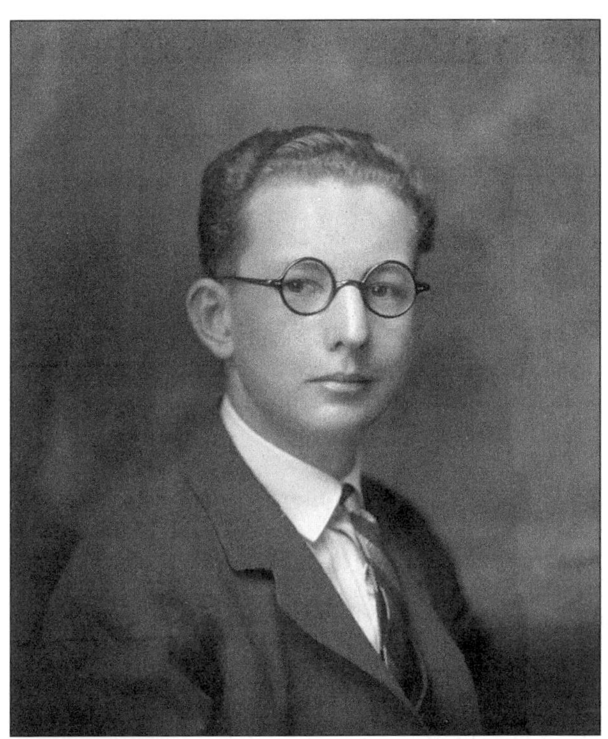

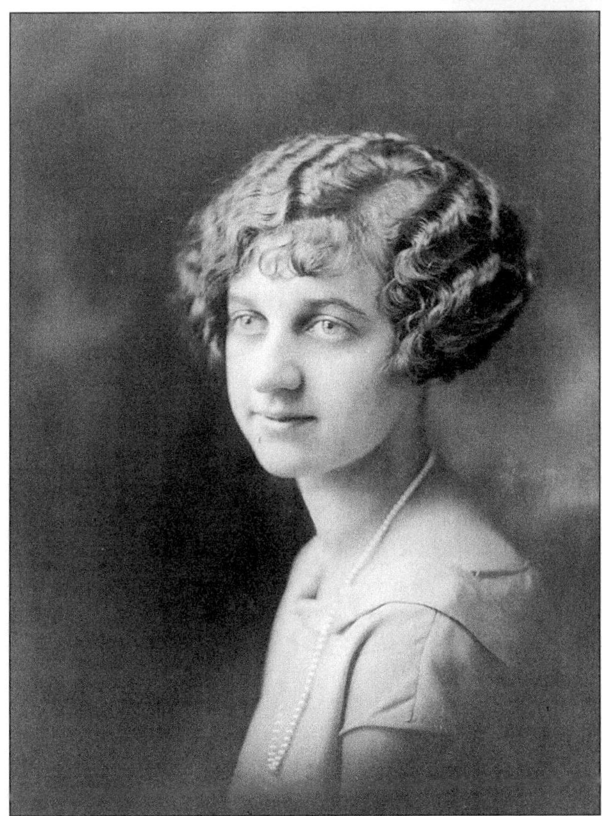

This photograph of Evelyn Florence Benson (1904–?) was taken in 1925 when she graduated from Greenfield High School. Her envious schoolmates wrote in her yearbook notes that she "travels to school rain or shine via the four-wheeled vehicle, which is a 'king' among cars." They hinted that she had a "well-off" boyfriend from Deerfield.

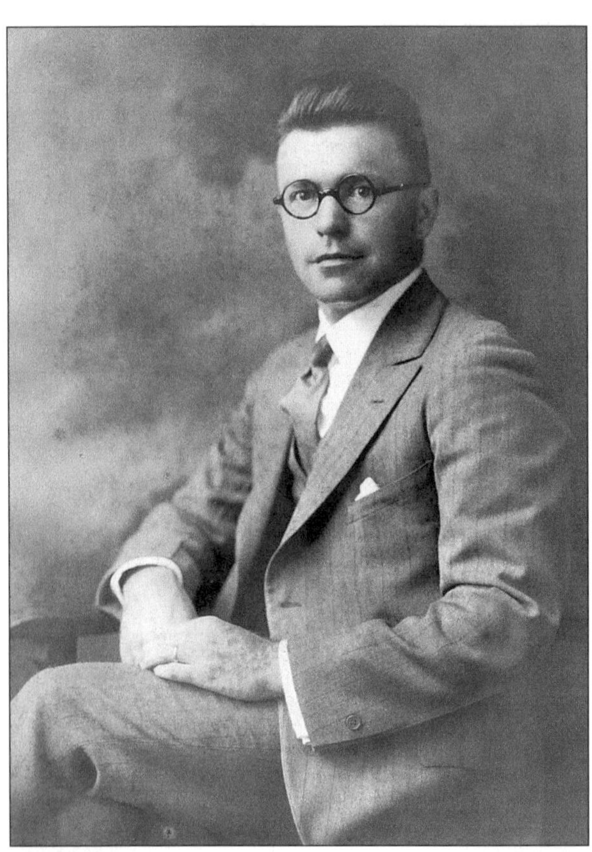

Benjamin C.L. Sander, a much beloved math teacher at Greenfield High School, died in 1960.

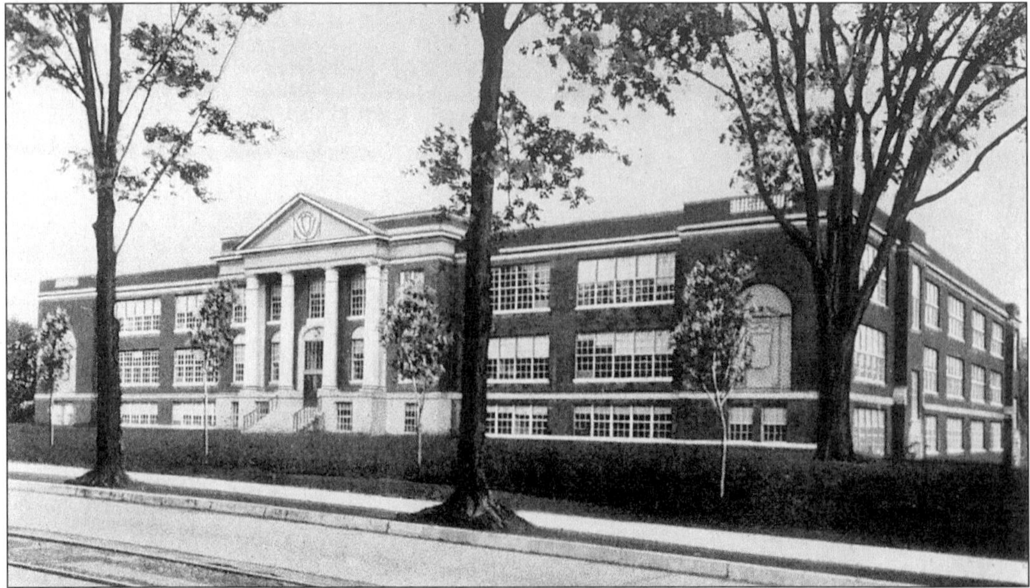

This is the fourth Greenfield High School, which was built on the site of the Sanderson Farm and the home of Anna Pierce Judah. Built in 1924, the school became the junior high in 1958 and was later renamed the Greenfield Middle School, for grades six through eight. The school was renovated in the early 1970s and again in 1998.

This photograph shows students in the machine shop at Greenfield High School in 1947. Students such as these two often went to work for Greenfield Tap & Die, Millers Falls Tool Company, or the Threadwell Company and were set with good jobs for life.

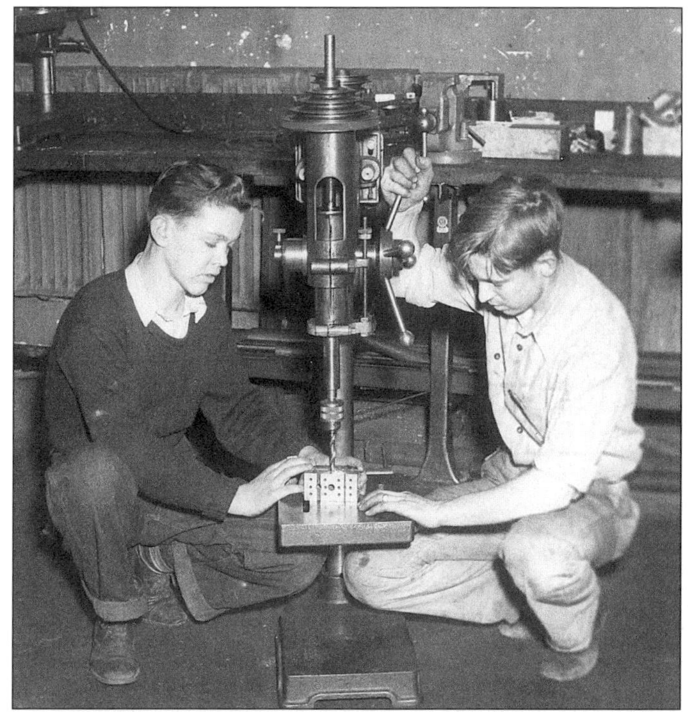

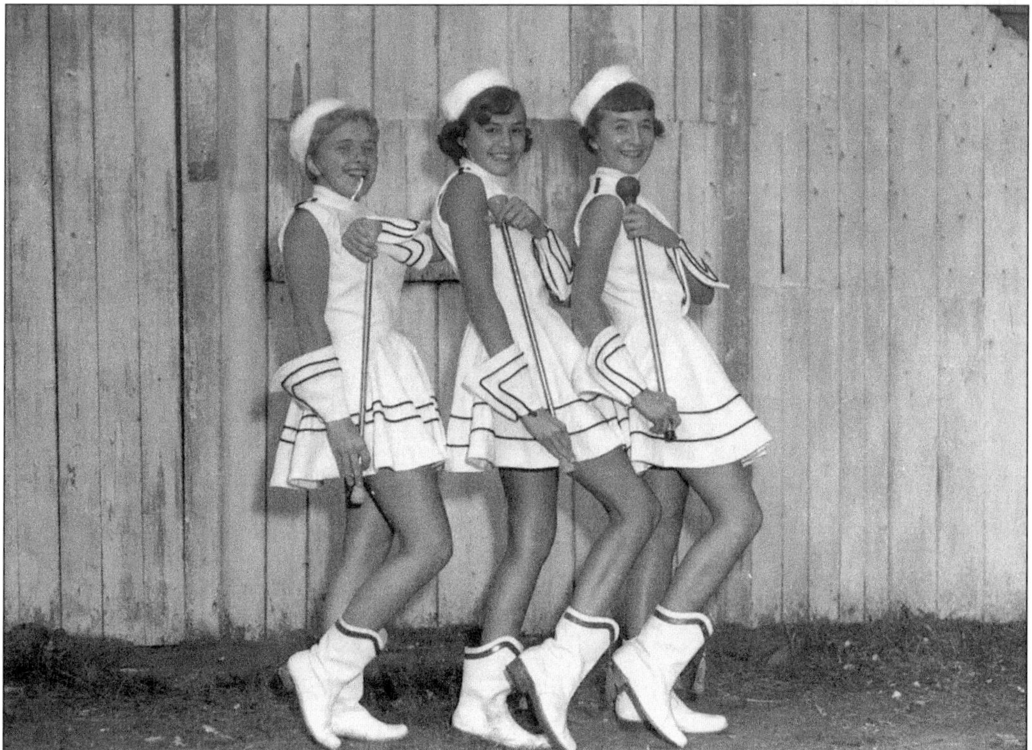

Three majorettes pose during one of the athletic competitions held between area high schools. These events were held at the Franklin County Fairgrounds during the 1940s.

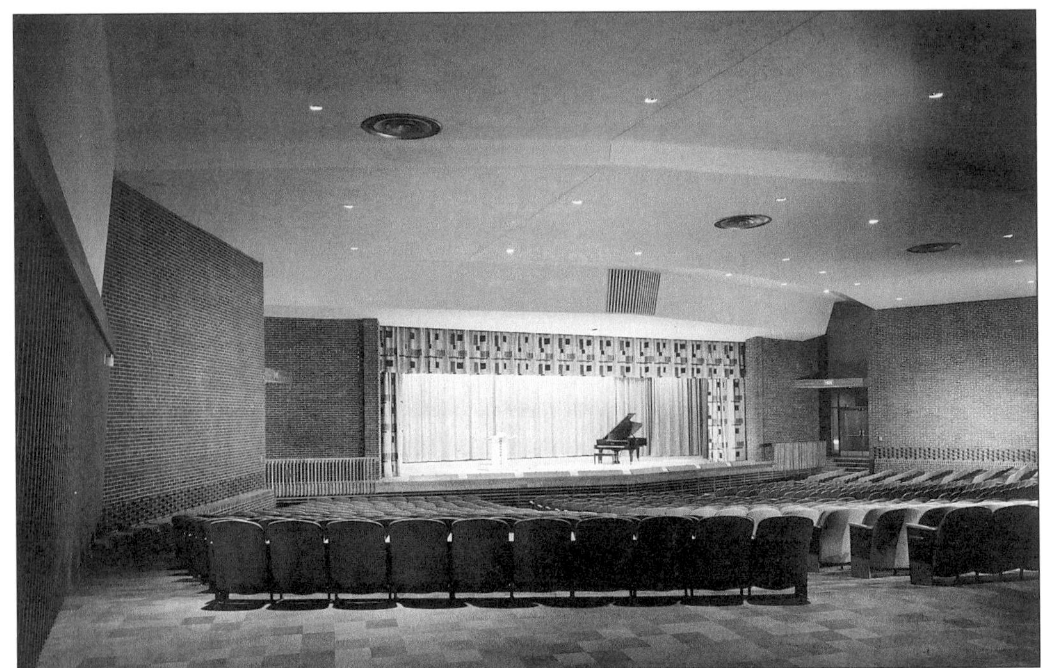

The Greenfield High School auditorium has been used since its construction in 1958 for a wide variety of community events, such as concerts by the Pioneer Valley Symphony, Jaycee Miss America pageants, and school plays. From 1958 to 1983, the auditorium also hosted the town's traditional New England-style town meetings. In 1983, Greenfield changed to a town manager-board of selectmen form of government.

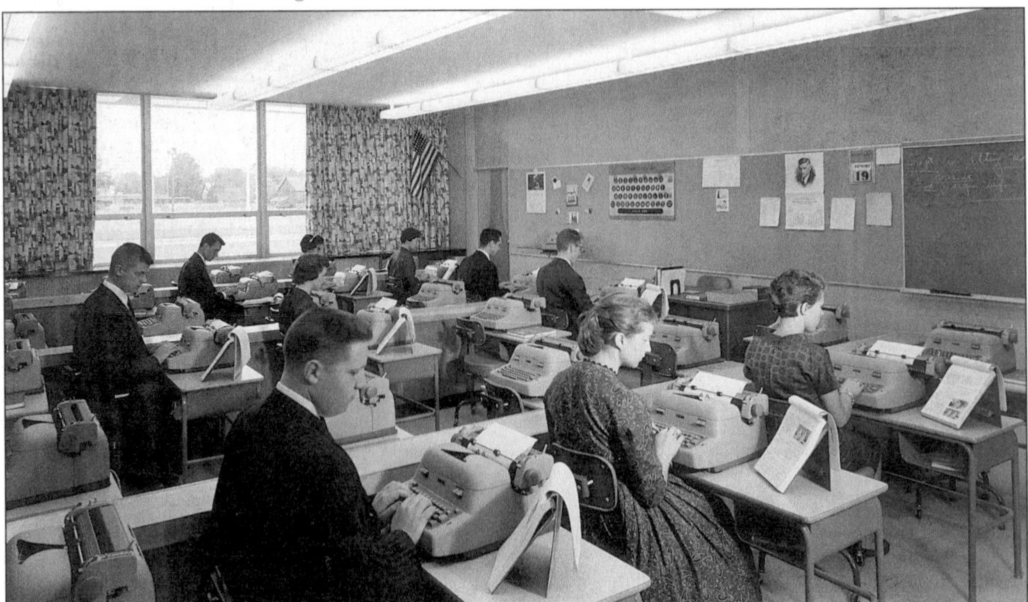

This carefully posed shot of a class at the recently built Greenfield High School on Silver Street was taken in 1958. It shows students learning to use up-to-date technology—electric typewriters. This is one of a series of publicity photographs taken for James Britton, the architect who designed the new school.

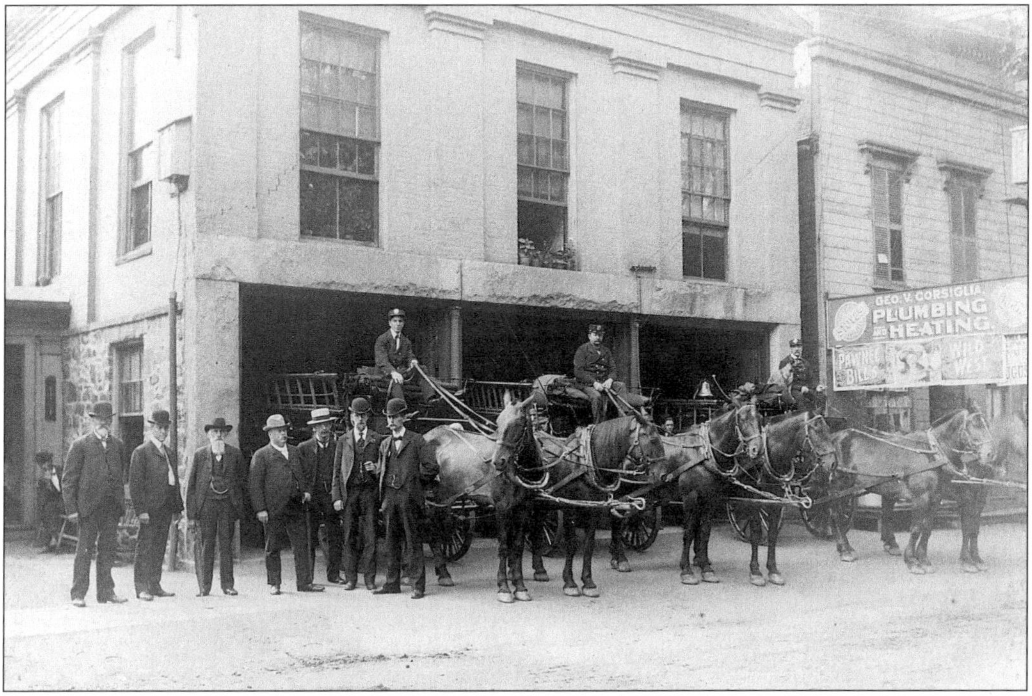

Three horse-drawn fire wagons wait in front of the old fire station on Federal Street. Note the poster advertising Pawnee Bill's Wild West show. This photograph dates from the 1890s.

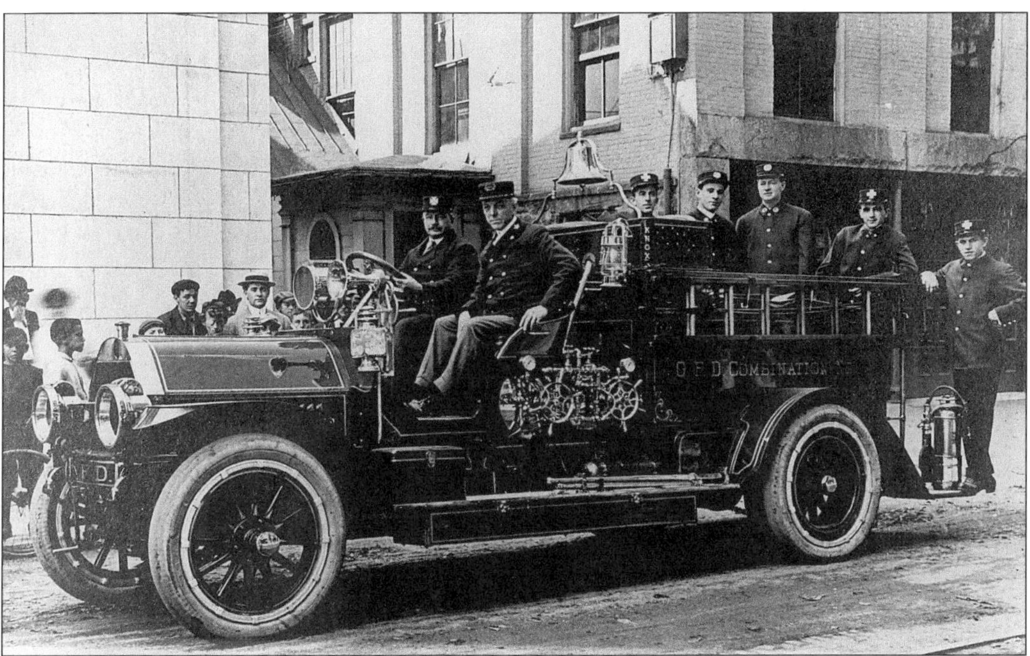

Greenfield's first mechanized fire truck was a 1909 Knox. It was used until 1921. Posing in front of the fire station on Federal Street are driver John C. Plumley and passenger Chief Philip Partenheimer, with the following men in back, from left to right: Frank Bulman, George Pfersick, Ed Harrison, Fred Rist, and George Patnode.

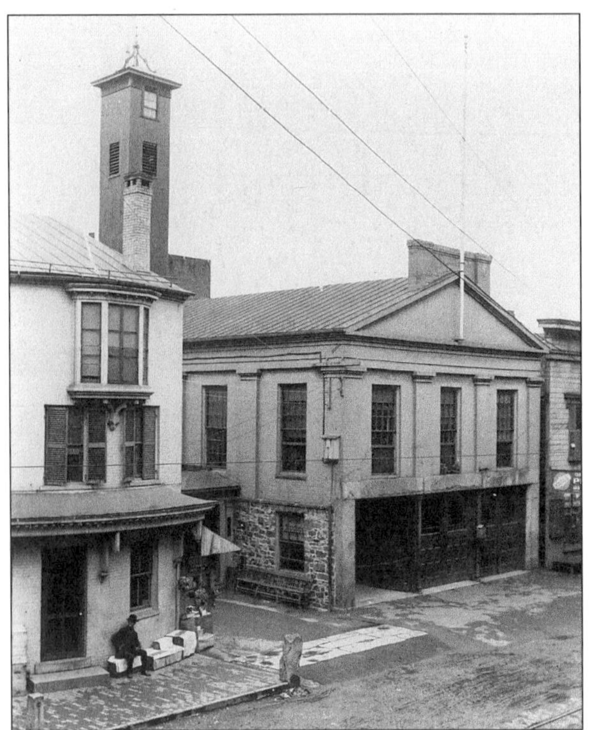

Greenfield's first fire station was originally built in 1849 by Henry Wells Clapp for use as Greenfield's first town hall. The building was converted to a fire station in 1854 when Washington Hall was constructed on Main Street. It remained a fire station until 1937. Shortly after the fire trucks were moved to the present location, the station was destroyed by fire. The new section of the Franklin Savings Institution replaced the station.

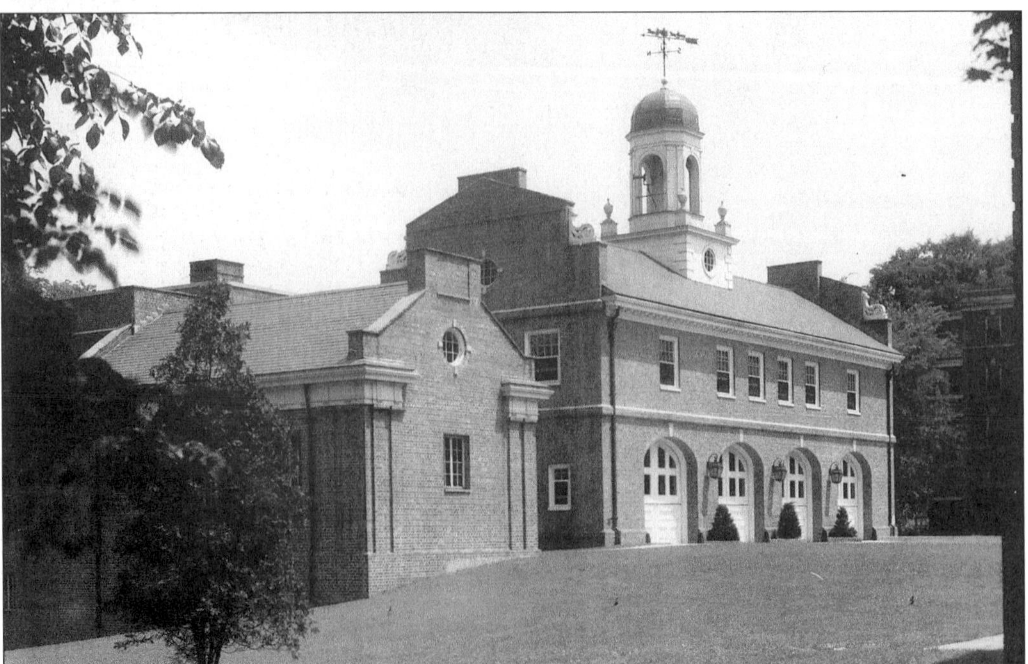

This 1937 view shows the second Greenfield Fire Station, designed by James Britton of Greenfield. On top of the cupola is a weather vane in the shape of a horse-drawn fire wagon, donated by Dr. John C. O'Brien. Housed in the cupola is an original 1800 Paul Revere bell, donated to the town by Daniel Wells. In 1999, a new wing was added on the east side to house a large ladder truck.

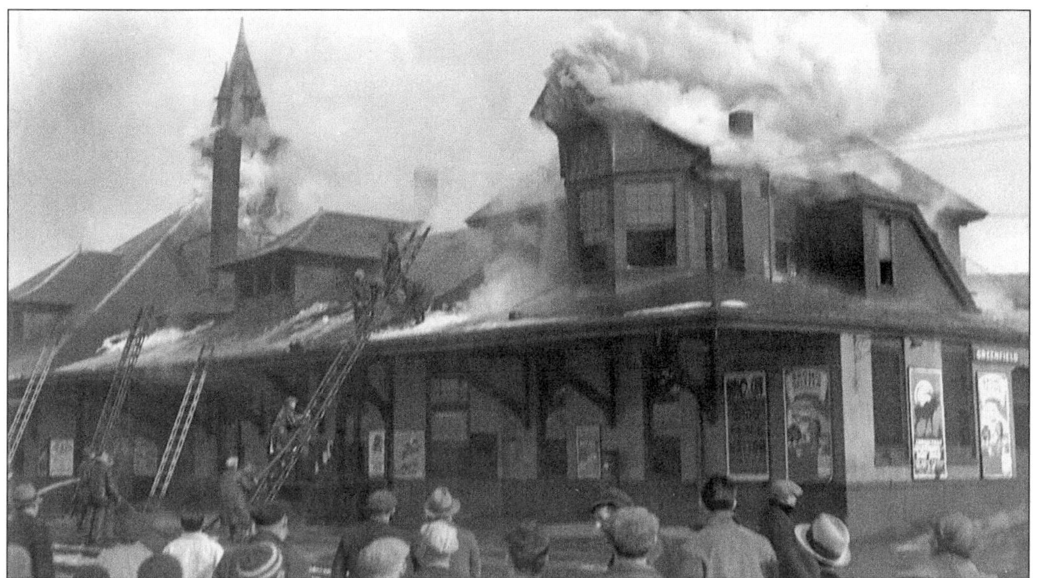

This photograph shows the Greenfield Fire Department in action at the southeastern corner of the railroad station on October 24, 1947. The original part of the station, built in 1881, was removed, but the remaining section continued to be used for some years.

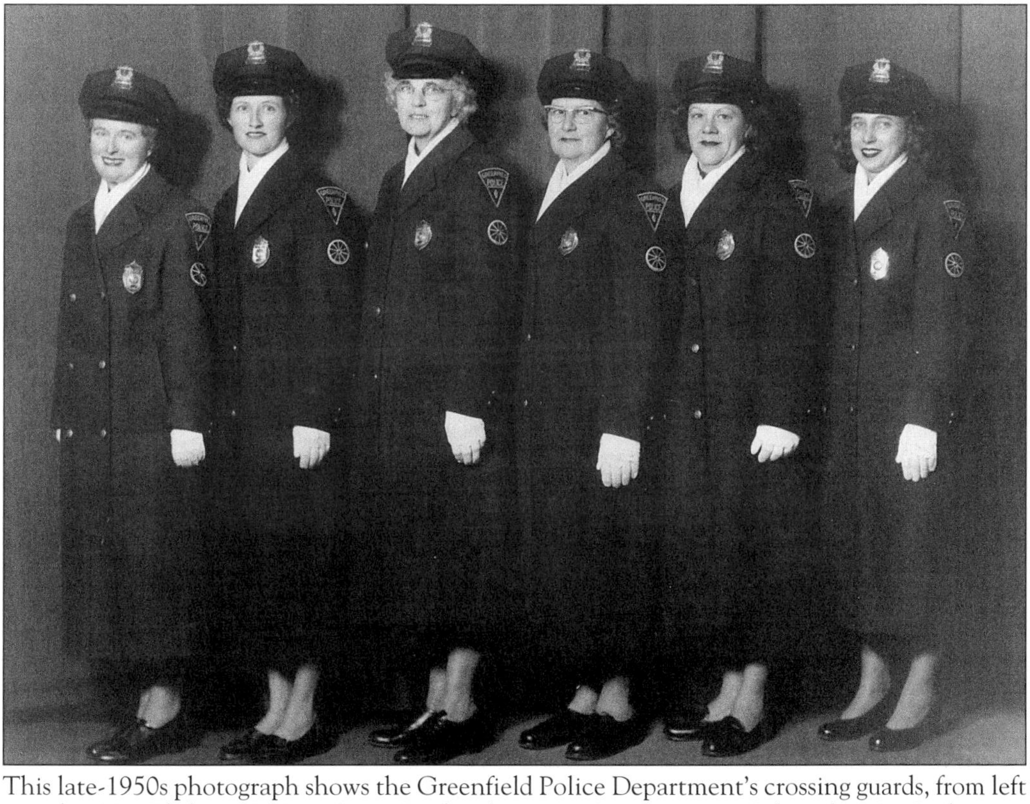

This late-1950s photograph shows the Greenfield Police Department's crossing guards, from left to right: Mrs. Philip J. O'Hara, Mary Fairbrother, Mrs. Brooks, Irene Galipault, Mrs. Budrewicz, and Jane Dow.

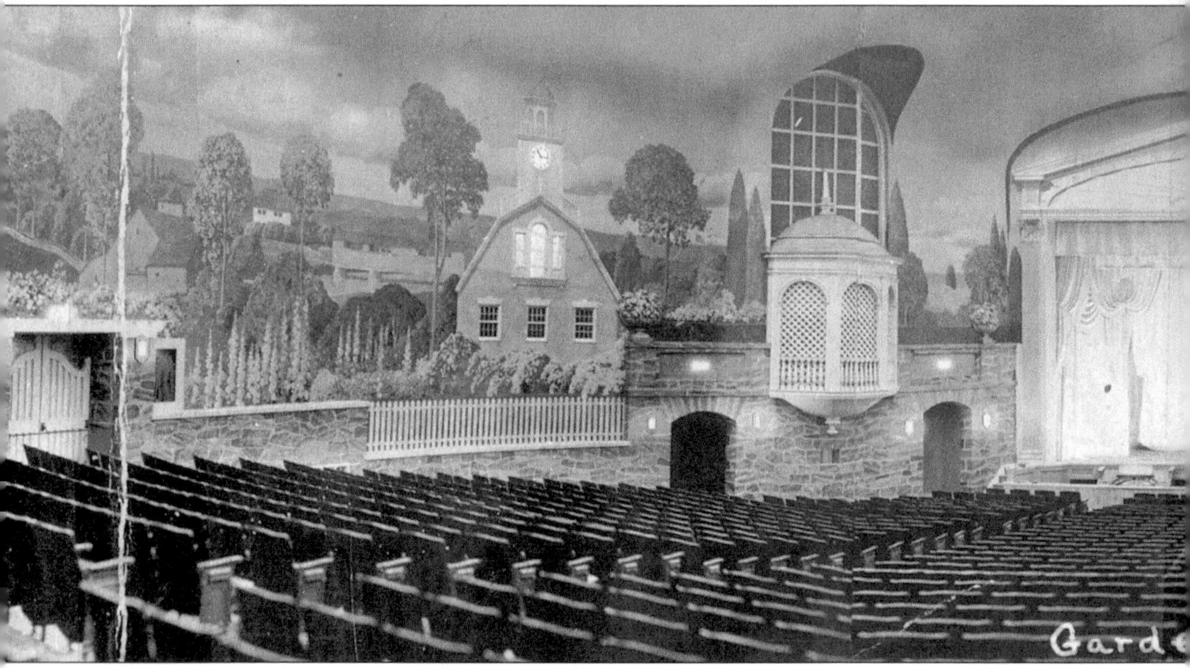

With its village scenes, lighted stars on the ceiling, and projected clouds, the Garden Theater was well named. This 1,900-seat theater opened on March 11, 1929 with an elaborate program including a "technicolor novelty," the Pathe Sound News, and *The Home Towners*, described as

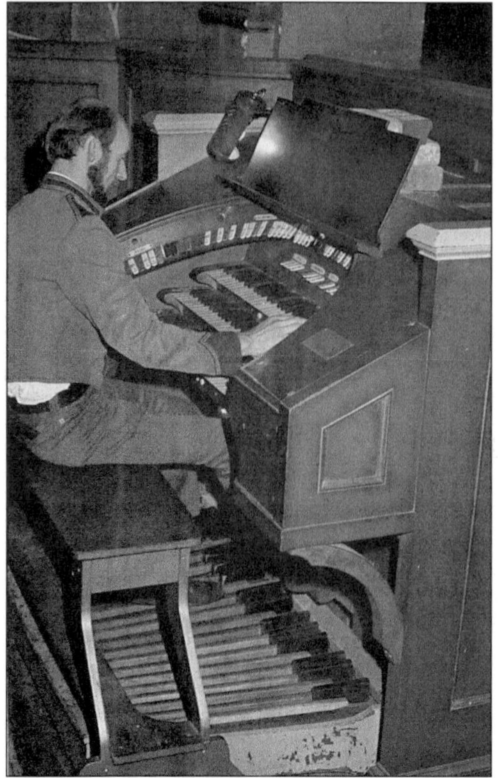

This photograph shows Ted Hausman playing the Marr-Colton organ at the Garden Theater in the 1980s. This organ was installed to provide short concerts before the movies. Hausman was the caretaker for both the Garden and the Showplace Theaters.

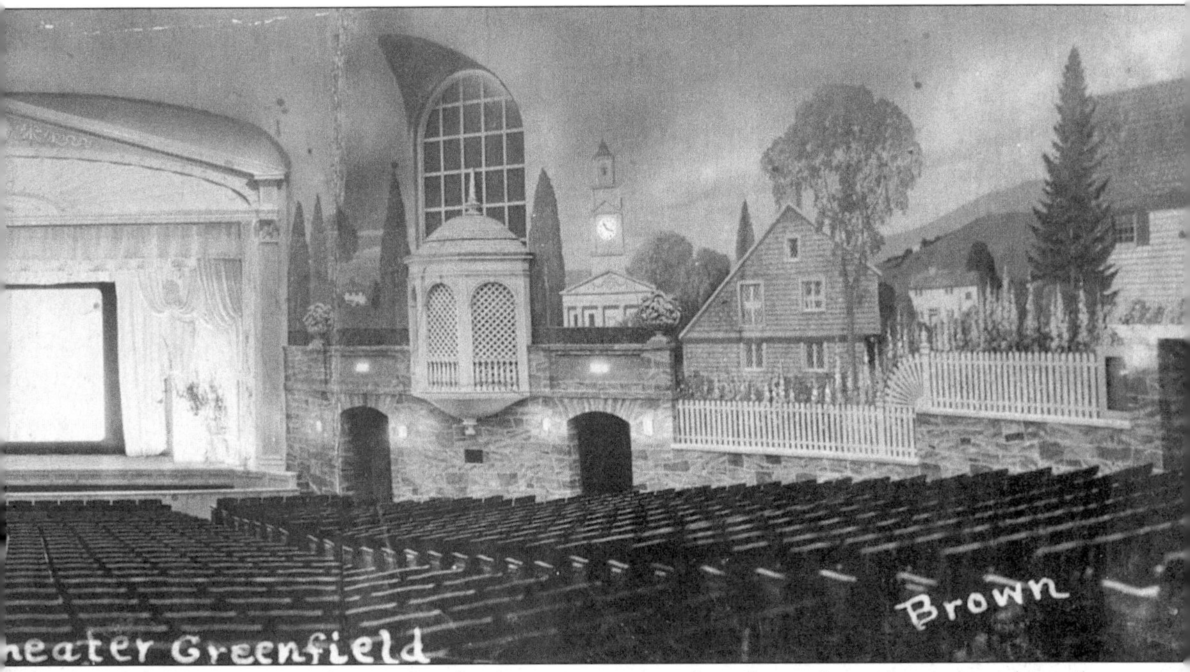

"an all-talking picture." On weekends, shows consisting of a talking photoplay, a comedy, and cartoons, started at 2:00 p.m. and ran continuously. Patrons could stay as long as they wished.

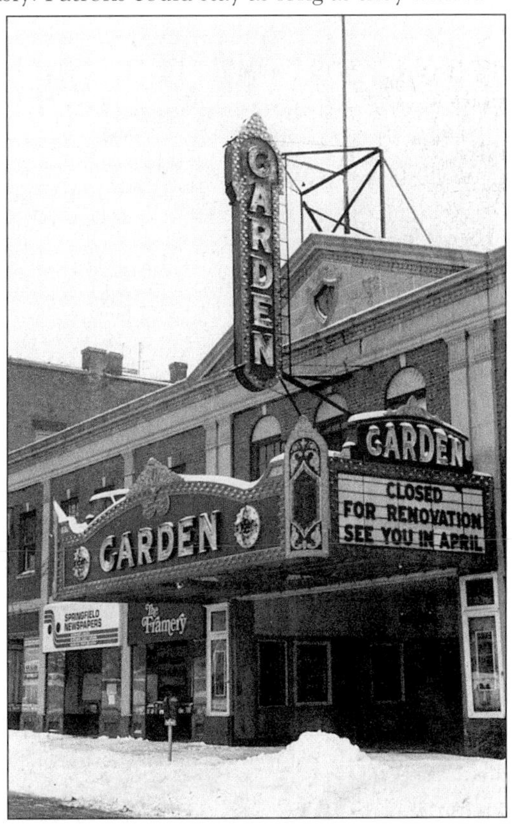

Here is the original marquee of the Garden Theater, just before the 1986 renovation. All that remains today are the Tiffany-style corner decorations. The theater was divided into seven smaller theaters: two on the stage, two in the balcony, and three on the main floor. The Garden Theater is still owned by the G-B Theatres Corporation, which once operated many large theaters such as the Showplace (formerly the Victoria), the Calvin in Northampton, and the State in Springfield.

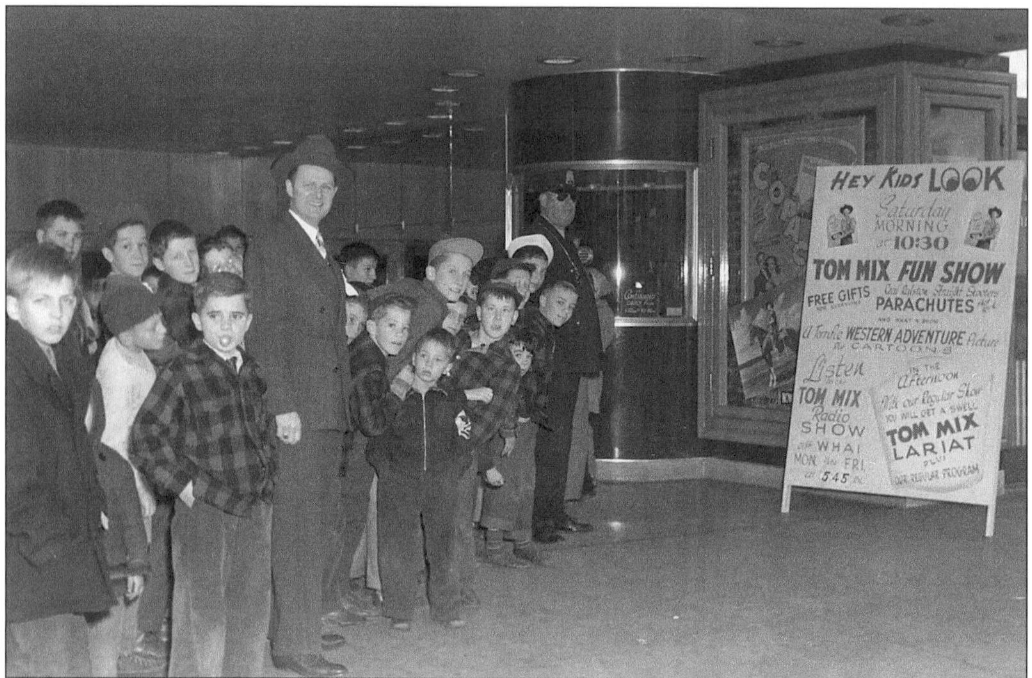

Children line up for a Saturday movie event at the Lawler Theater on Federal Street in 1947. The policeman is John O'Hara, who was also the crossing guard at the Federal Street School. The boy to the right of the tall man wearing the hat is James Karner. The boy wearing the plaid coat leaning on the boy with the baseball jacket is Robert Atwood. During this era, children could see two movies, a cartoon, a newsreel, previews, and a serial—all for 15¢.

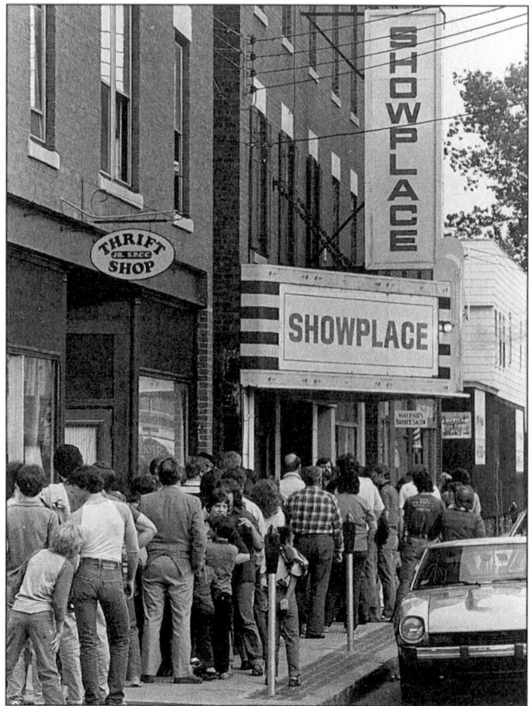

Here is the Showplace Theater, formerly the Victoria. This building fell into disrepair and was demolished in 1998. This photograph was taken in 1983 at the opening of *The Return of the Jedi*.

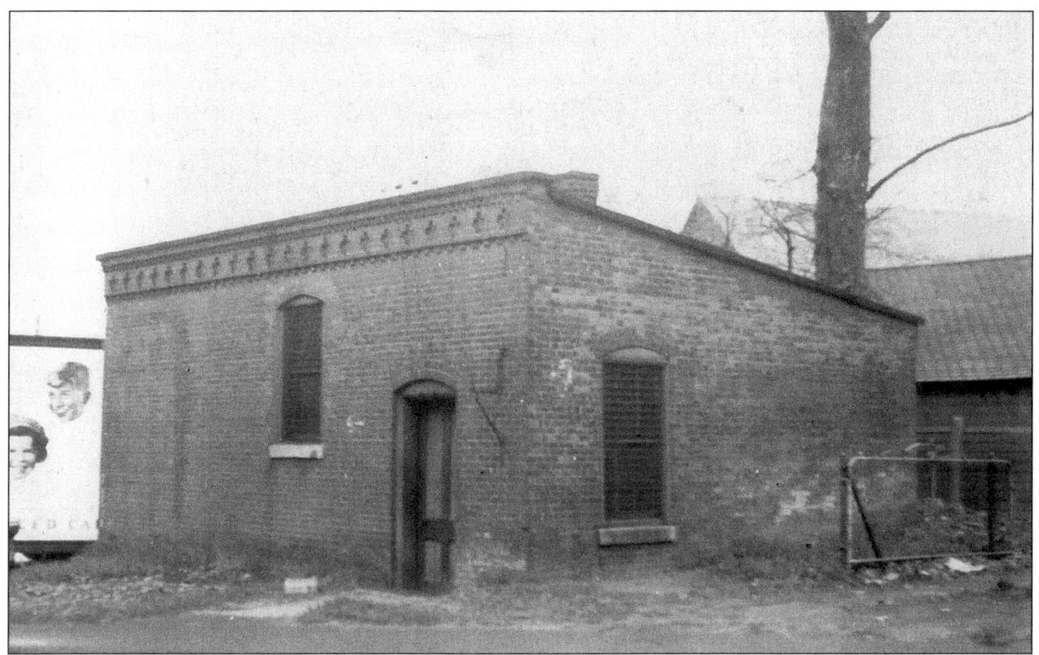

The old Greenfield town lockup was located on the west side of Miles Street, just south of the Miles Hotel. It was used by the Greenfield Police Department until *c.* 1935, when the town built the station in the rear of Washington Hall. This photograph was taken *c.* 1930.

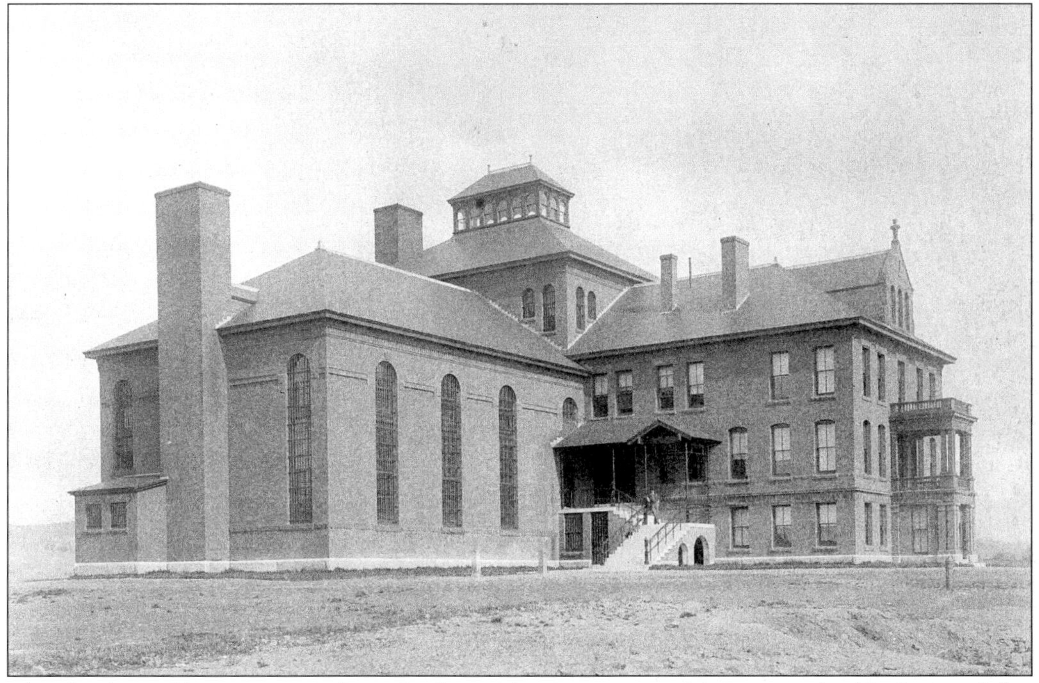

The third Franklin County Jail was built on Elm Street in 1886. Despite the bleakness of this photograph, the jail had its own dairy farm for many years. The first jail was located on upper Deerfield Street and the second on Hope Street near the intersection with Prospect Street. This photograph was taken *c.* 1910.

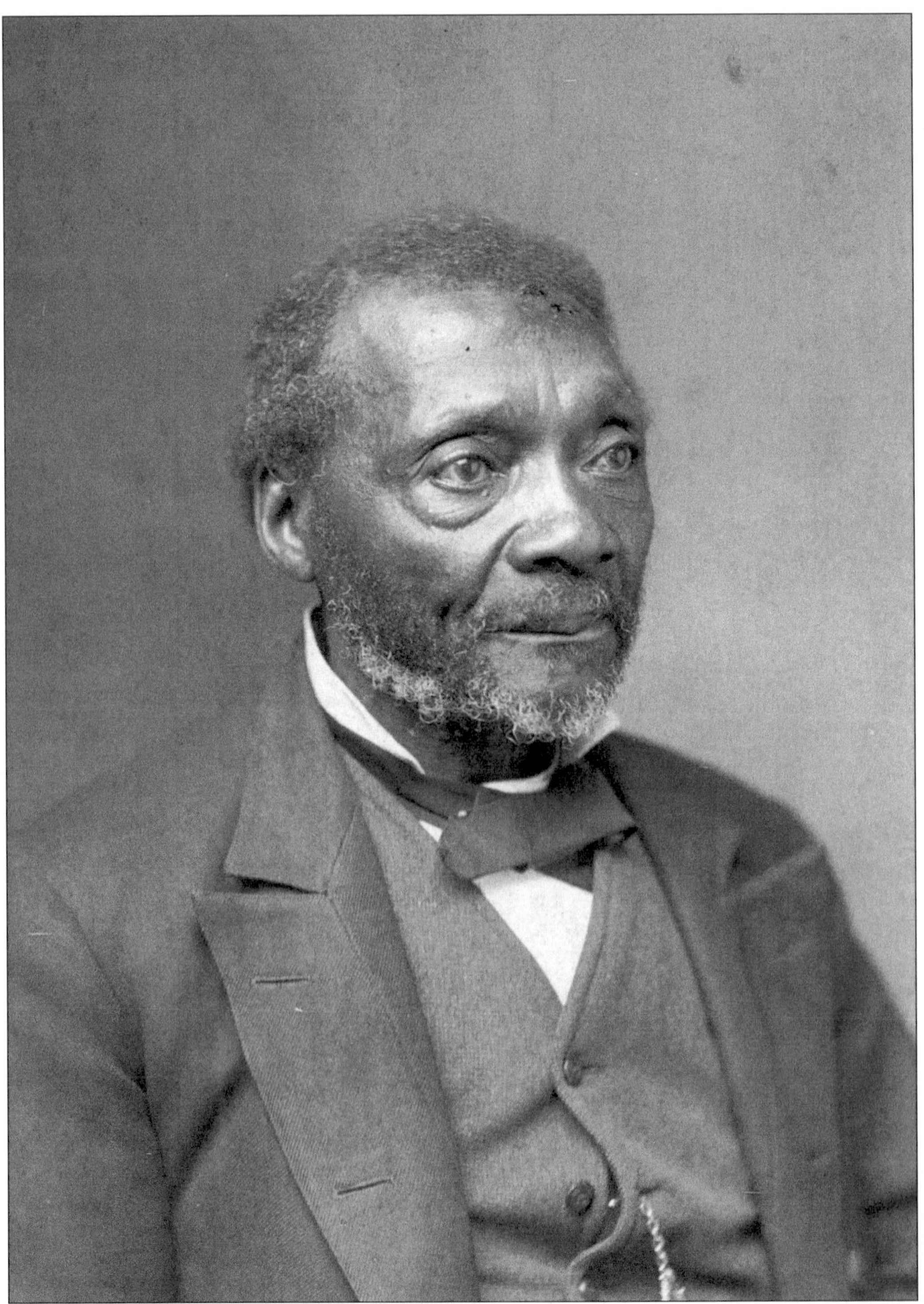

John Putnam (1817–1895) was well known in Franklin County as a fiddle player and dance caller. By trade a barber, Putnam lived on Wells Street above Arch Street, in a house which may have been part of the Underground Railroad.

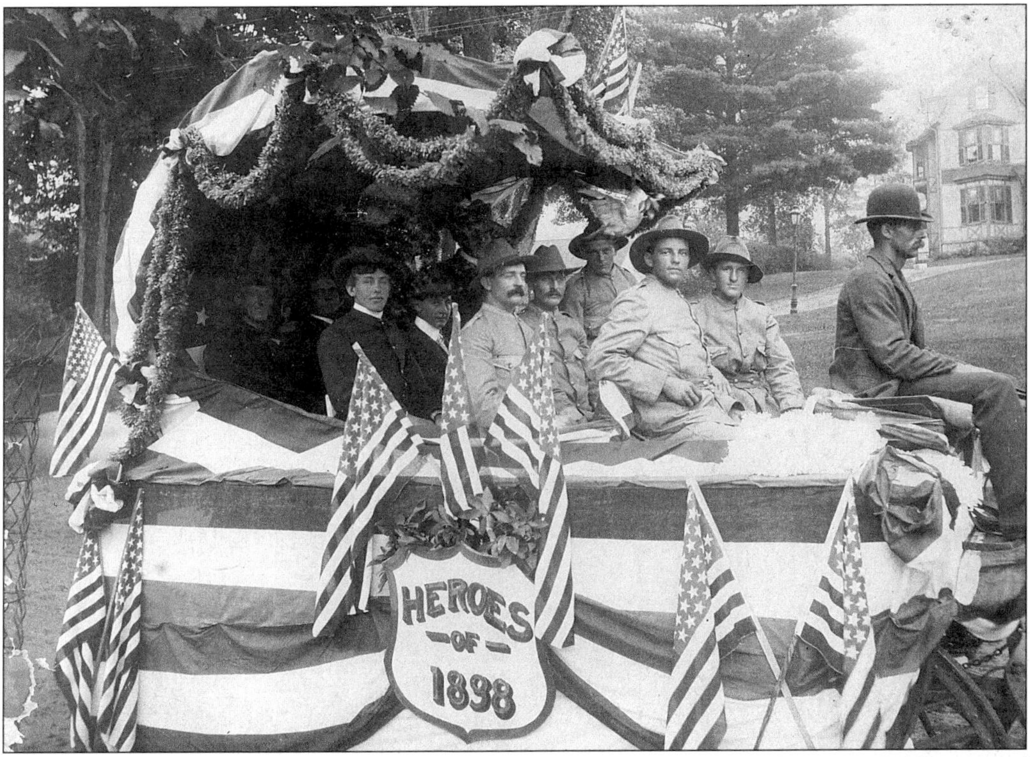

This float in front of the Cutler house on Highland Avenue honored the Greenfield troops of Company L who fought in the Spanish-American War in Cuba. The driver is Fred Schiller. Behind him is H.L. Woodard. The man with the mustache in the middle of the third row is Alston Salisbury. To Salisbury's left is Henry Graves.

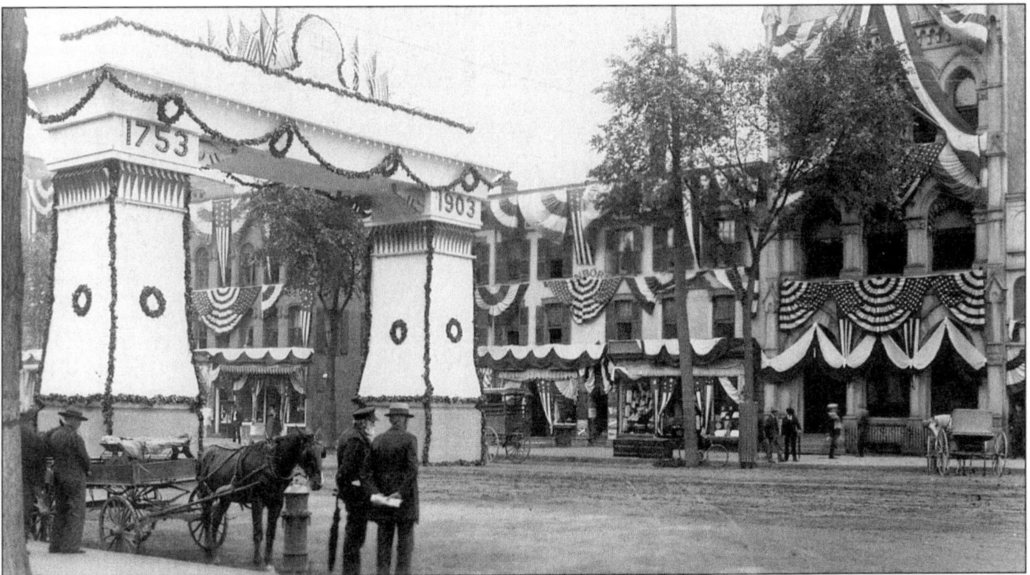

The 1903 sesquicentennial celebration of the founding of Greenfield was marked by this elaborate arch just north of the town common. The town had a large parade, commissioned a granite horse trough, and published a two-volume history by Judge Francis M. Thompson.

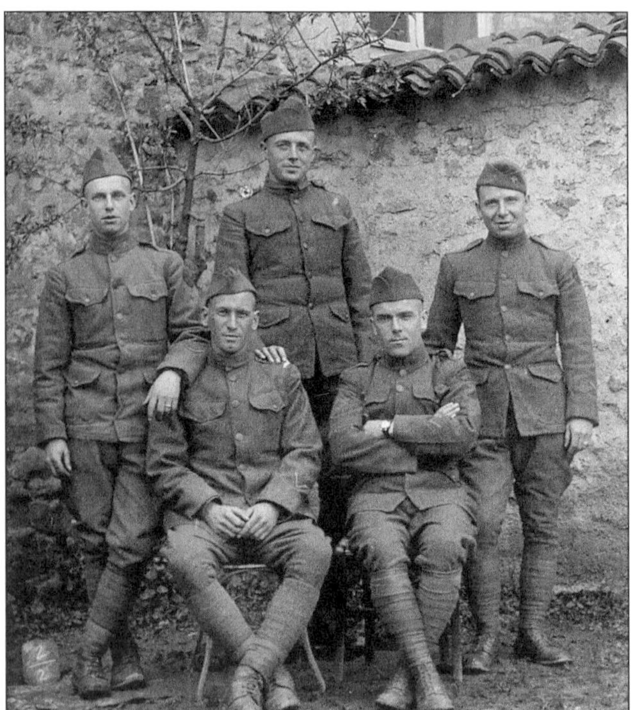

Donald Parker is shown here, seated on the left, while serving in France during World War I. On the back of the photograph, Parker wrote, "Taken at Nogent—The detail I had in the dugout for four months. Just back from the hospital." The Parker family had a farm on Shelburne Road, but Donald moved to Seattle after the war.

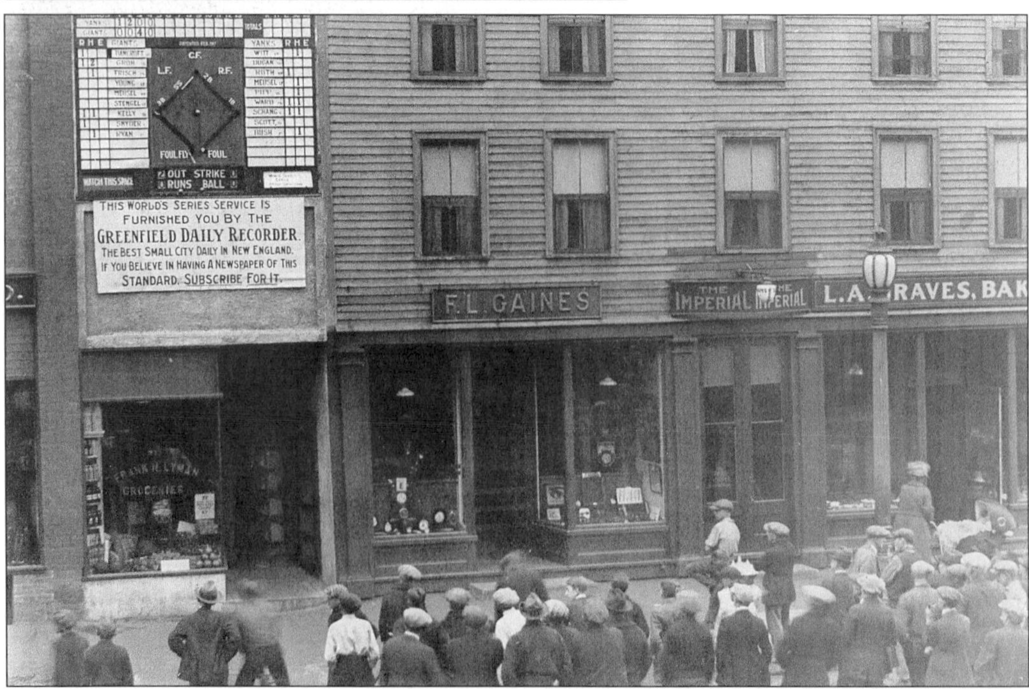

The Standard Ball Player above Lyman's grocery store was used to describe the October 10, 1923 World Series game play-by-play. It informed passersby, with only a three- or four-play delay, of the baseball game. Runners dashed from the Associated Press teletype at the *Greenfield Daily Recorder* newspaper office less than a block away to the operators behind the board. Note the players listed on the sign—there are some great names up there.

This photograph shows Jane Taylor Adamoyurka during her service in the U.S. Marine Corps. Adamoyurka enlisted March 17, 1943, as the first woman marine from Franklin County. After boot camp she trained to be an aviation machinist. While serving in an otherwise all-male engine overhaul unit for Services Squadron 46, she was promoted to sergeant and married another marine sergeant, Michael Adamoyurka Jr. After the war the Adamoyurkas operated Negus & Taylor Inc., a monument company. (Photograph courtesy of Jane Adamoyurka.)

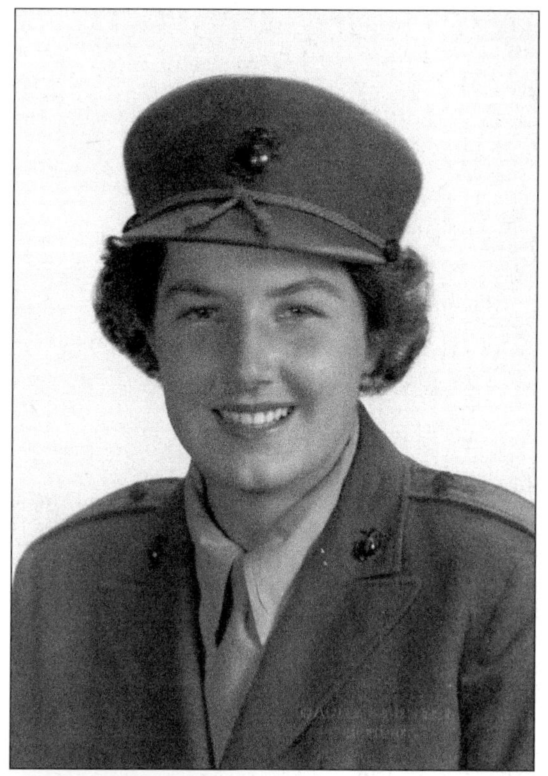

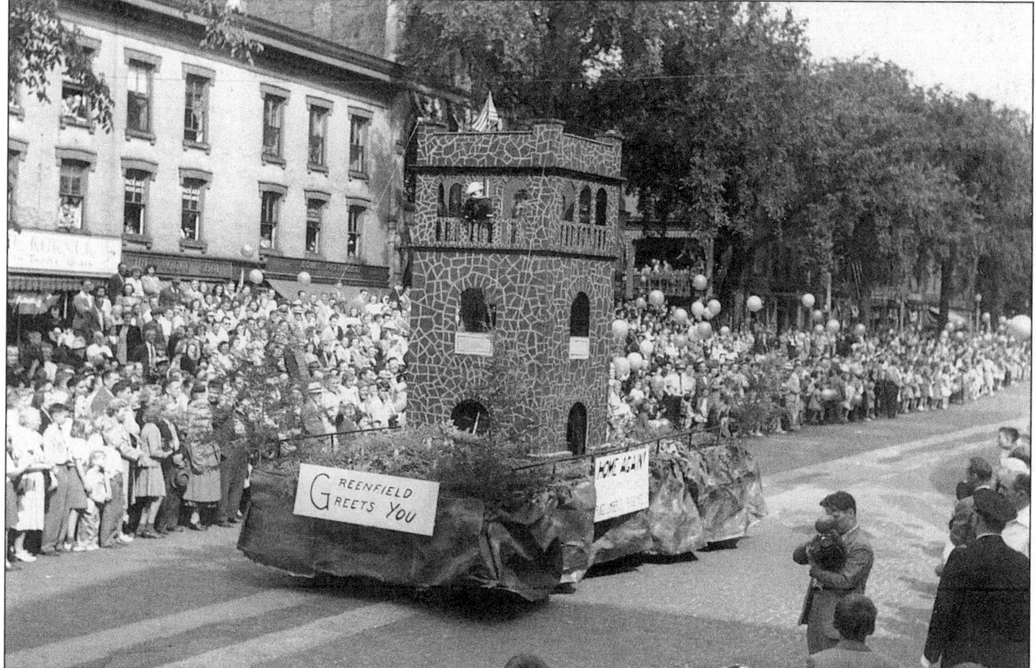

This scene shows the Welcome Home Parade held in 1946 for veterans of World War II. These photographs were taken on Main Street, just north of the town common. Note how the trolley tracks had recently been dug up—probably as part of a scrap drive—and replaced by concrete.

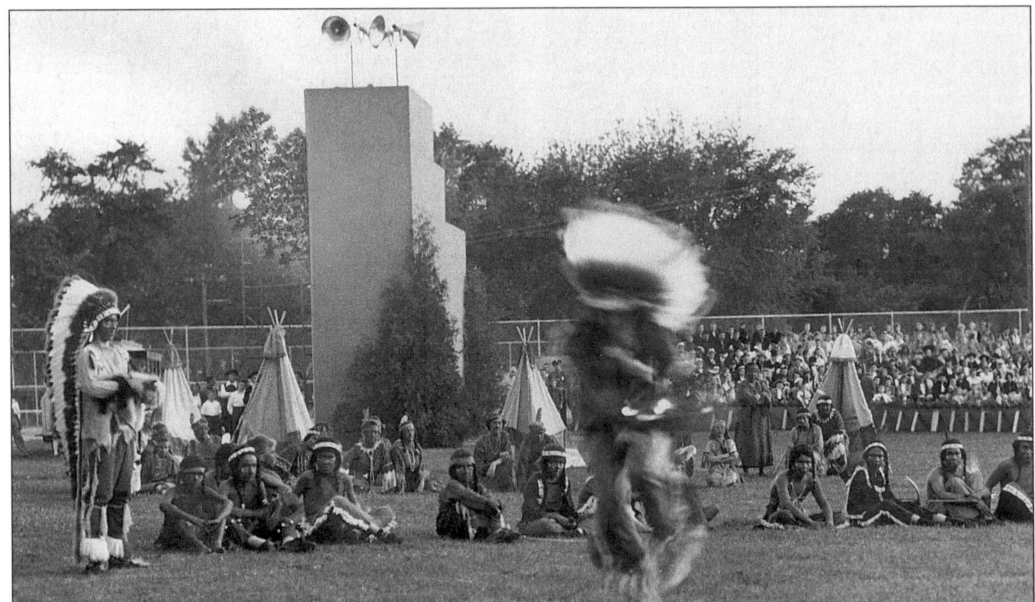

This was the opening scene at the evening pageant to celebrate Greenfield's bicentennial in 1953. Some of the actors were from Boy Scout Troop 2. The boys made their own costumes. The event was held at Beacon Field, with Rocky Mountain and Poet's Seat Tower as a backdrop. (Photograph by Al Daigle.)

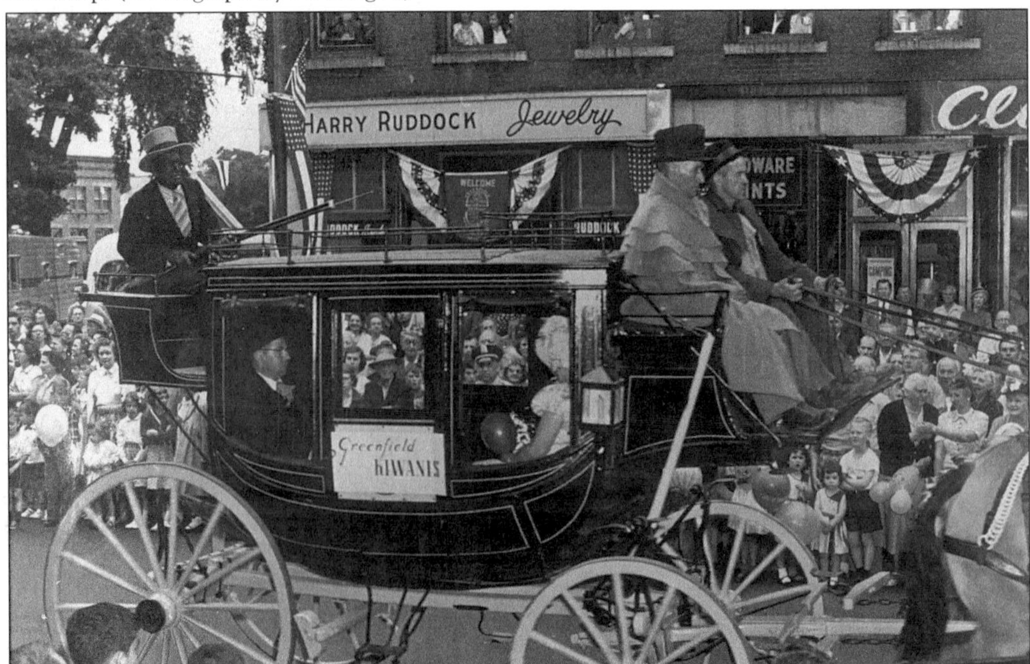

Clarence Strecker is seated in the Greenfield town stagecoach in the Bicentennial Parade in June 1953. There has not since been a parade as elaborate as this one. The Greenfield Kiwanis Club sponsored the stagecoach entry. The coach, which still exists, was made in Concord, New Hampshire, and has been used in many parades through the years. It was nearly identical to one built for Buffalo Bill and is similar to hundreds built in Concord and used all over the country.

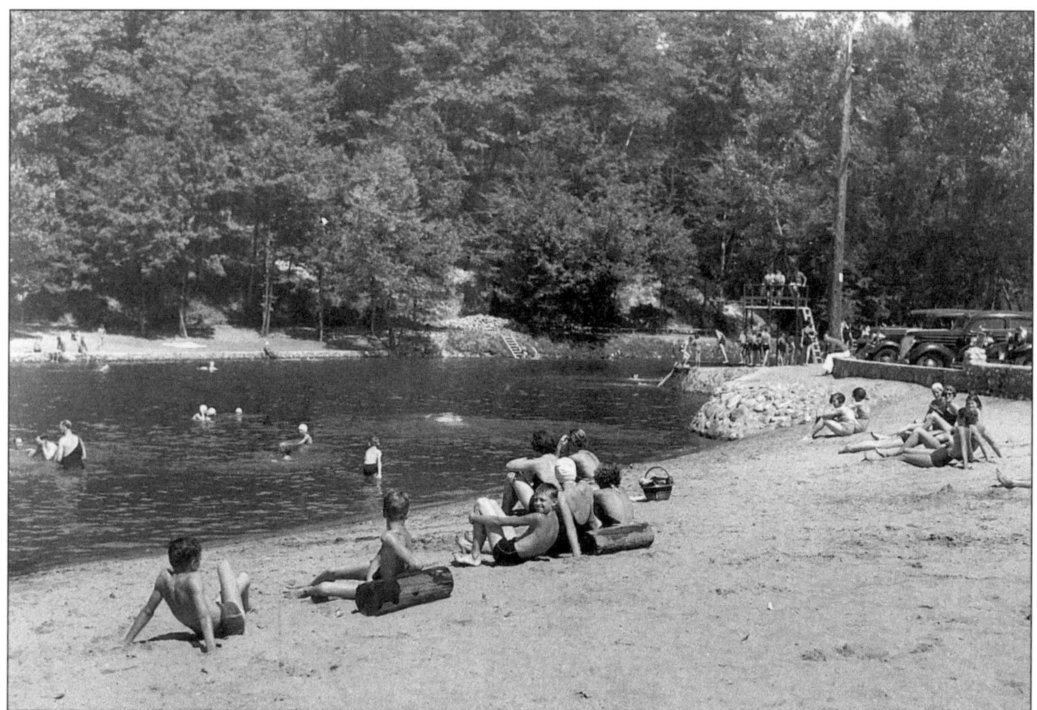

This view, looking toward the diving boards, shows the middle beach of the Greenfield Swimming Pool. The photograph was taken in the mid-1940s, at the peak the pool's popularity.

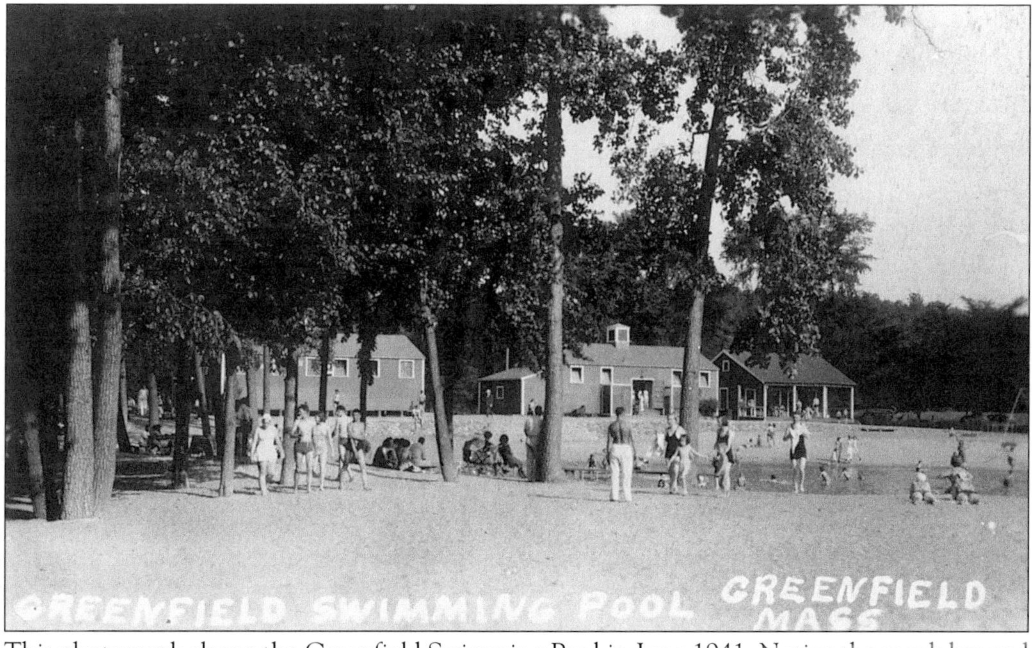

This photograph shows the Greenfield Swimming Pool in June 1941. Notice the snack bar and the men's and women's changing rooms in the background. In the foreground is the kiddie pool.

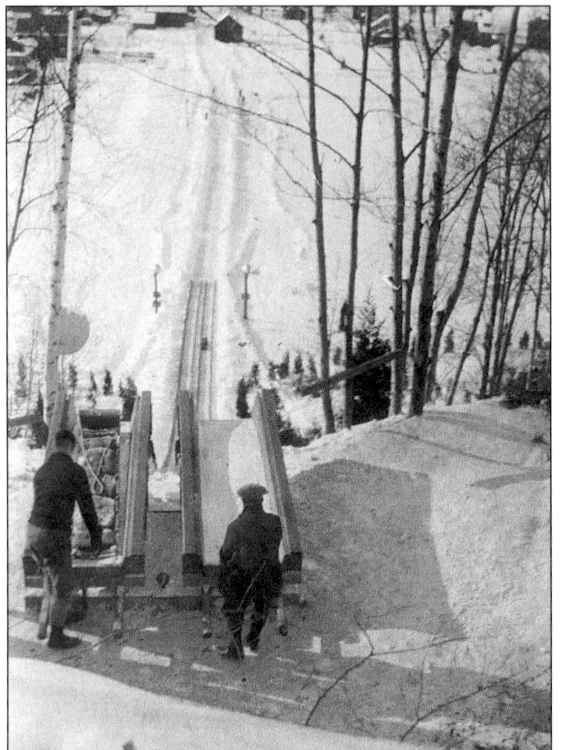

This view was taken from the top of the double-barreled toboggan run on Rocky Mountain, just below Poet's Seat Tower. The run went west over Beacon Field, and the bottom curve was just to the east of Garrett Street. It was in use during the 1920s and 1930s. This photograph was taken in 1922.

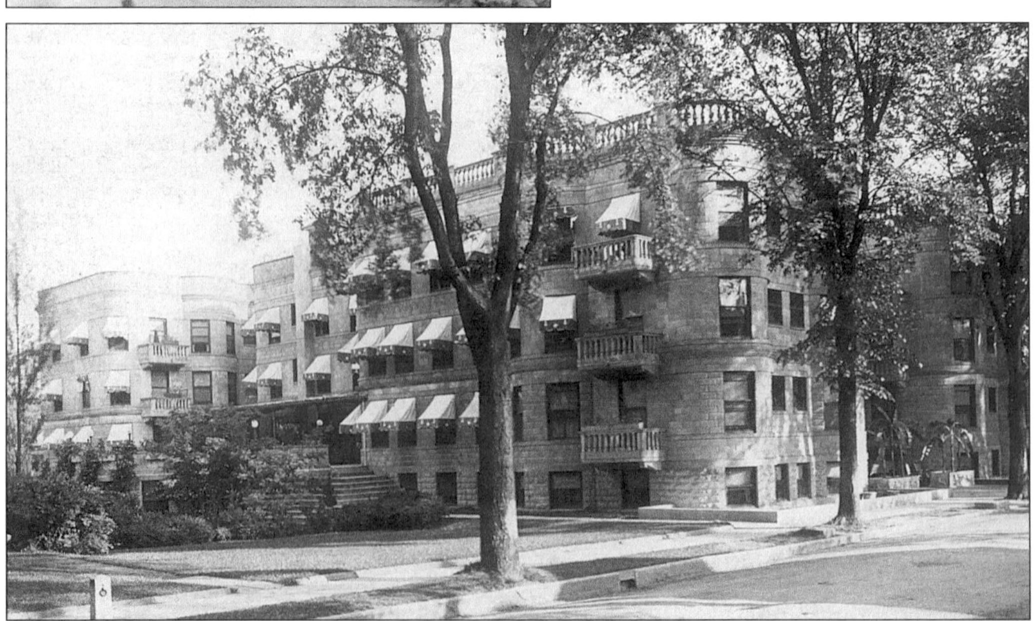

The Weldon Hotel was built in 1905 by F.O. Wells as an apartment building, but it was soon converted into one of New England's premier hotels. The Weldon promoted the area as a winter sports mecca, and had a beginners slope built on the north side where patrons could learn to ski. Wells was the first to use reinforced concrete construction on a hotel. The re-routing of Route 2 took away the hotel's travel trade, and it closed in the 1970s. It was rehabilitated in 1981–82 as subsidized apartments and the Greenfield Senior Center.

This photograph of champion ski jumper Strand Mikkelson of the Greenfield Outing Club was taken *c.* 1928 at the Shelburne Mountain ski jump. Mikkelson was the ski pro at the Weldon Hotel.

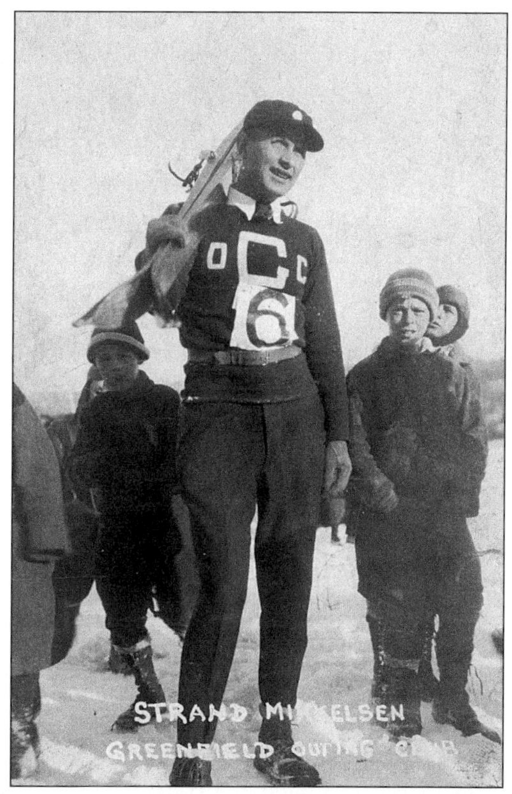

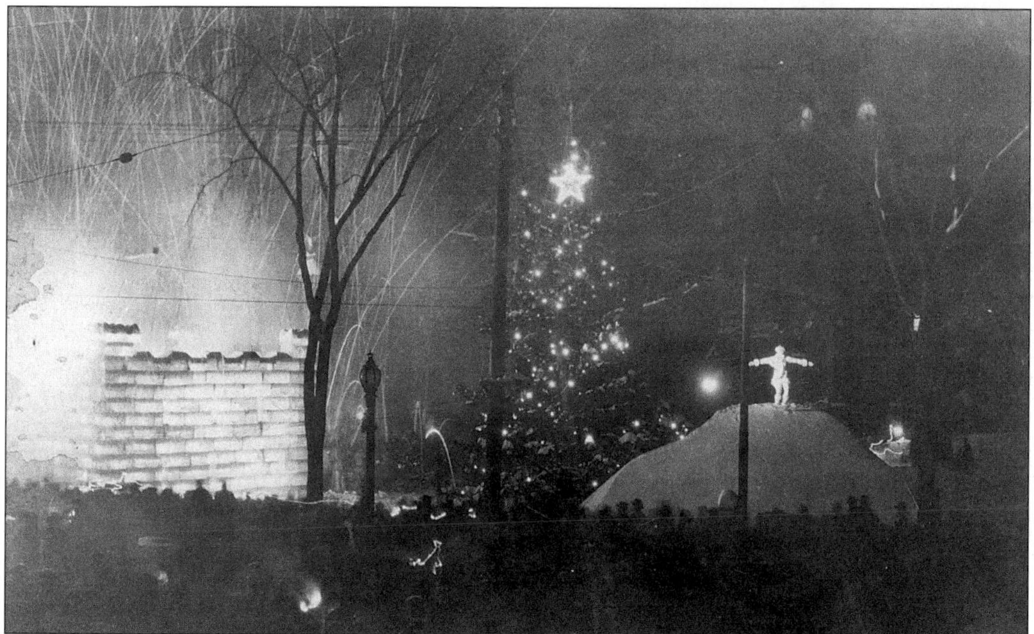

This night shot shows an ice castle created on the common for a winter carnival. Winter carnivals started in 1922 to promote Greenfield as a tourist destination. They took place during one winter week each year. Note the snow sculpture of a ski jumper in the background.

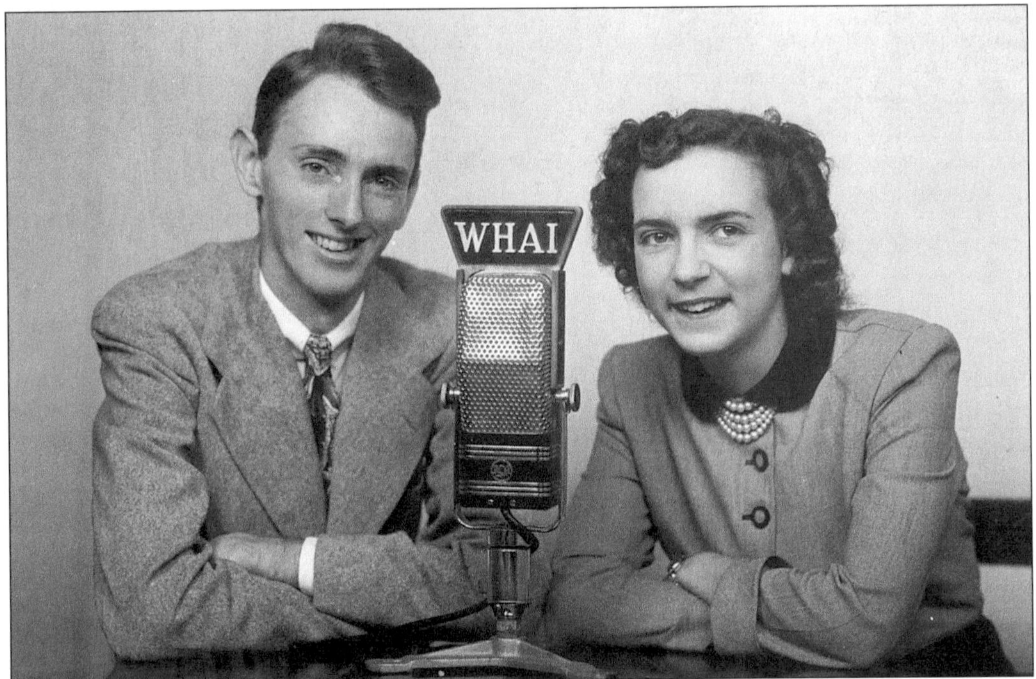

Here are Donald Tuttle and Audrey Clark, personalities of local radio station WHAI. This photograph was taken in the early 1950s, when the station was still located on the second floor of the Mansion House. Tuttle was farm editor of the radio station.

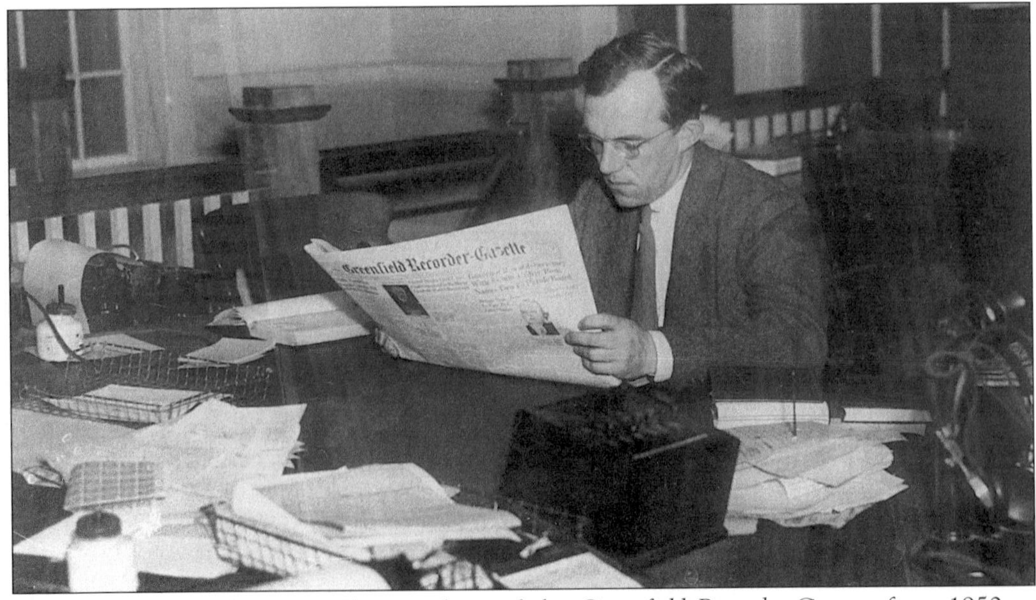

Harold LeVanway (1909–1997) was editor of the *Greenfield Recorder-Gazette* from 1950 to 1974. He was also a local historian, contributing to two volumes of Greenfield history. The *Recorder-Gazette* was formed in 1900 by the merger of two weeklies: The *Recorder*, owned by John W. Haigis, and the *Courier & Gazette* owned by E.A. Hall Company. The *Courier & Gazette* was descended from a paper started in 1792 by Thomas Dickman, the *Impartial Intelligencer*.

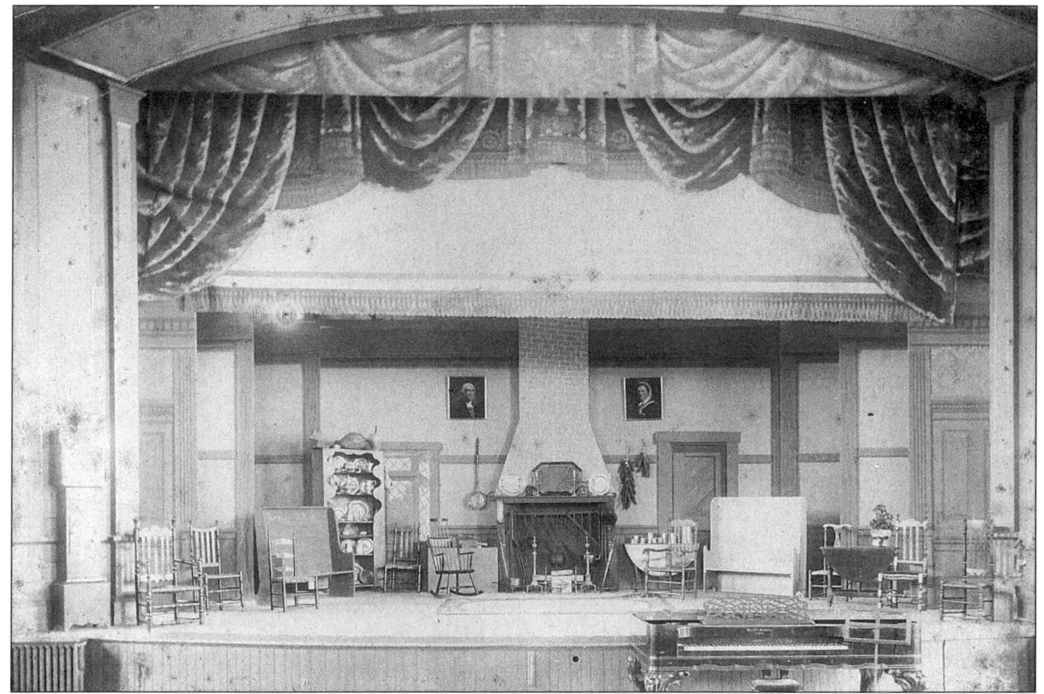

The stage of Washington Hall on Main Street was a combination town hall and entertainment venue. The props for the play shown here are almost a perfect collection of Colonial Revival objects, lacking only a spinning wheel. The building was used for town meetings and other community events. The photograph was taken *c.* 1890. The play may have been *Priscilla, or the Pilgrim's Proxy*.

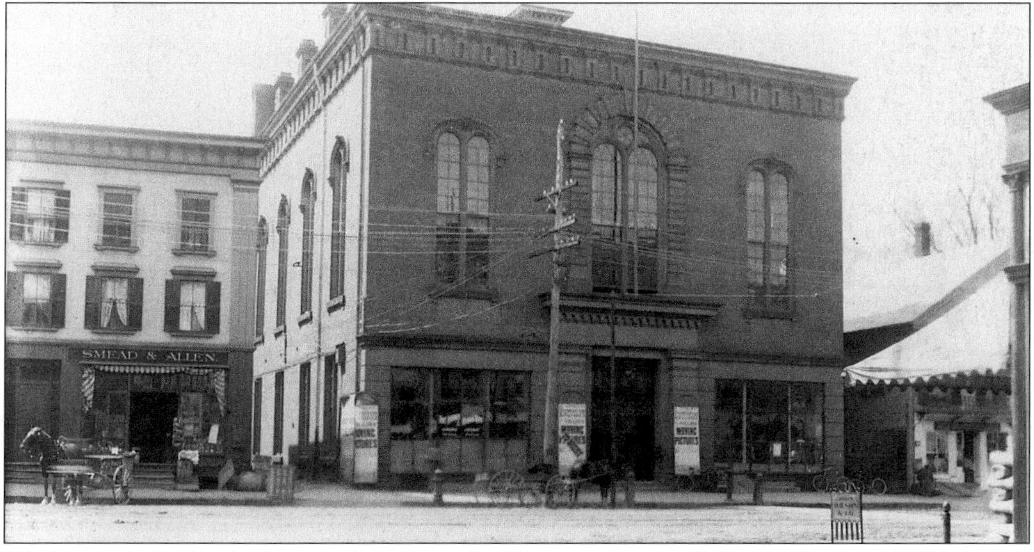

Washington Hall, which served as Greenfield's second town hall, was built in 1854. It was located on the present site of the Veteran's Mall. On the second floor was a large auditorium. In 1935, the police station was added at rear, where it remained until the department moved to High Street in 1999. Washington Hall was torn down in 1964 and later replaced by the Veterans' Mall war memorial.

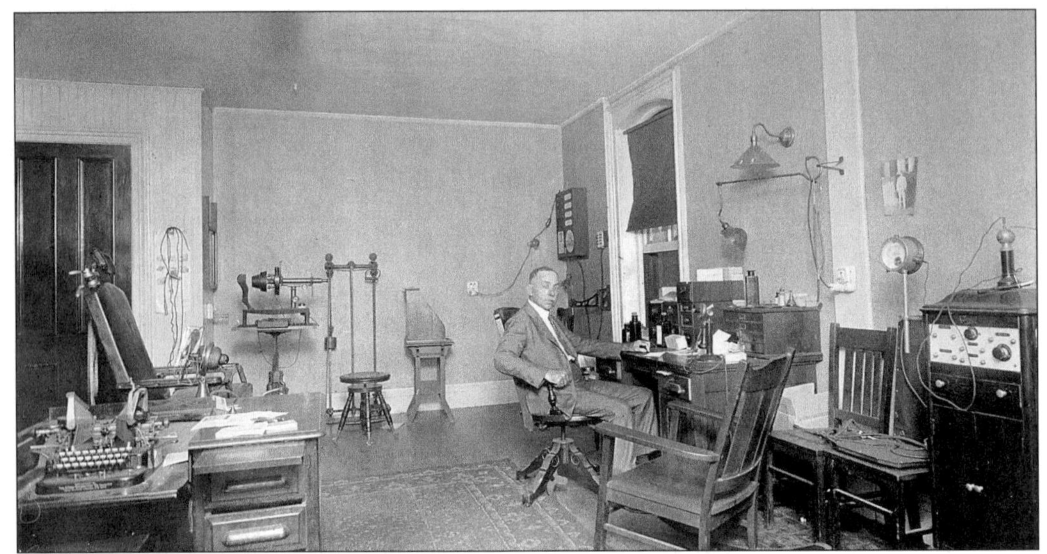

This photograph shows physician and surgeon Dr. John C. O'Brien (1863–1948) in his office on Main Street, *c.* 1910. O'Brien also had an office in his home on Federal Street, north of the Elks building. A graduate of the University of Vermont, O'Brien also studied in Paris and London.

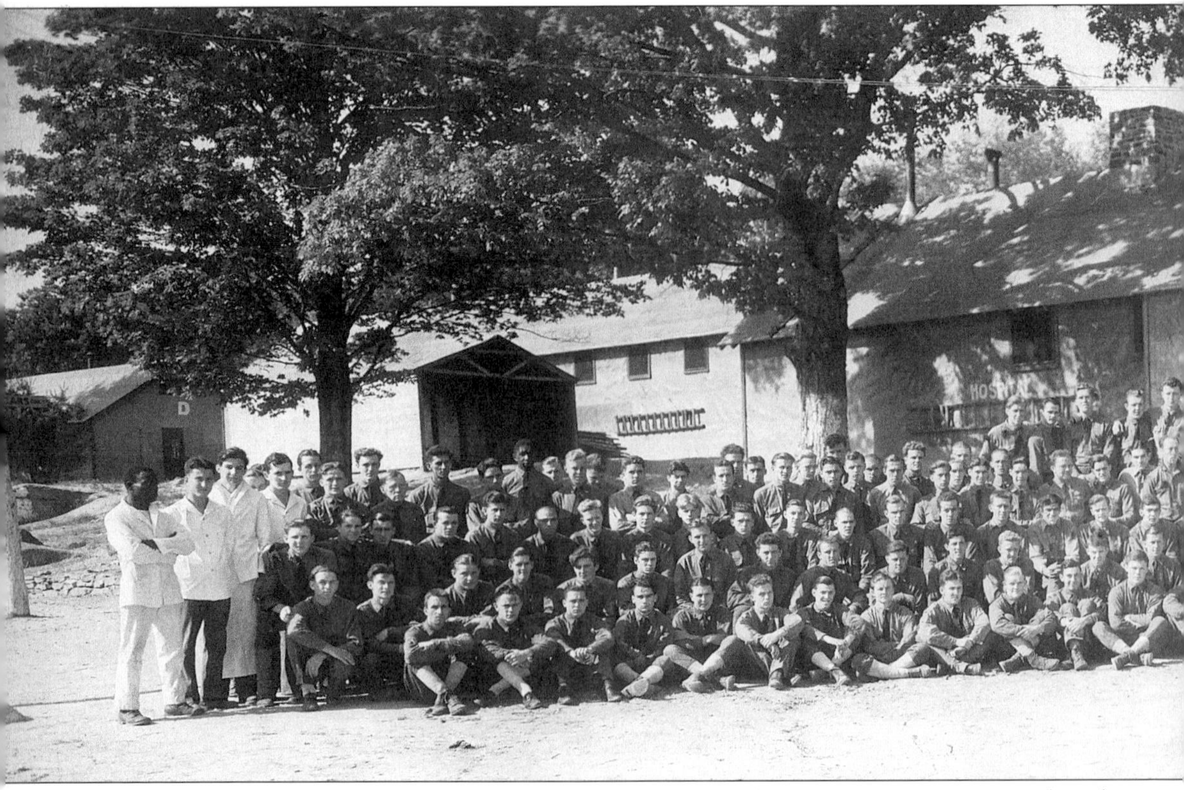

This 1932 photograph depicts Company 116 of the Civilian Conservation Corps, based in Greenfield. The grounds were located off the upper Green River Road, near the intersection with Plain Road. The CCC was a depression-era attempt to provide employment for thousands

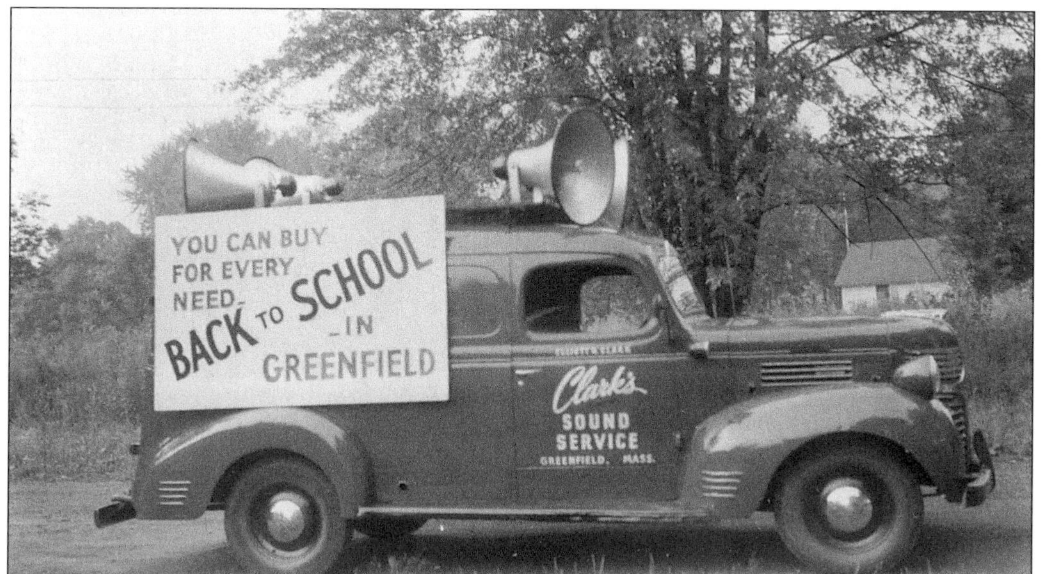

Here is Elliott E. Clark's Sound Service truck, *c.* 1940. Sound trucks were used to advertise local businesses and political campaigns until the 1970s. Bill Gribbon was probably the last to use a sound truck when he ran for town treasurer in the 1970s.

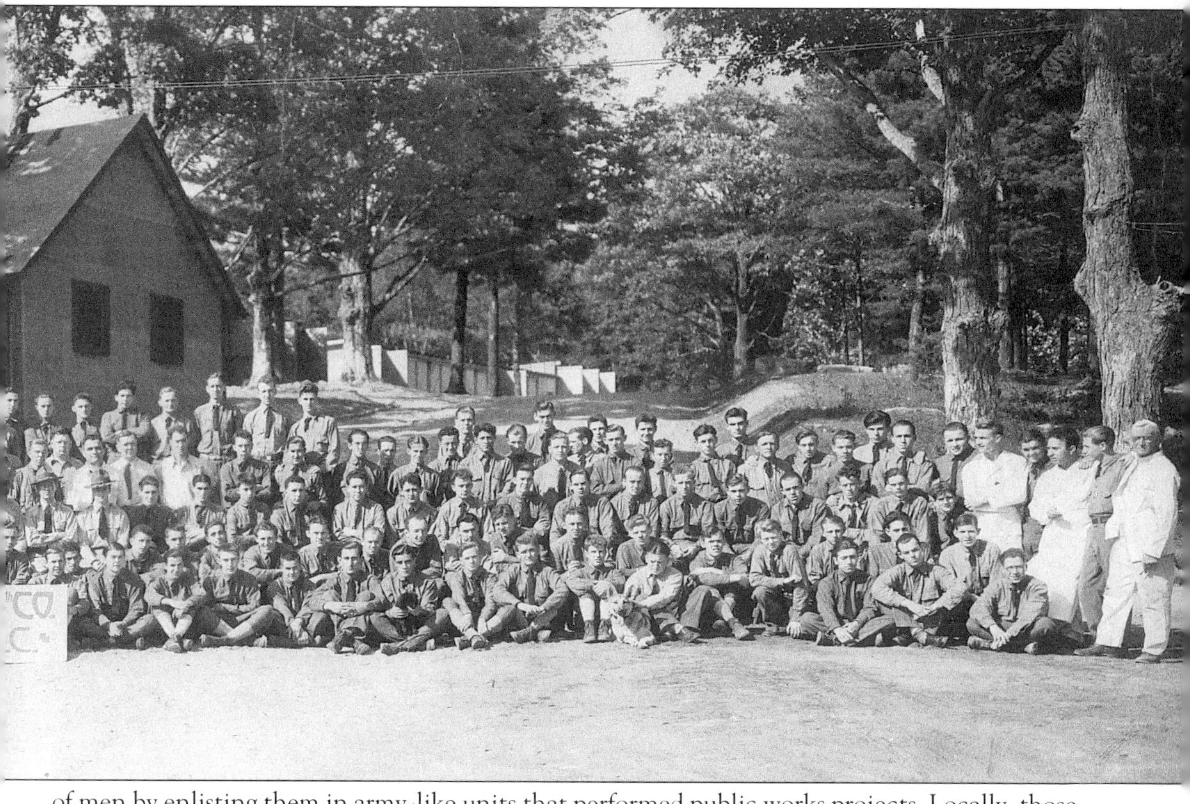

of men by enlisting them in army-like units that performed public works projects. Locally, those projects included tree planting and forest work.

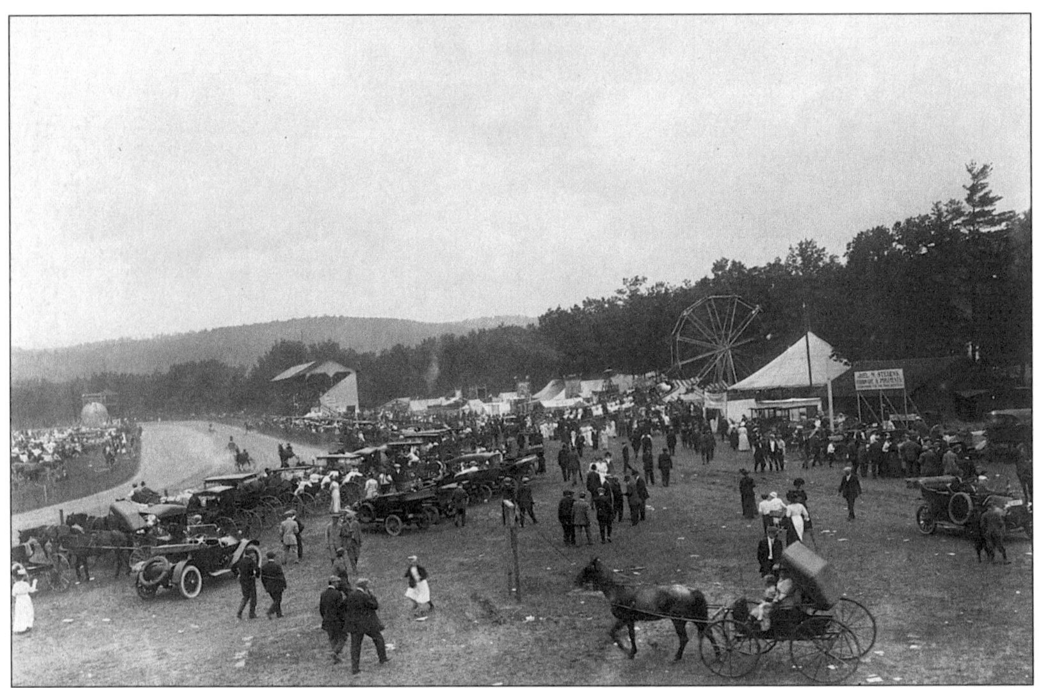

This photograph was taken looking west toward the grandstand at the Franklin County Fair, where a sulky race is under way.

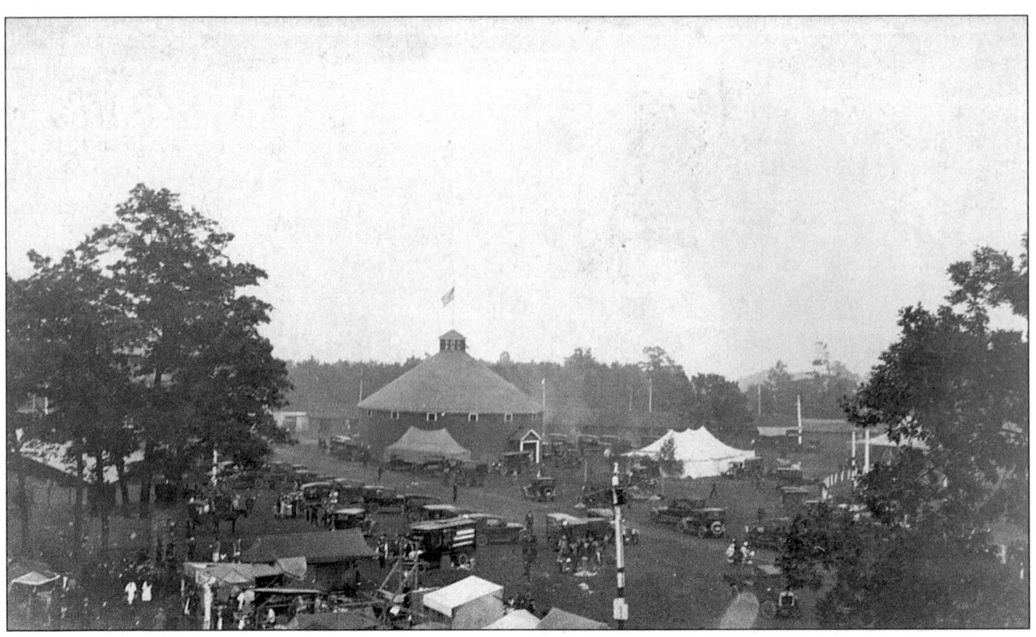

This *c.* 1910 view of the fairgrounds shows the Roundhouse and the carnival midway.

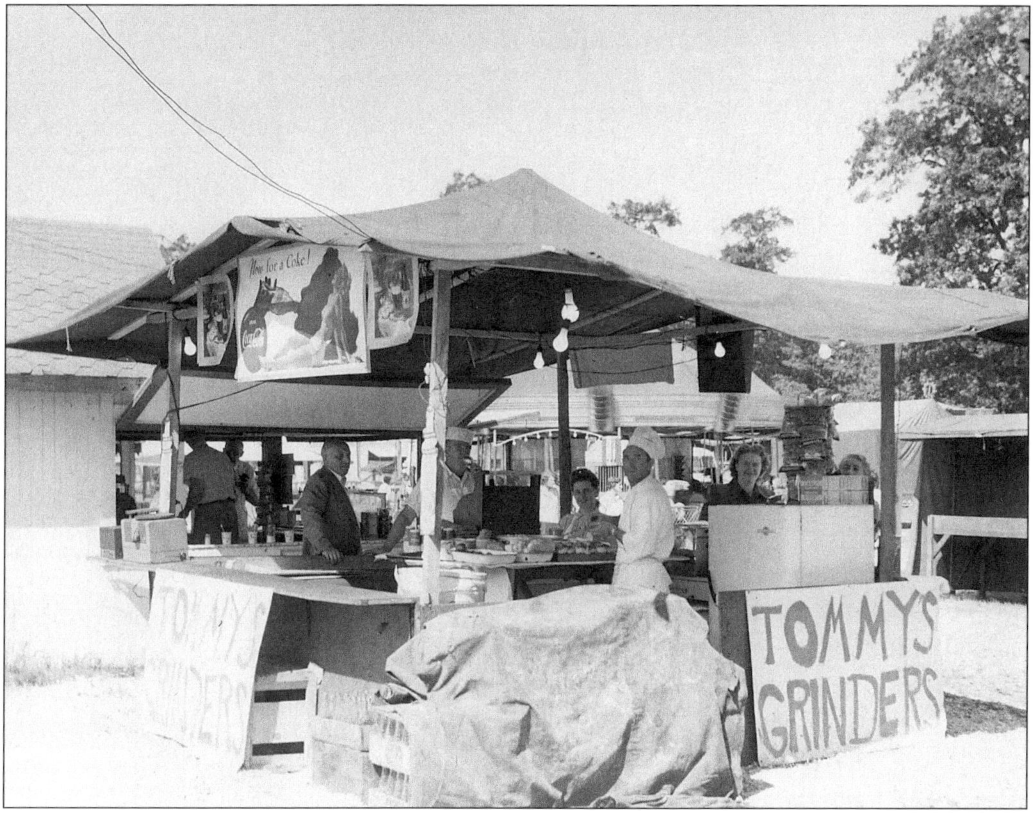

Tommy Maratea's Grinders was a feature at the Franklin County Fair during the 1940s. Maratea is the one wearing the white hat.

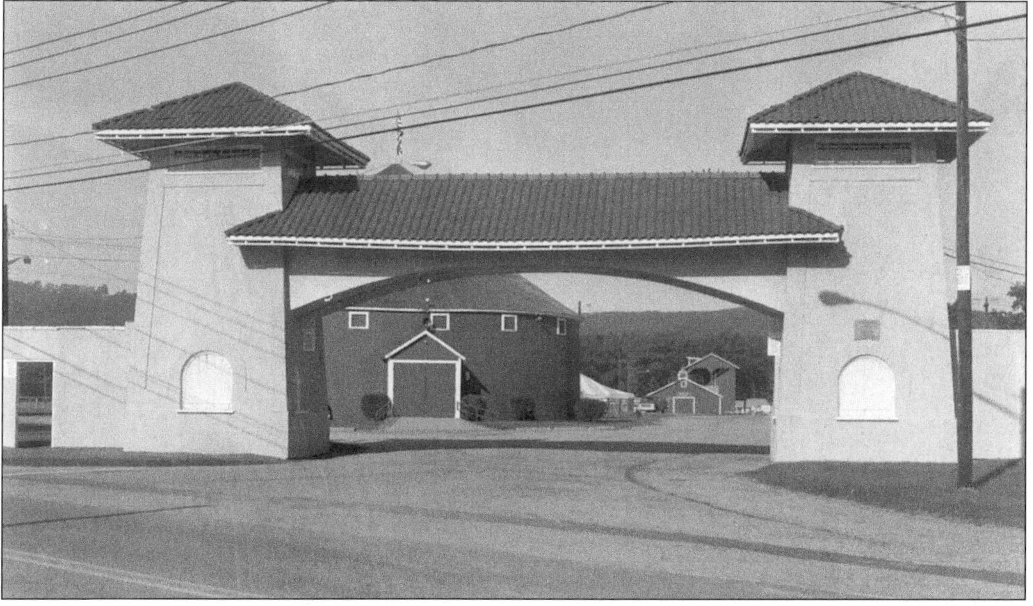

This is a 1980s view of the fairground gates and the Roundhouse. The Roundhouse was built in 1899 by F.W. Wells.

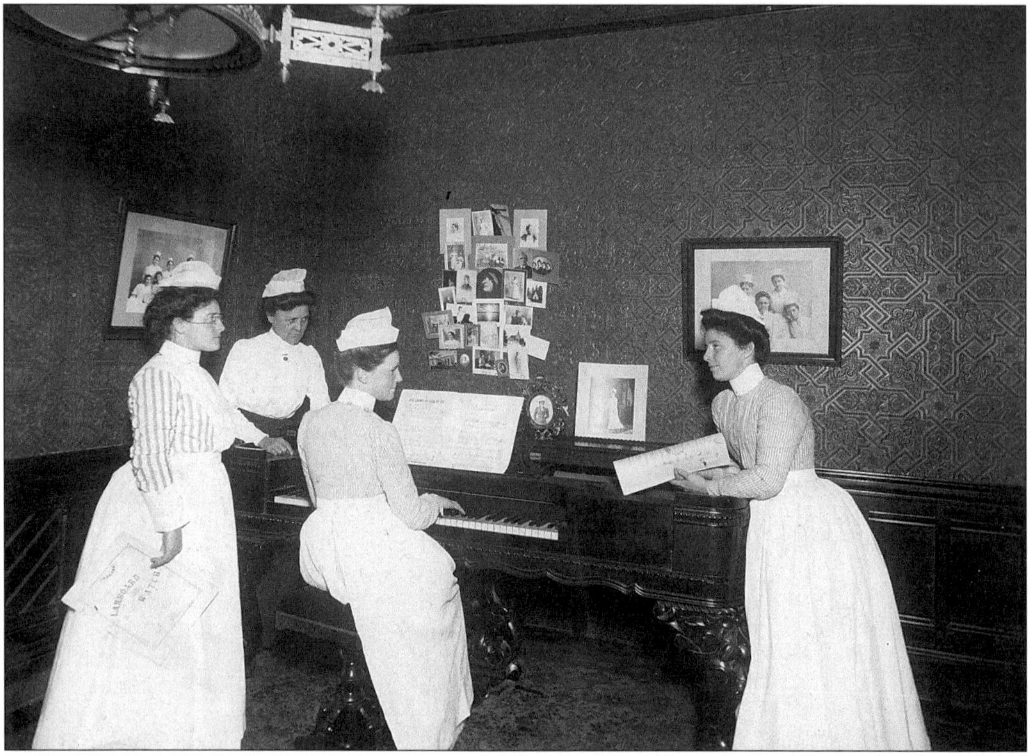

Nursing students sing around the piano in the second Franklin County Public Hospital in 1903. Behind the piano is Anna M. Sweeney, superintendent. Ethel McLean is playing, and the other two students are unidentified.

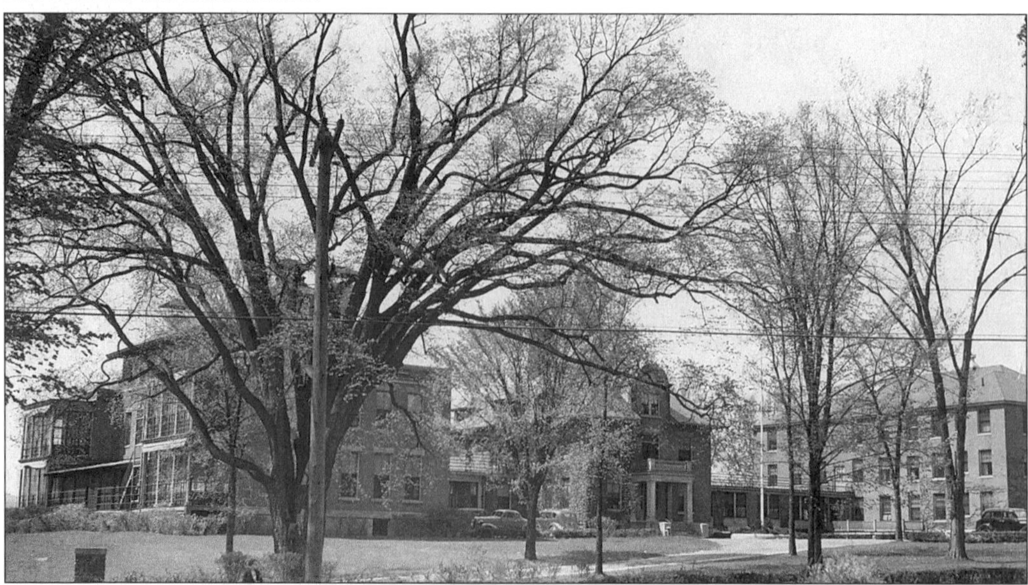

This early view of the Franklin County Public Hospital was taken *c.* 1930. The older wing on the left has since been demolished; the right wing is now the oldest part of the sprawling Franklin Medical Center on High and Sanderson Streets. The hospital moved to this High Street location in 1910. The earlier hospital was located at Main and Conway Streets.

Three

Homes and Citizens

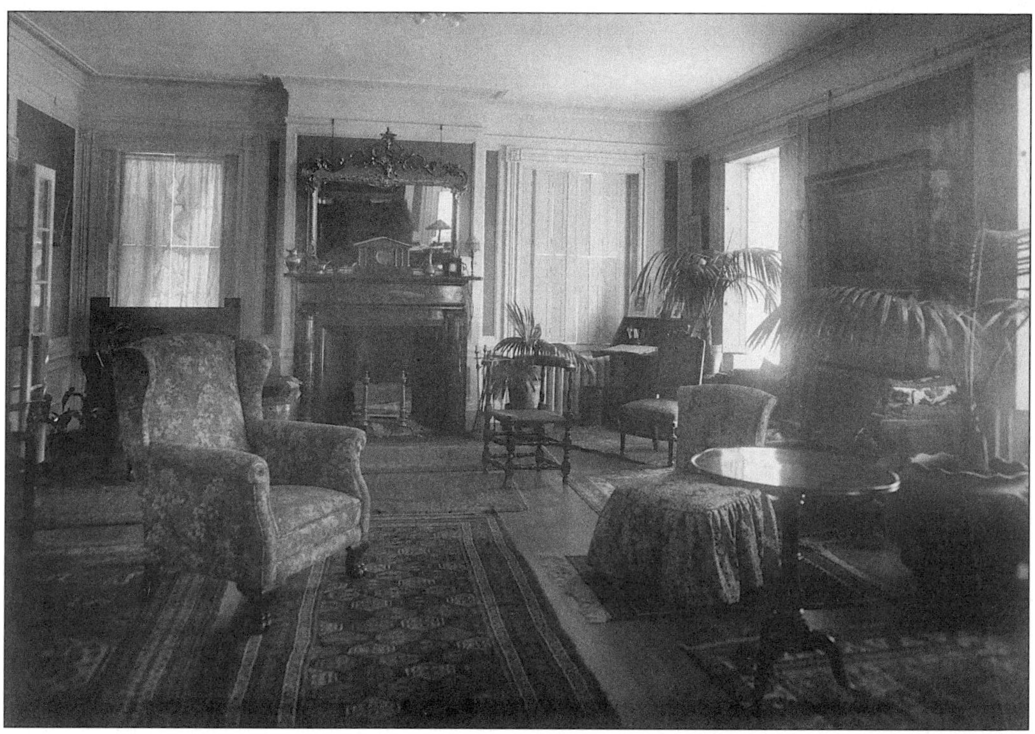

This is a 1912 photograph of the Gould-Clapp-Potter House. The hall was greatly expanded in a 1910 renovation. John W. Haigis Sr. purchased the house in 1955 and then converted it into professional offices with a studio in the upstairs ballroom for his radio station, WHAI.

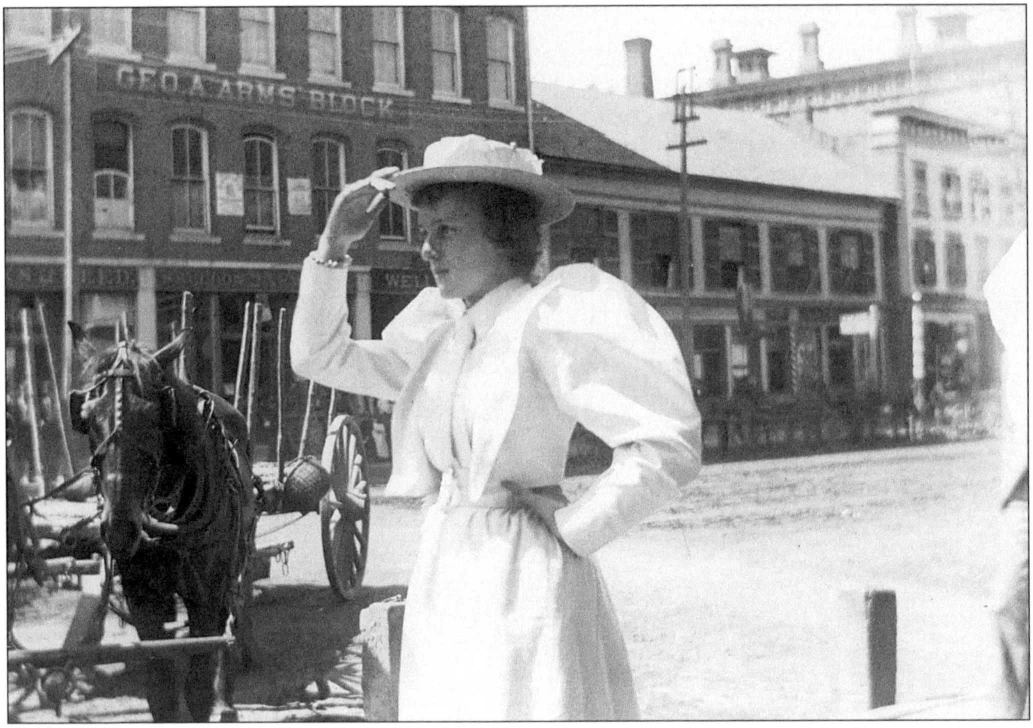

A young lady stands across Main Street from the George Arms Block in this photograph from *c.* 1900.

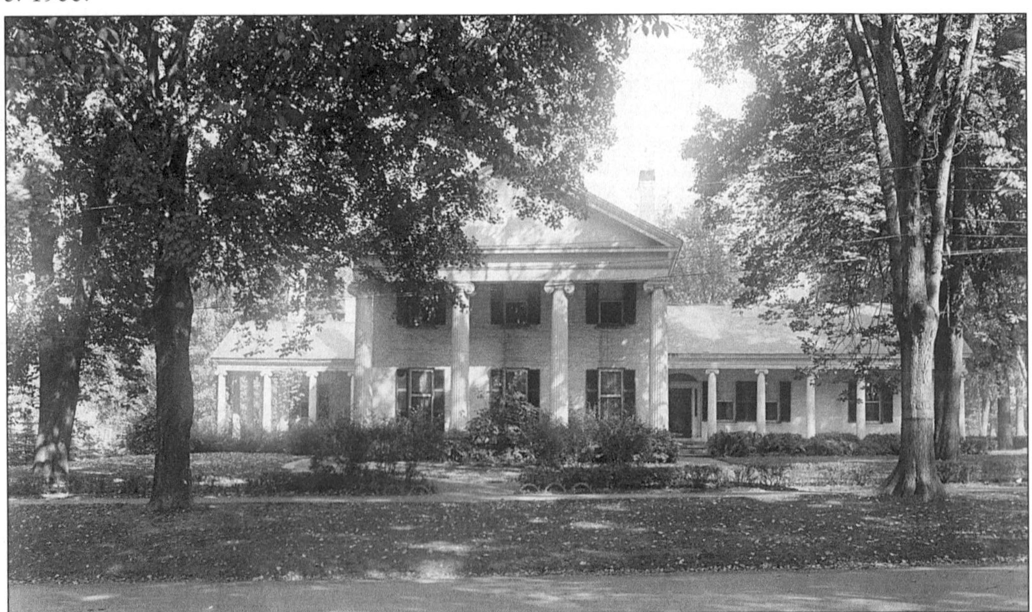

The Gould-Clapp-Potter House, at the corner of High and Main Streets, is an excellent example of Greek Revival architecture. The house was built in 1827 by merchant Elijah A. Gould, but this is not its original appearance. After Gould ran into debt and lost the property, Henry Wells Clapp purchased the house in 1834. The house lot once encompassed all the land between Main, Church, Franklin, and High Streets and had a statuary garden in the back.

Anson K. Warner, a successful farmer, held various town offices until he was killed in the Bardswell Ferry railroad crash in 1886. After his widow, Esther Warner, died in 1915, the A.K. Warner Fund for American Boys and Girls was established for the education of indigent Greenfield residents between the ages of 14 and 20. The fund is still active. This cabinet-card photograph was taken in Petaluma, California, *c.* 1880.

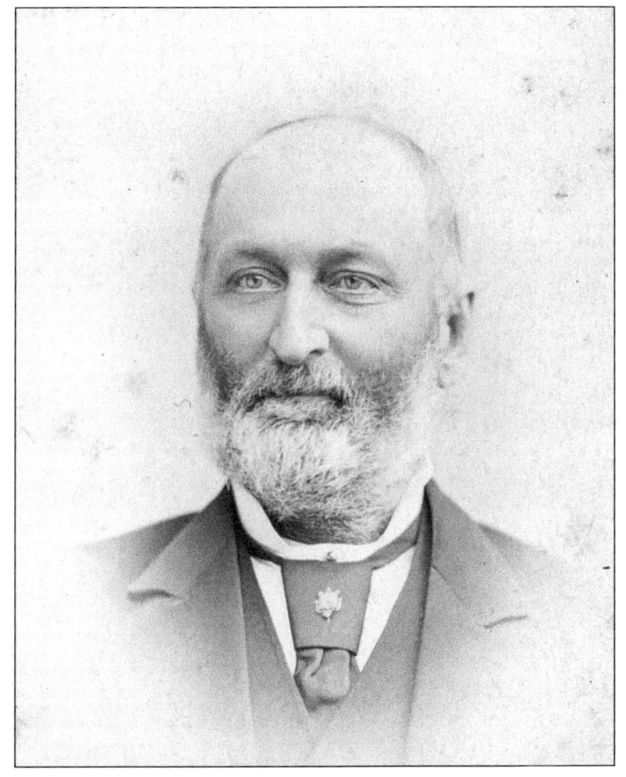

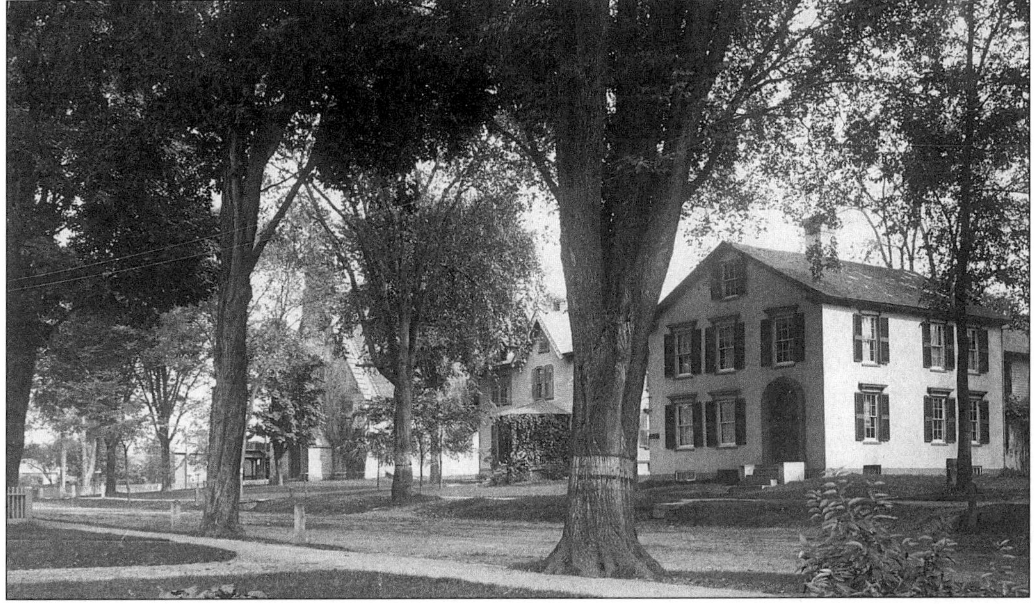

This 1880s photograph shows Federal Street just south of Church Street, an area that has changed a great deal over the years. The house in the foreground has been replaced by the Greenfield Cooperative Bank. The next house, which serves as a parsonage for the Episcopal church, now has stucco siding. In the background is St. James Church. The elm trees are gone, and the street has been widened.

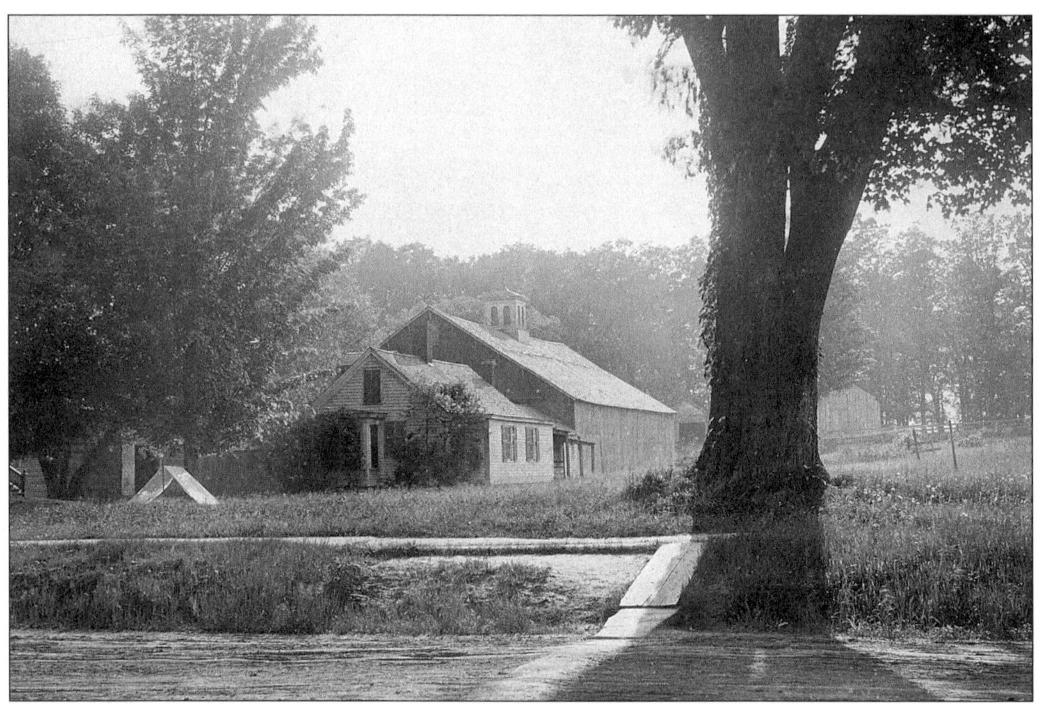

The old Pierce farmhouse and barn were on the west side of Federal Street, where the Fleet Bank is now located. This huge farm extended from Garfield Street north to middle of the Lunt Silversmiths Block and west beyond the railroad tracks. The wooden path leads across Federal Street to Anna Pierce Judah's house.

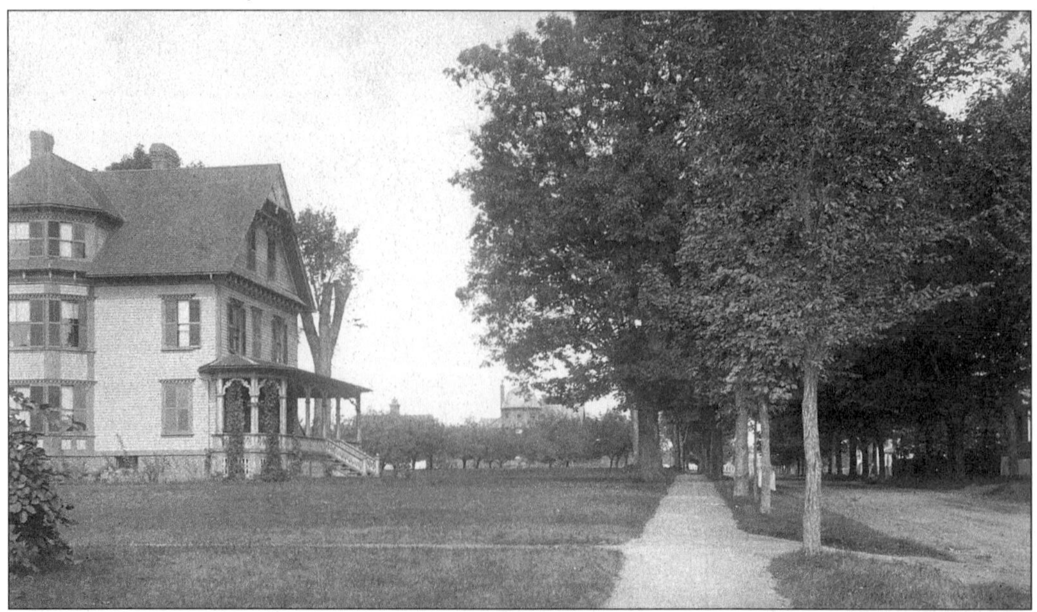

This 1890s photograph shows the John Joyce Pierce House at the corner of Abbot and Federal Streets, across from the Greenfield Middle School. The Pierce family lived in this house from 1886 to 1978. The very large Pierce farm building was just north of the house. The property was sold over the years to developers for house lots.

Theodore Dehone Judah (1826–1863) was one of the originators and promoters of the transcontinental railroad. Only his untimely death from yellow fever prevented him from being one of those who profited greatly from this achievement.

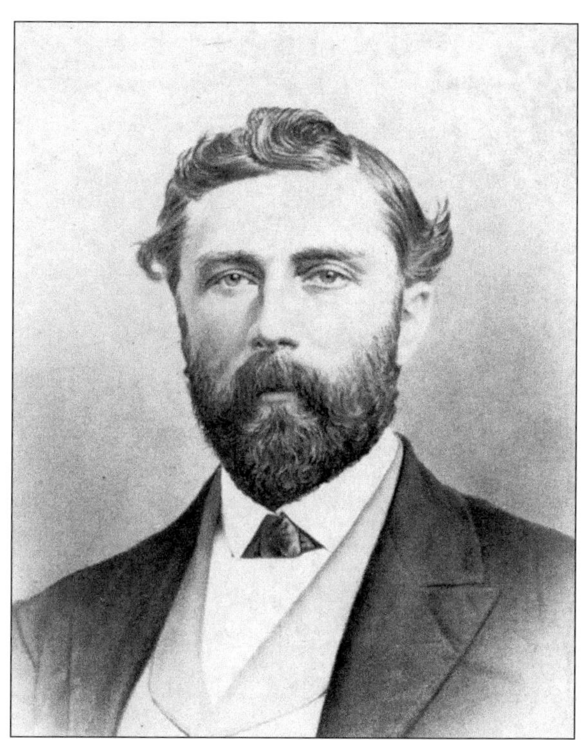

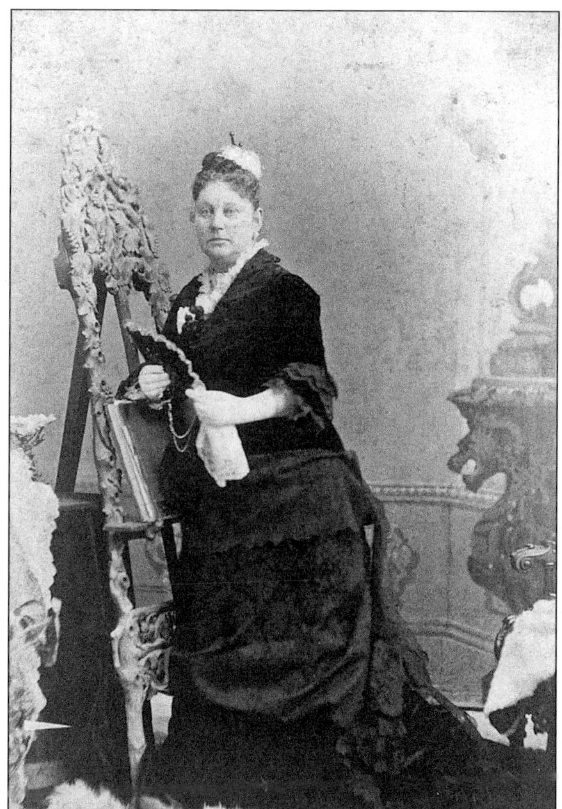

Anna Feron Pierce Judah (1828–1895) was the wife of Theodore Dehone Judah, an originator of the transcontinental railroad. Her parents were John Joyce Pierce and Eliza Dwight Field Pierce. An artist in her own right, she traveled extensively with her husband, journeying into the Colorado mountains to help scout routes for the transcontinental railroad.

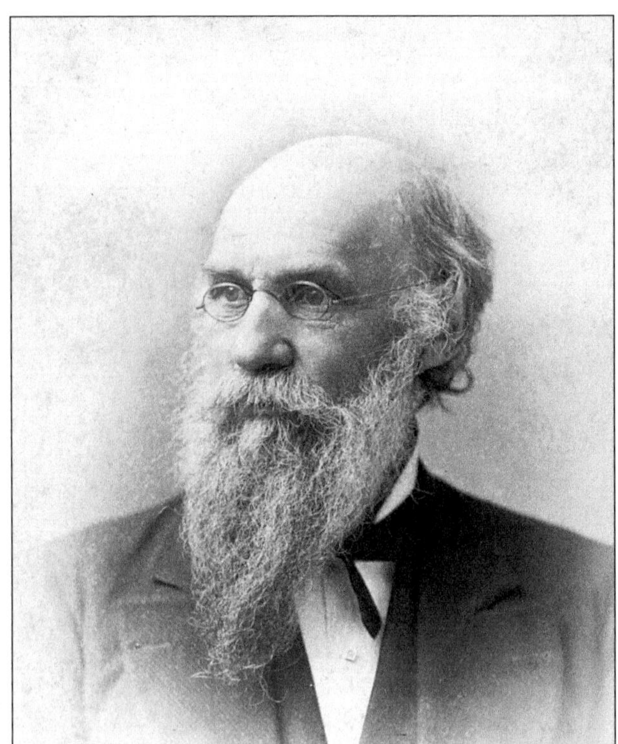

This portrait of Dr. Joseph Beals was taken *c.* 1880 by Benjamin Popkins, a longtime Greenfield photographer with studios at the corner of Main and Federal Streets. Dr. Beals was an early dentist who also briefly had a photograph studio. He was a founder of the Greenfield Public Library and an early spiritualist at the Lake Pleasant retreat in Montague.

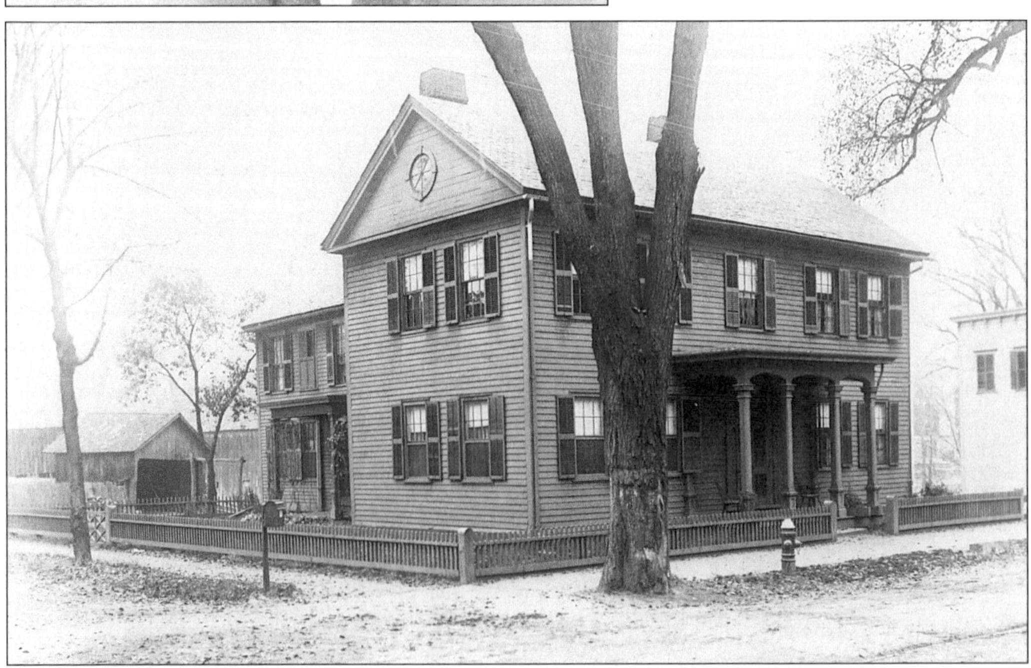

This photograph shows the Ambrose Ames House, built in 1793 at the corner of Ames and Federal Streets as part of a dairy that operated into the 20th century. Its pastures were located where Madison Circle is now. These buildings were removed in order to make way for what is currently Bill's Restaurant. Ambrose Ames served as postmaster from 1804 to 1841 and was also a selectman and volunteer fireman.

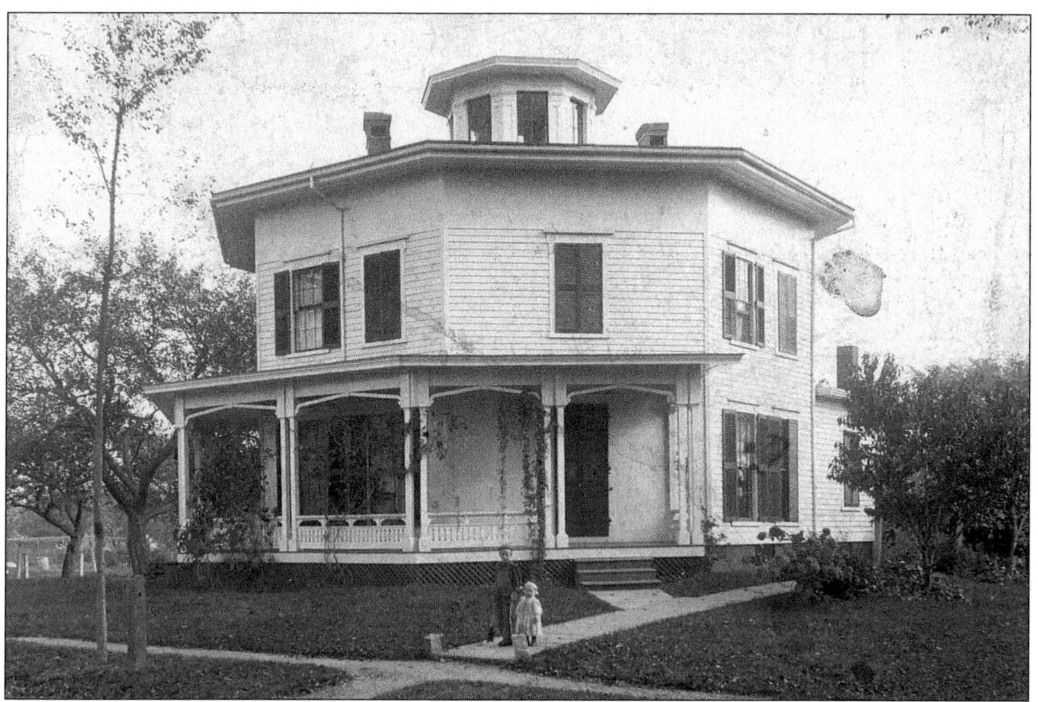

This octagon house is located at 117-119 Conway Street. It was built by Elias B. McClellon in 1858. (Howes Brothers photograph.)

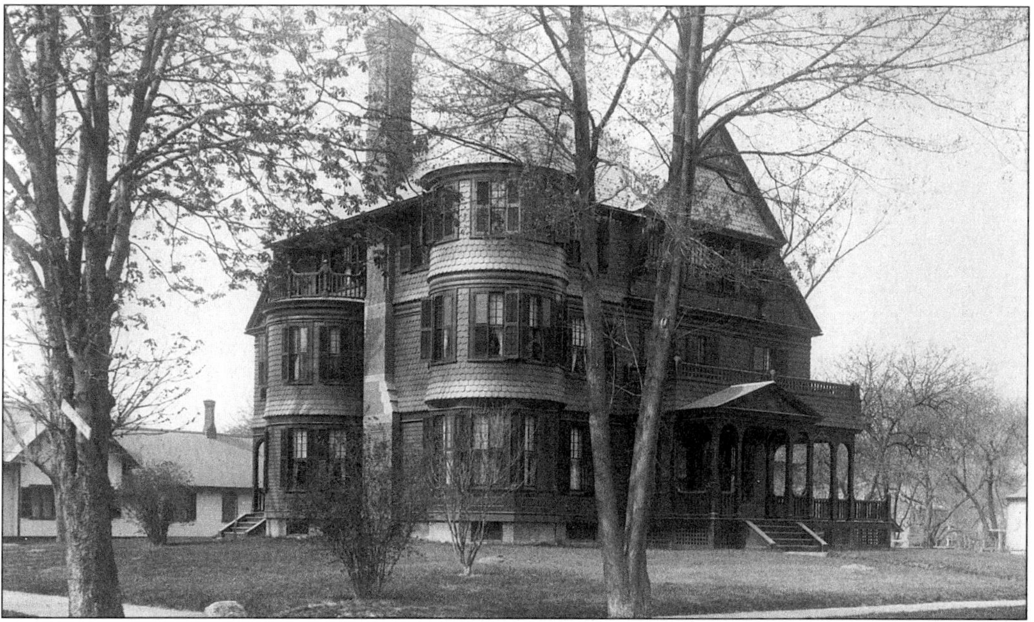

The W.N. Potter House was built in 1888 at the corner of Church and Franklin Streets, replacing a house that was moved to Union Street. A wonderful example of Queen Anne architecture, the Potter House is now a home for elderly women, each of whom have their own room and eat in a common dining room.

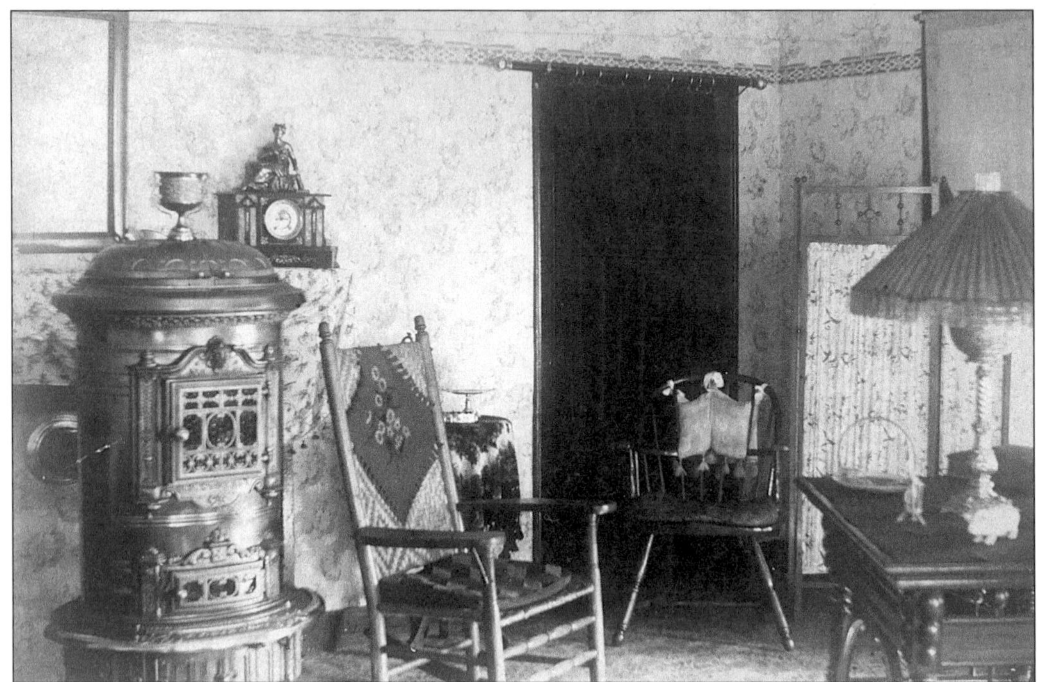

This photograph shows the sitting room in the Old Tavern Farm house in 1892, when it was a private residence. Today, owner Gary Sanderson runs a bed and breakfast, continuing the old building's tradition of hospitality to travelers.

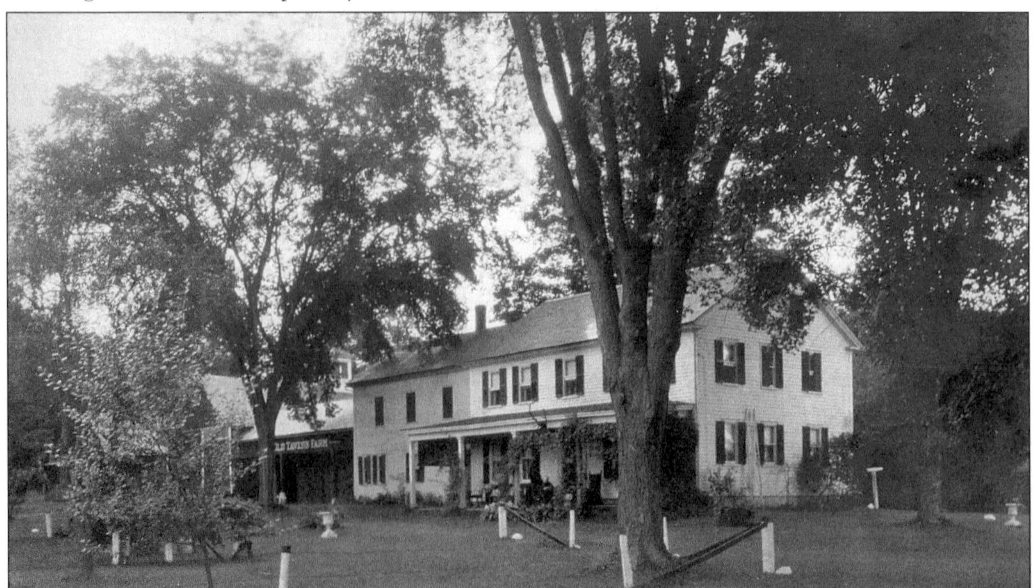

The Old Tavern Farm is located at the intersection of Colrain and Green River Roads. Originally built in the 1740s by Samuel Hinsdale as a tavern, the farm also served as a stagecoach stop. On the second floor is a large ballroom with a "spring" floor that was specially constructed to add bounce for dancing. In more recent years, Frank Gerrett and his daughter Helen Gerrett lived here. Although they used the building as a private residence, the Gerretts left much of the original tavern intact.

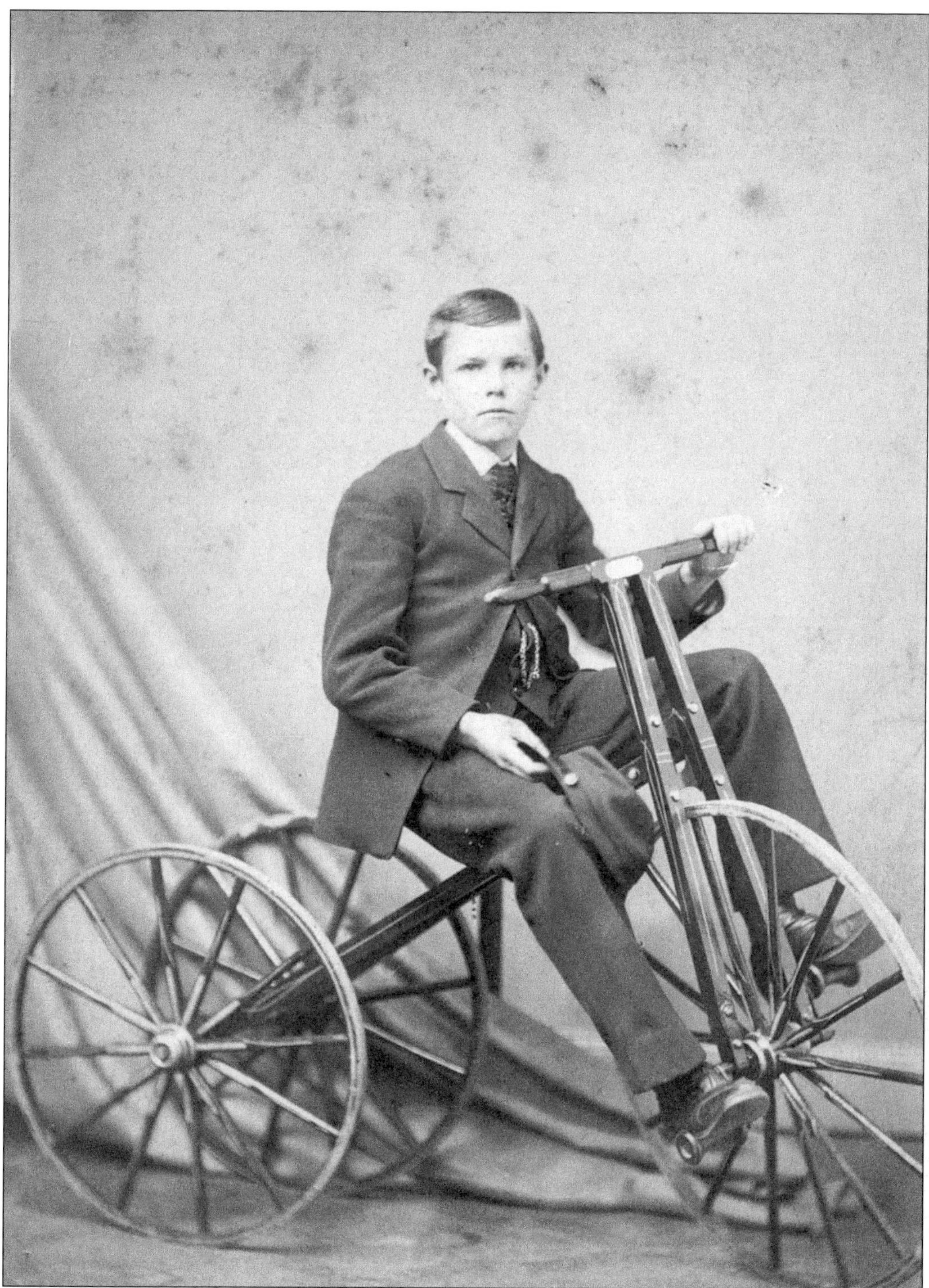

Frederick Russell Hollister (1865–1927) was the son of early Greenfield jeweler J.H. Hollister. The younger Hollister was a member of an early Greenfield Penny Farthing cycling club and went on to establish his own jewelry business in Providence, Rhode Island. His uncle was the photographer Benjamin F. Popkins. (Photograph courtesy of the Hollister family.)

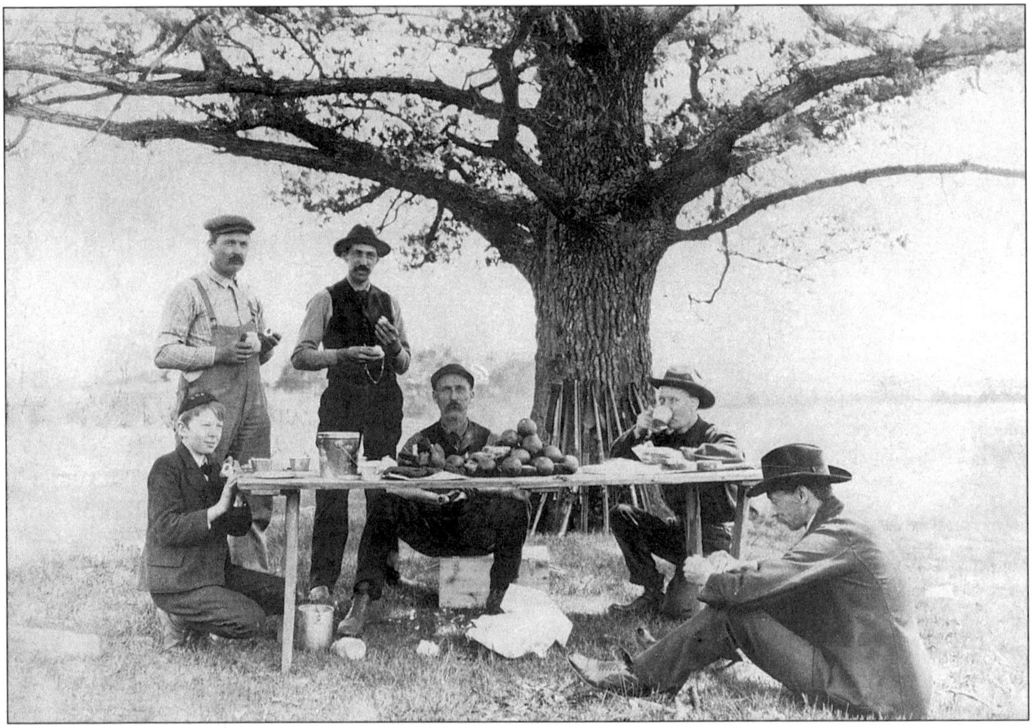

The Woodchuck Gang (c. 1899) included, from left to right, Phil Foster, Thad Parmenter, ? Tryon, Cliff Goodnow, Wendell F. Foster, and Arthur Waite. The details of this informal club have been lost to history. The group obviously enjoyed being together and getting out into the countryside.

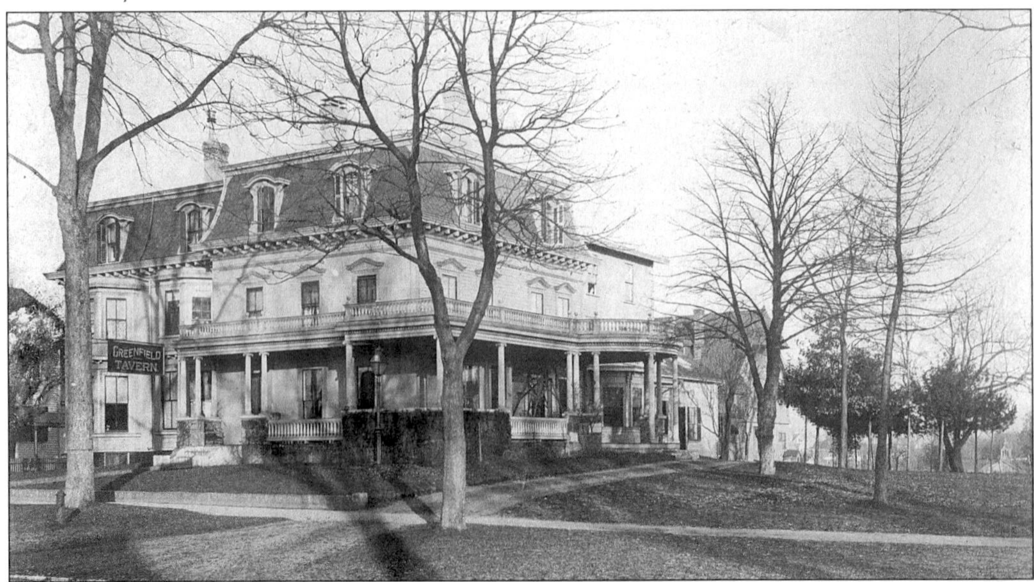

The Converse House was built on the corner of Conway and Main Streets in the 1890s. It later served as the second Franklin County Public Hospital from 1898 to 1910. After the hospital moved to its present High Street site, the Converse served as a rooming house until it was demolished in the 1950s.

Mary Prudence Wells Smith (1840–1930) was the first female bank employee in Massachusetts. Smith wrote a series of children's books, including *The Boy Captive of Old Deerfield*. She was the founder of both the Historical Society of Greenfield and the Greenfield Women's Club in the early 20th century. She grew up in the Meadows with roots deep in local history and she was an active Unitarian.

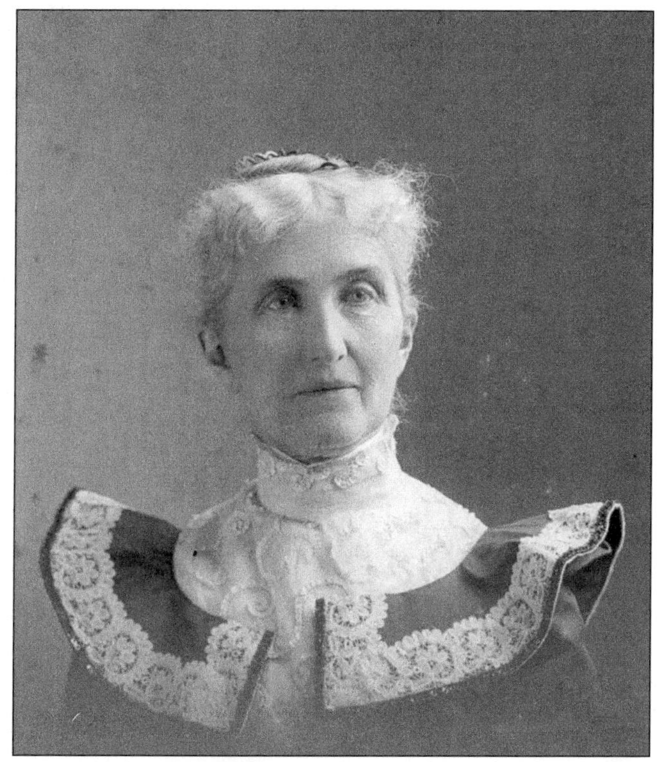

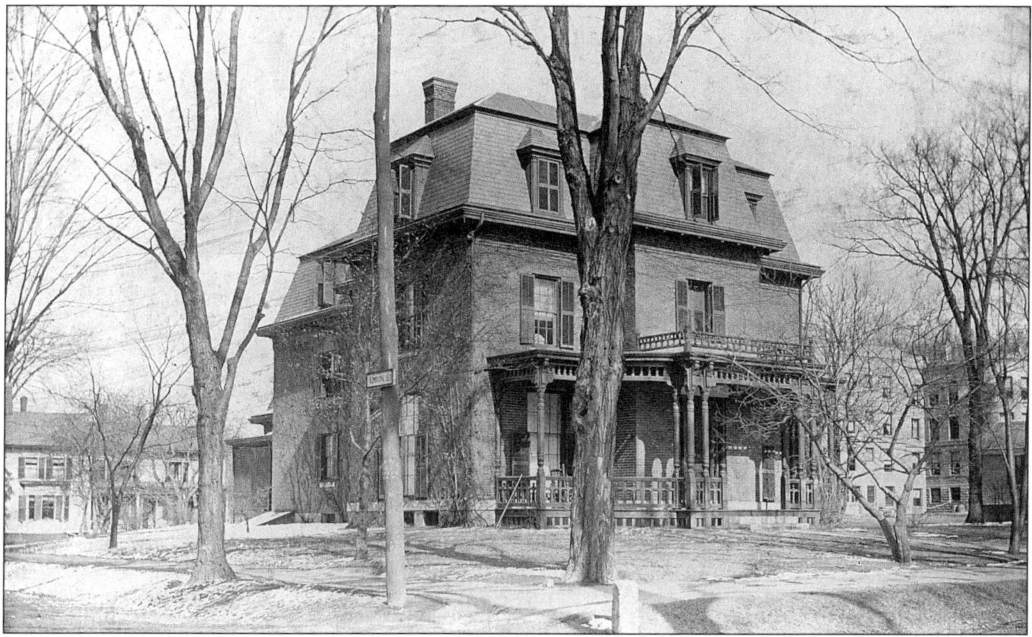

The original part of this house at the corner of Church and Union Streets was built for Thomas Wait in 1851. The third floor and the mansard roof were added in 1883 by a new owner, John E. Devlin. The front porch was added in 1886. The Historical Society purchased the building in 1914 to use as a museum. This photograph was taken *c.* 1910. Behind the house is the rear of the Weldon Hotel.

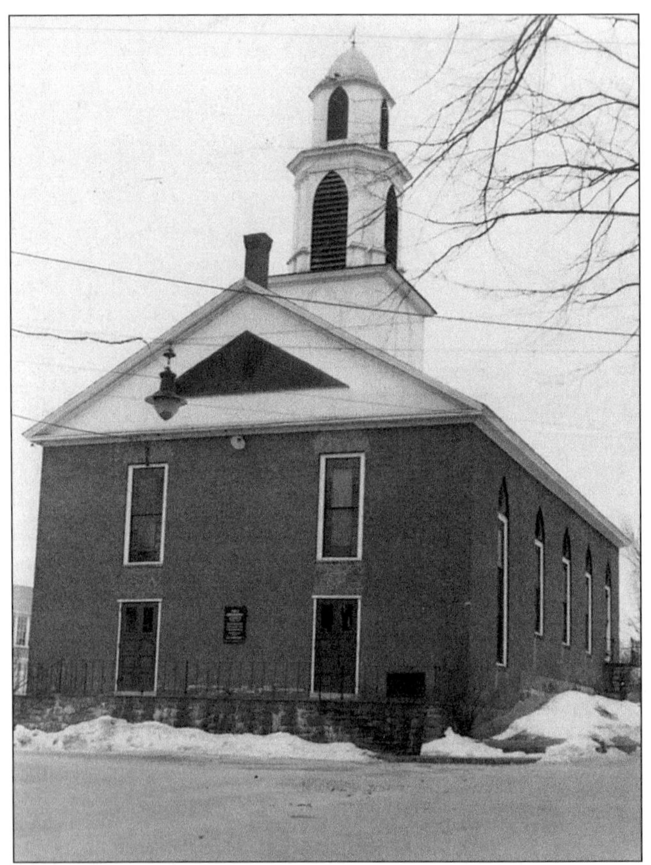

The First Congregational Church and Parish Hall at Nash's Mills was often referred to as the North Parish. The church was designed and built by Isaac Damon of Northampton in 1832. The church was located in the middle of the northern end of Conway Street, where it joins Silver Street. The parish hall is visible on the right and Leyden Road is visible between the two buildings in this photograph taken in the early 1960s. Due to construction of Interstate 91 in this area, the historic old church was given up by its congregation in 1963. The First Congregational Church is now located on Silver Street, near Federal Street.

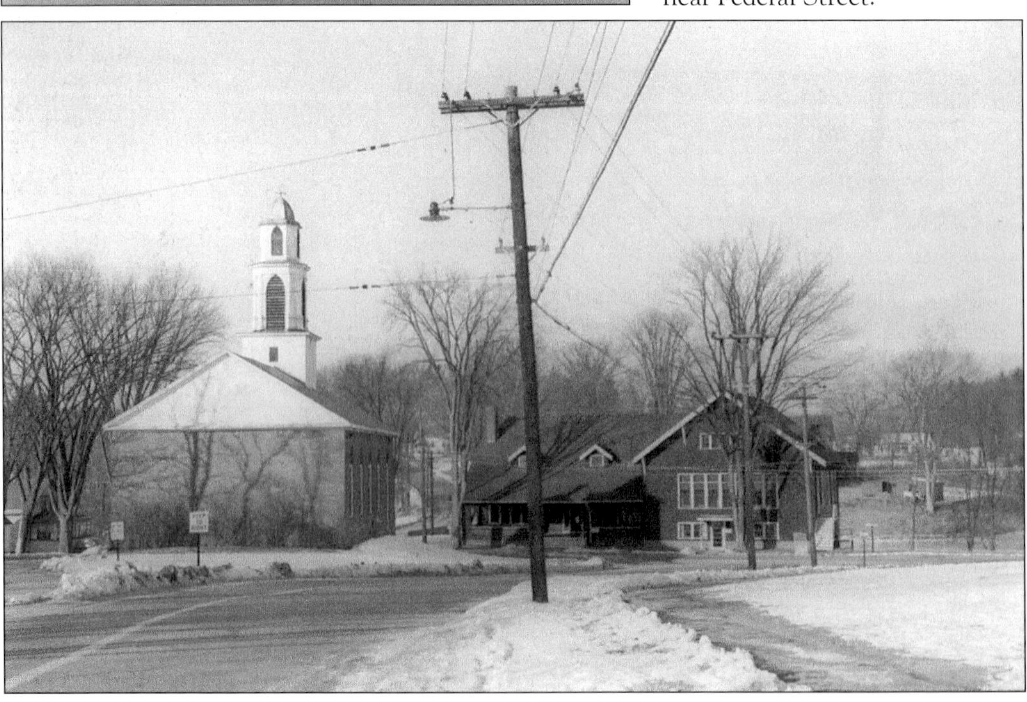

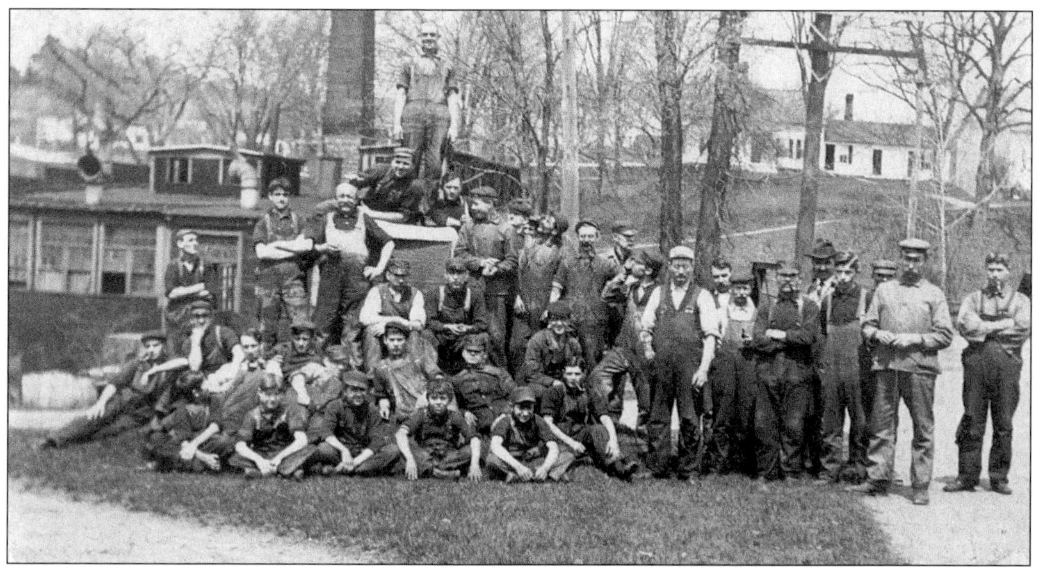

Workers pose in front of the Warner Manufacturing Company's cutlery factory on Leyden Road at Nash's Mills. The Carpenter Farmhouse is in the background. This photograph was taken in 1910. Interstate 91 now goes through this site.

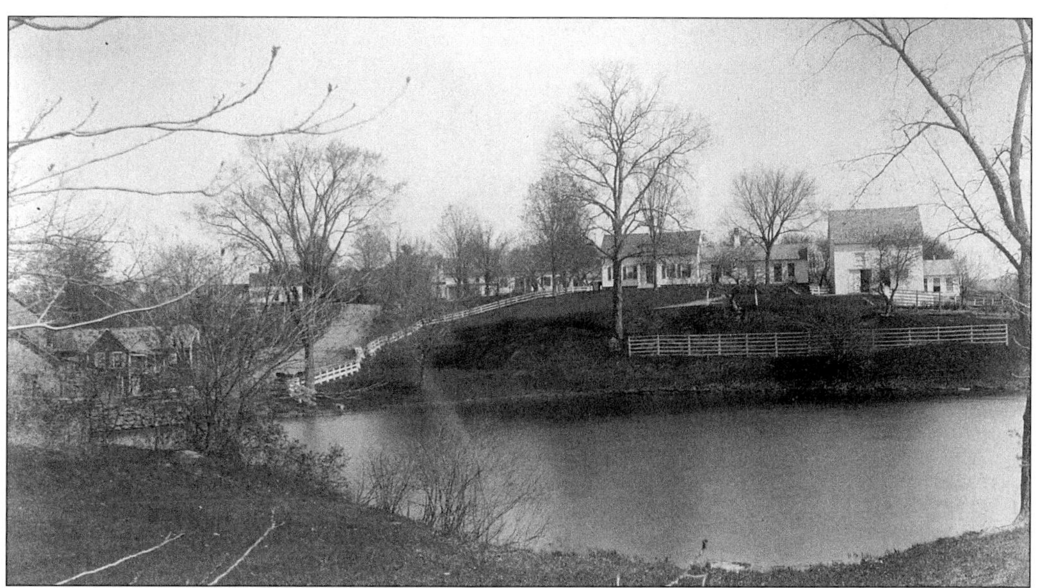

Nash's Mill Pond was located just east of the current bridge over Interstate 91 at the intersection of Leyden Road and Conway Street. This beautiful historical area disappeared in 1963 due to the construction of the interstate highway. The hamlet included a church, a small school, farms, and houses. The old Carpenter residence in the foreground was moved to another location. The mill on the left disappeared in the early 1900s.

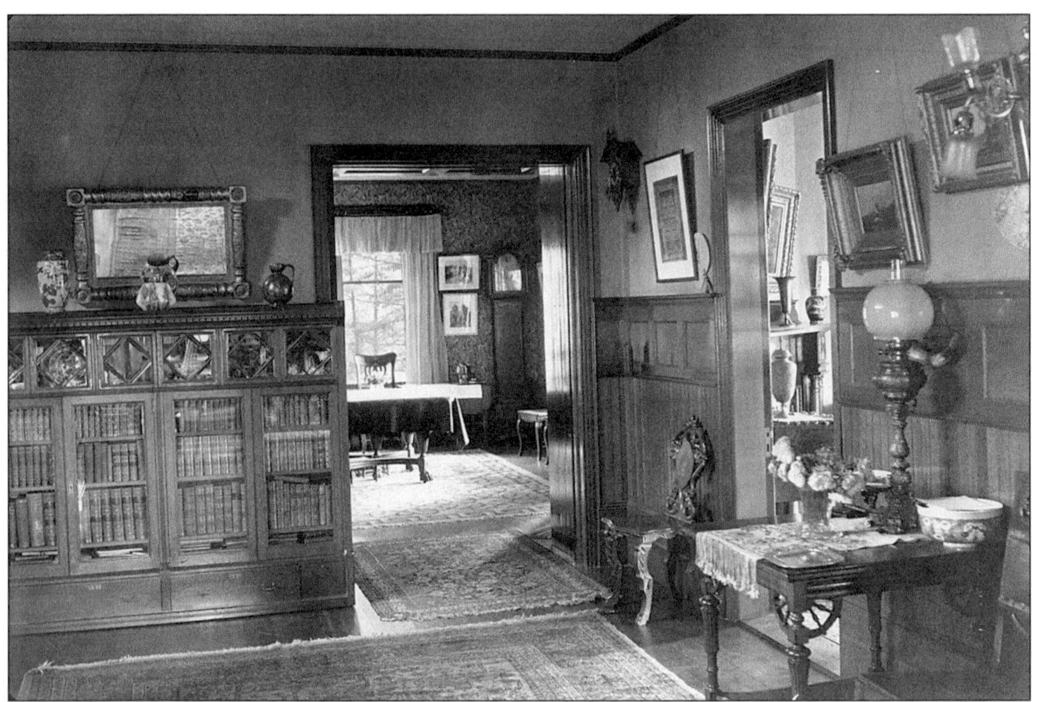

This photograph of the interior of Lupinwood, a house at the end of Highland Avenue, was taken when Fannie Stevens Peabody and Bertha F. Field lived here in the early 20th century. From this site there is a nice view of Deerfield to the south.

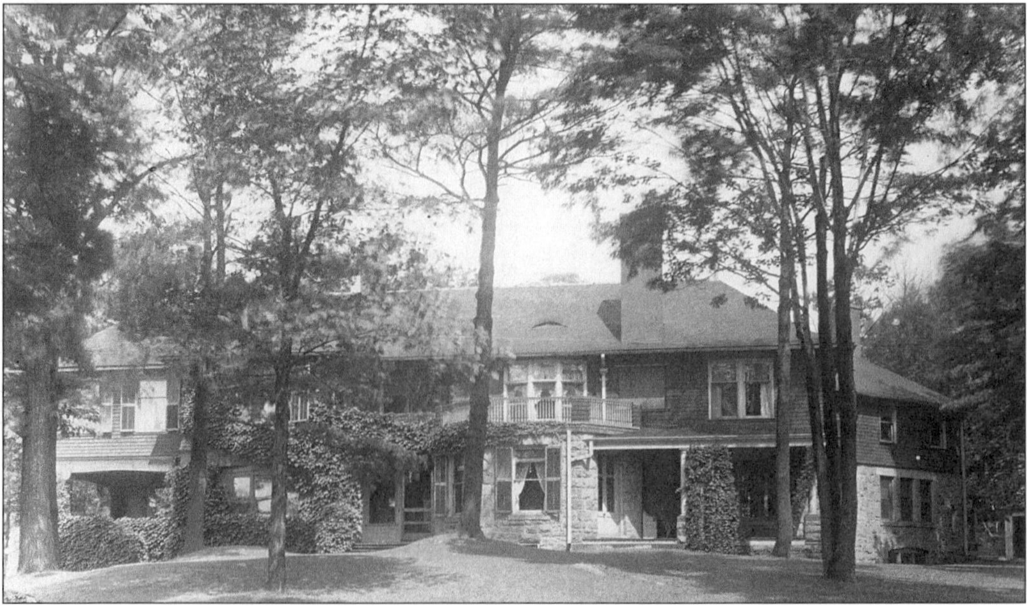

Lupinwood was built *c.* 1890 by Charles and Fannie Stevens Peabody as a summer home. Fannie Stevens grew up in Greenfield, married Charles Peabody (who had served as an officer in the Union army in the Civil War), and went with him to live in Philadelphia. This summer home, a shingle-style villa designed by the architectural firm of Cope and Sewardson of Philadelphia, was named Lupinwood for the flowers, lupins, that bloomed in the nearby woods.

Four

Trains to Automobiles

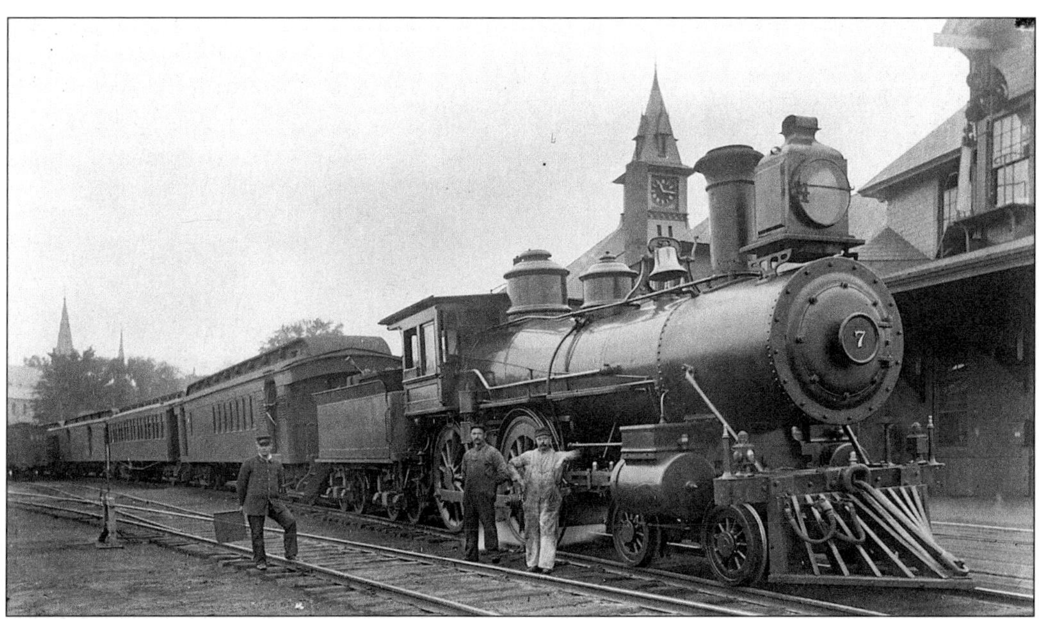

This photograph shows the crew of a passenger train on the west side of the railroad station in 1900. Note the lack of markings on the train. The two steeples in the background are the Second Congregational Church and the Unitarian church. The photographer was Orville C. Leonard of Greenfield, who worked for the railroad and shot a large number of excellent photographs.

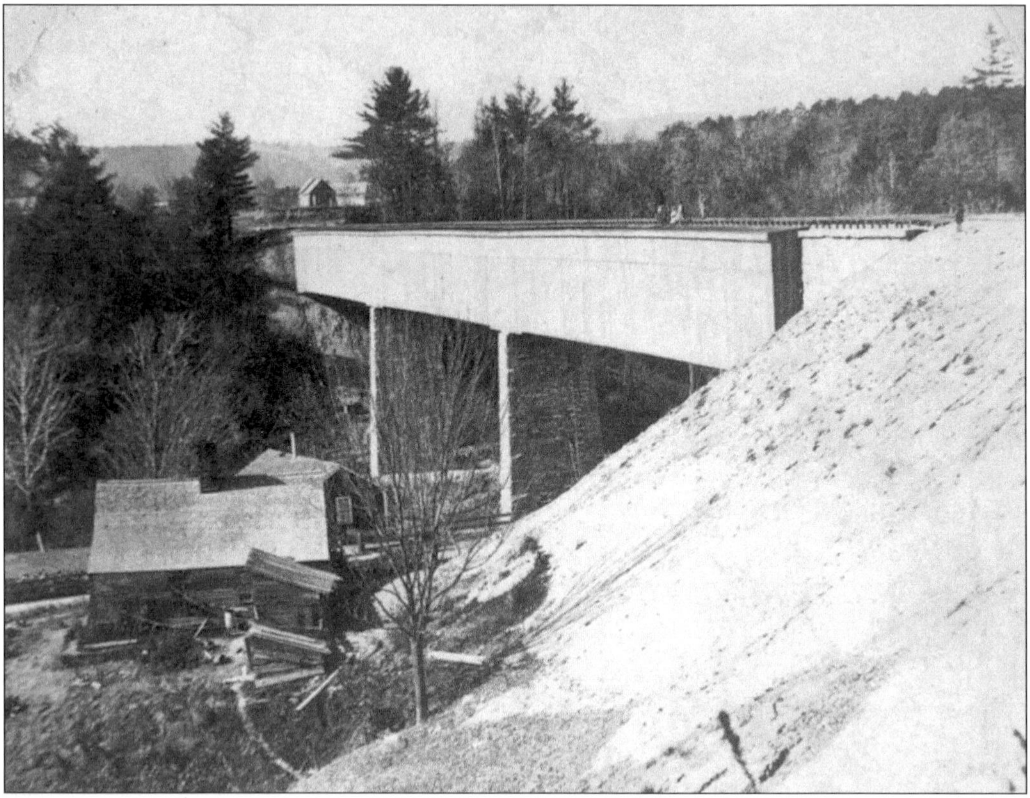

This is how Deerfield Street looked *c.* 1860. The Greenfield and Troy railroad bridge over the Green River was constructed just below the southern intersection of Washington and Deerfield Streets. The bridge was designed by Herman Haupt, later famous as the "railroad general" during the Civil War and as being the first contractor for the Hoosac Tunnel. This bridge was replaced later by an extension of the railroad through Greenfield center. (Photograph courtesy Peter Miller.)

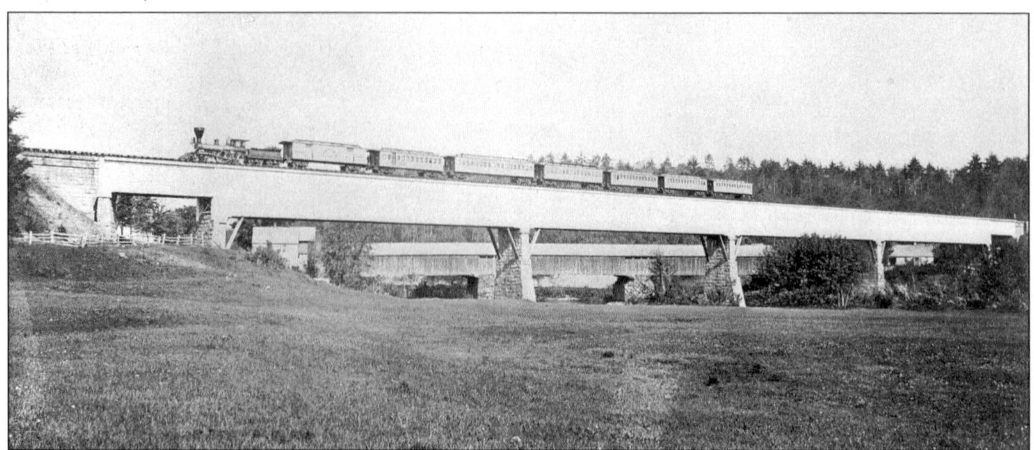

A train crosses the second Cheapside railroad bridge, *c.* 1875. The engine is named Holyoke and pulls wooden coaches and U.S. mail cars. This bridge replaced one that burned under mysterious circumstances during the Civil War. The double-barreled covered bridge is just east of it. The present concrete Routes 5 and 10 bridge is in front of this location.

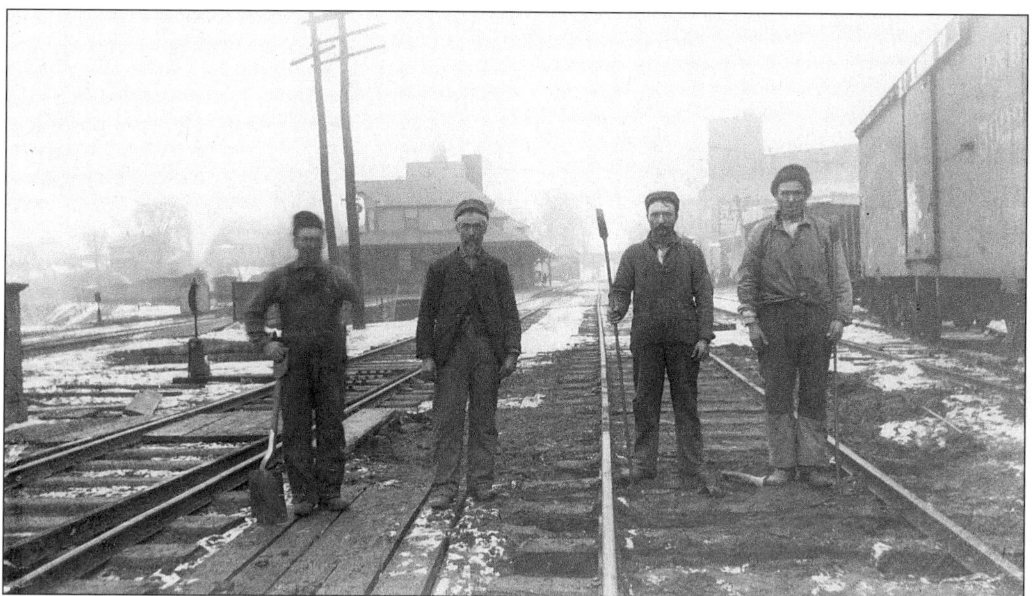

A railroad crew stands on the Connecticut River Railroad line of the Boston & Maine railroad tracks, which ran north and south through Greenfield. The railroad station is in the background. This photograph was taken *c.* 1900 by O.C. Leonard.

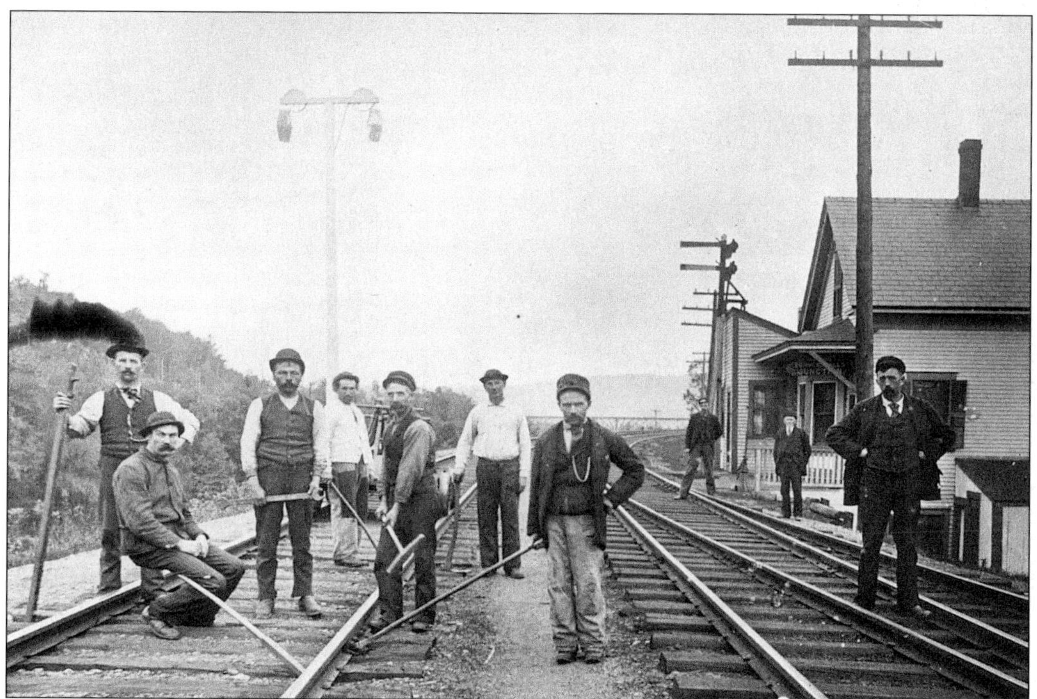

A track section gang works in East Greenfield *c.* 1900. For more than 100 years, Greenfield had large numbers of men working for the railroads. These tracks were laid west from the East Deerfield freight yards.

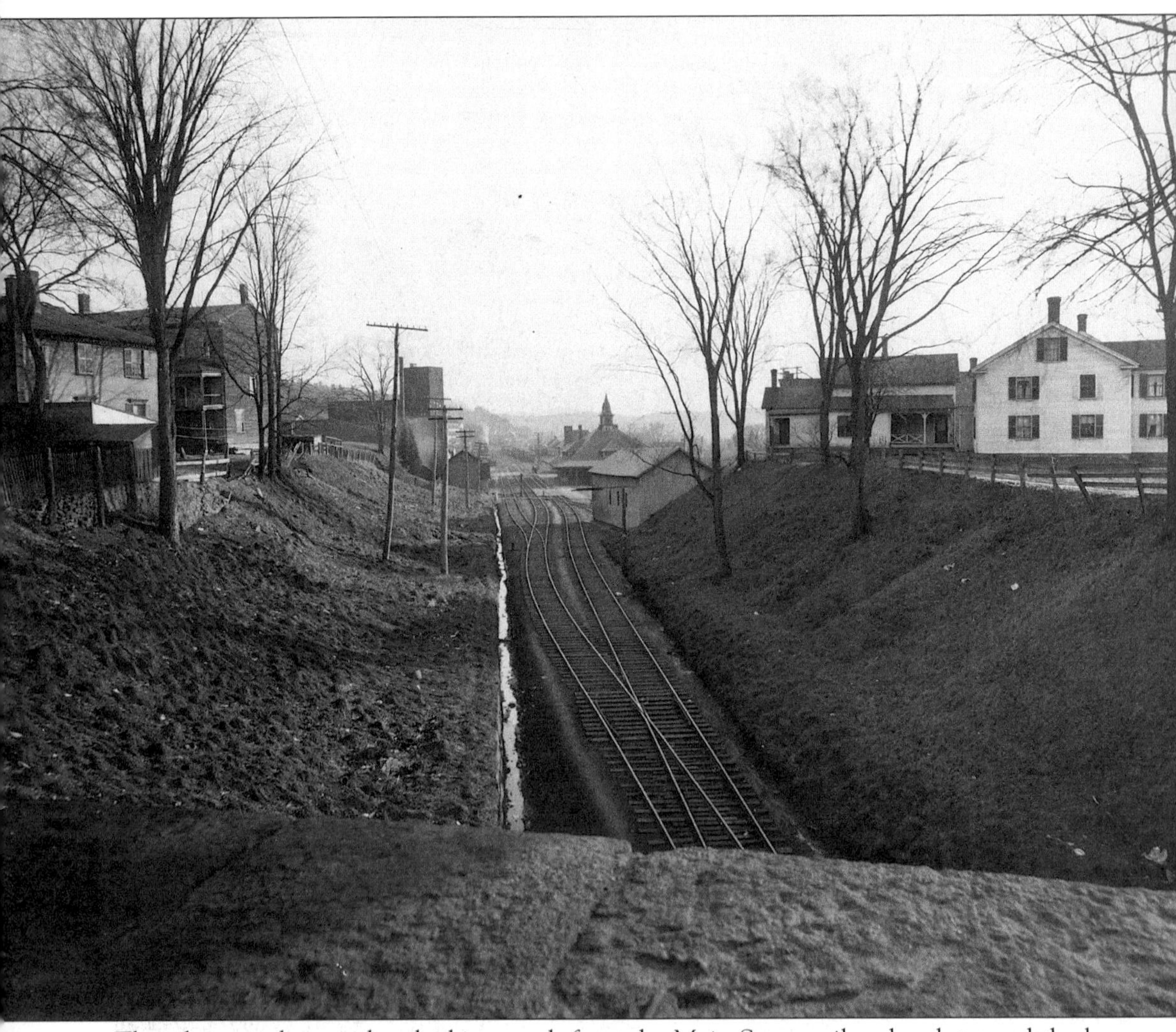

This photograph was taken looking south from the Main Street railroad arch toward the busy railroad station *c.* 1900. The first building on the left is the old Reverend Newton House and one of the wings of the High School for Young Ladies. Both buildings are now gone. The house on the right was removed to construct the Fiske Avenue and East Miles Street business complex. The town's first cemetery, known as the old burying ground, was located just south of this building, on the right. It was moved to make room for the railroad station.

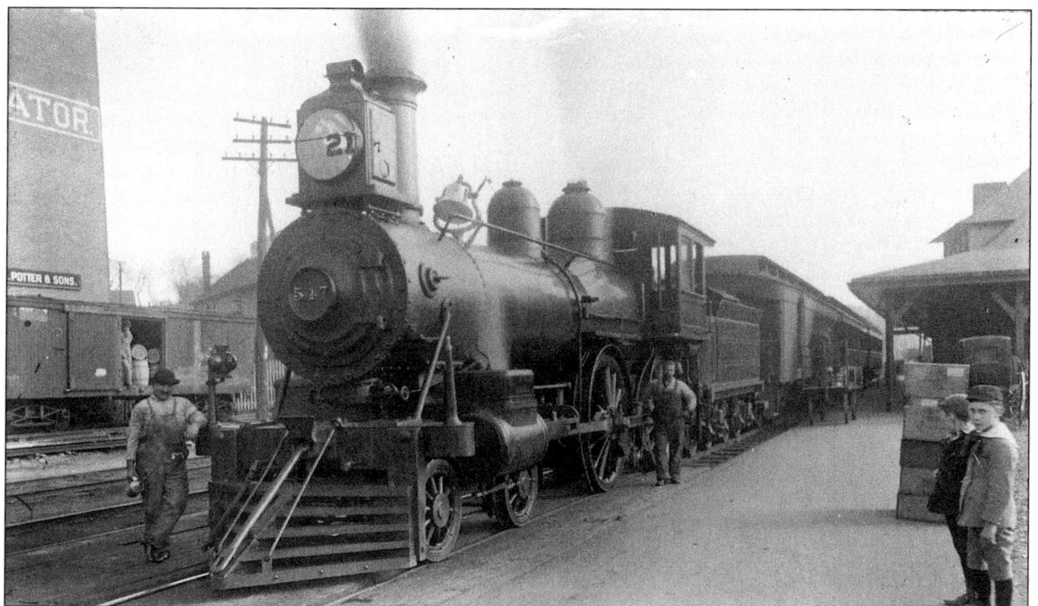

This was the engine crew for No. 547, probably of the Connecticut River Railroad, in 1900. Workers are unloading baggage from the passenger train and to the left, others are unloading a freight car.

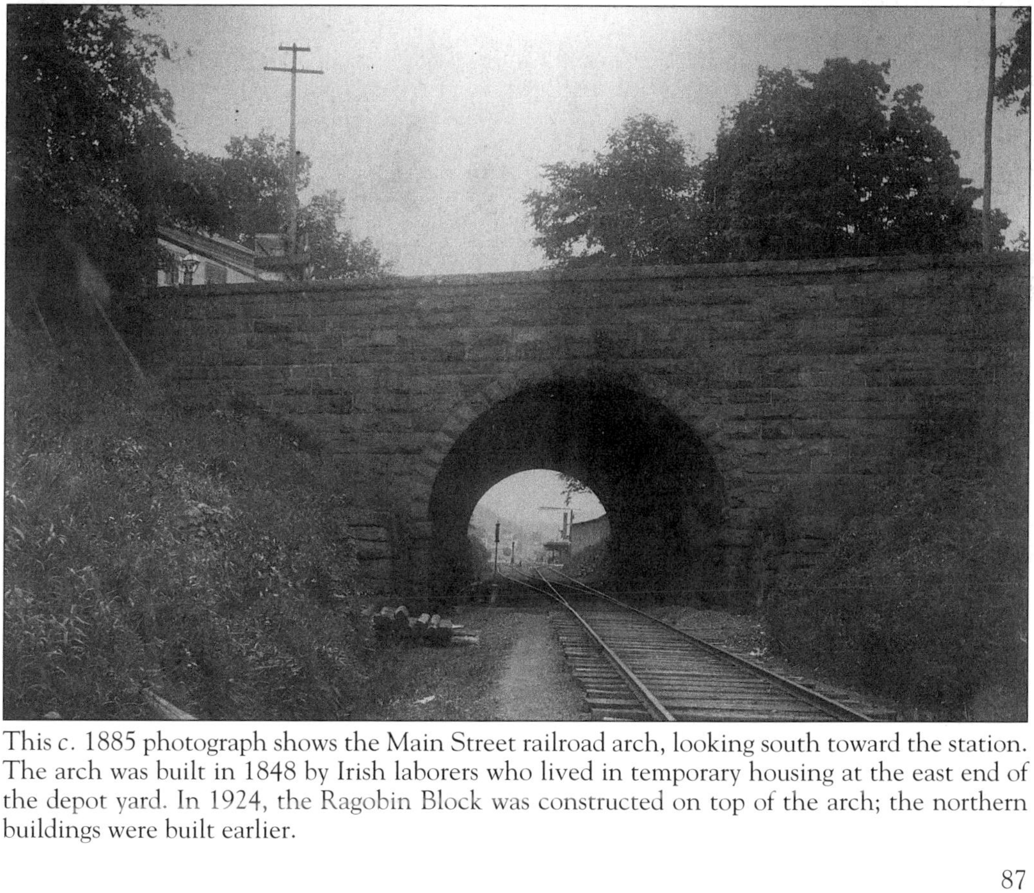

This *c.* 1885 photograph shows the Main Street railroad arch, looking south toward the station. The arch was built in 1848 by Irish laborers who lived in temporary housing at the east end of the depot yard. In 1924, the Ragobin Block was constructed on top of the arch; the northern buildings were built earlier.

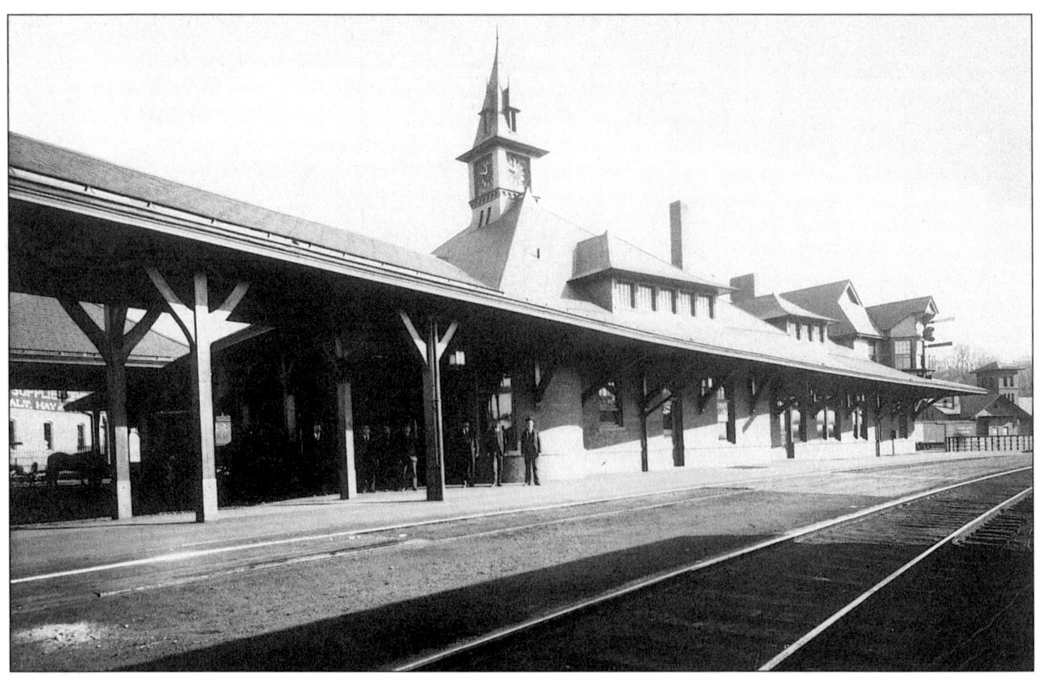

Greenfield's Union Station was built in 1881 and extensively remodeled in 1895. This photograph shows the western side, when the station was at its height *c.* 1900. The *porte cochere* on the front of the station did not remain long. Over the years, the station fell into disuse and disrepair, and in 1966, it was completely removed by the town.

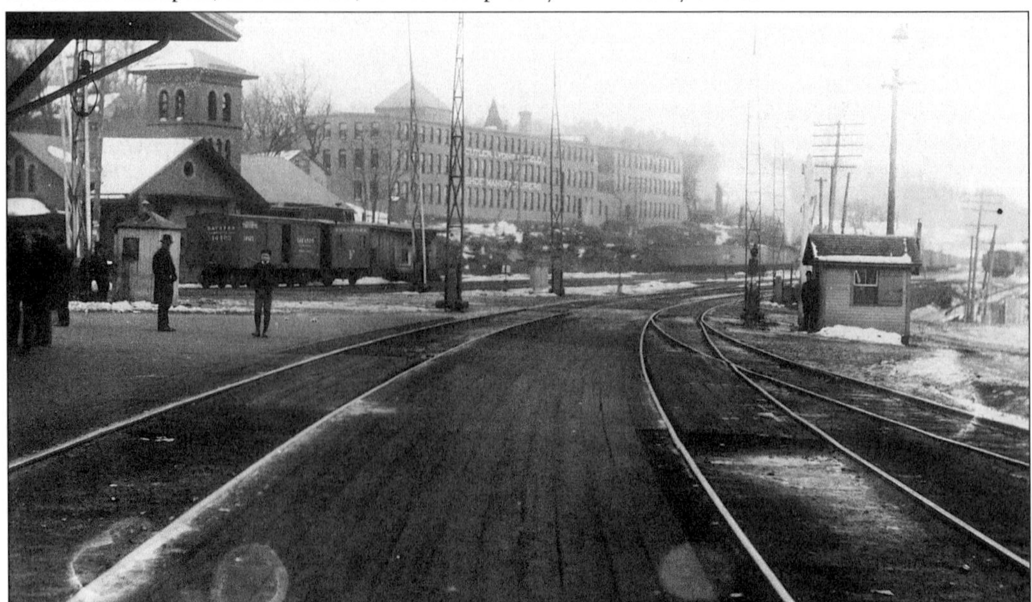

This photograph was taken in front of the new railroad station and shows the old station on the left. The newly constructed Cutler, Lyons, and Field Shoe Manufacturers factory is in the background. The photograph dates from 1892, the year the factory was finished and the at-grade crossing at the bottom of Bank Row, still visible here, was replaced by a railroad overpass that enabled trolleys to climb Bank Row.

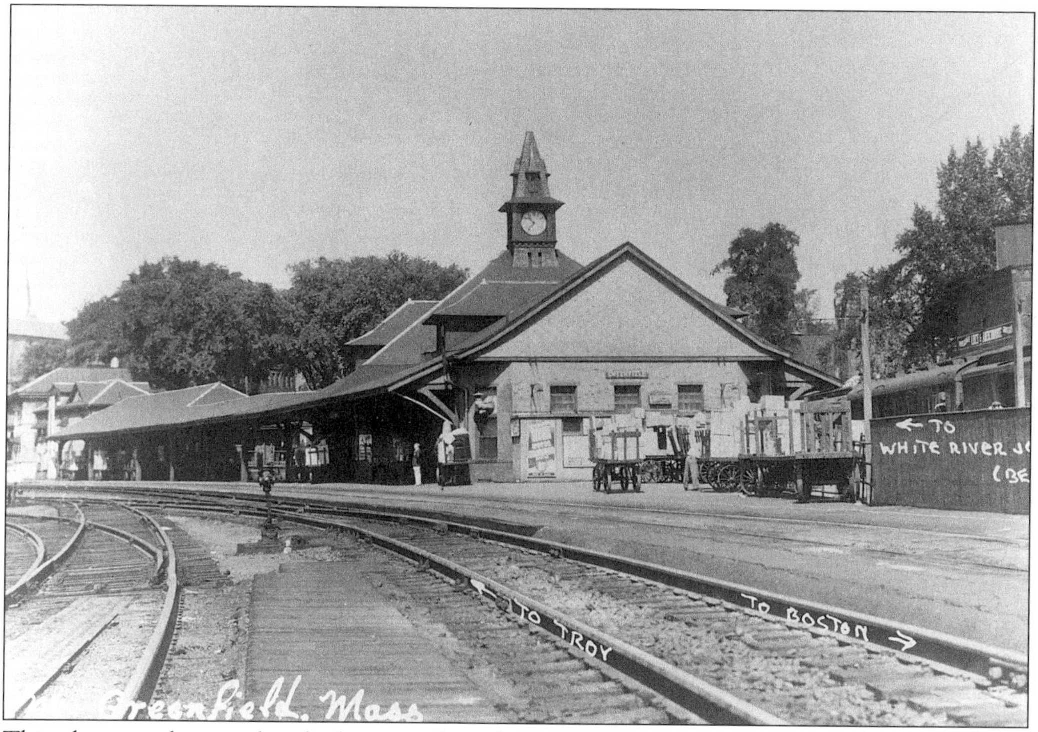

This photograph was taken looking north at the railroad station, *c.* 1949. Note that part of the station was already removed due to a 1947 fire. From right to left are the Luey & Abercrombie Warehouse, the station baggage room, the American Express office, and the Fitchburg Division office for the Boston & Maine Railroad. This area of town has recently been revived as the site of the new Greenfield Energy Park.

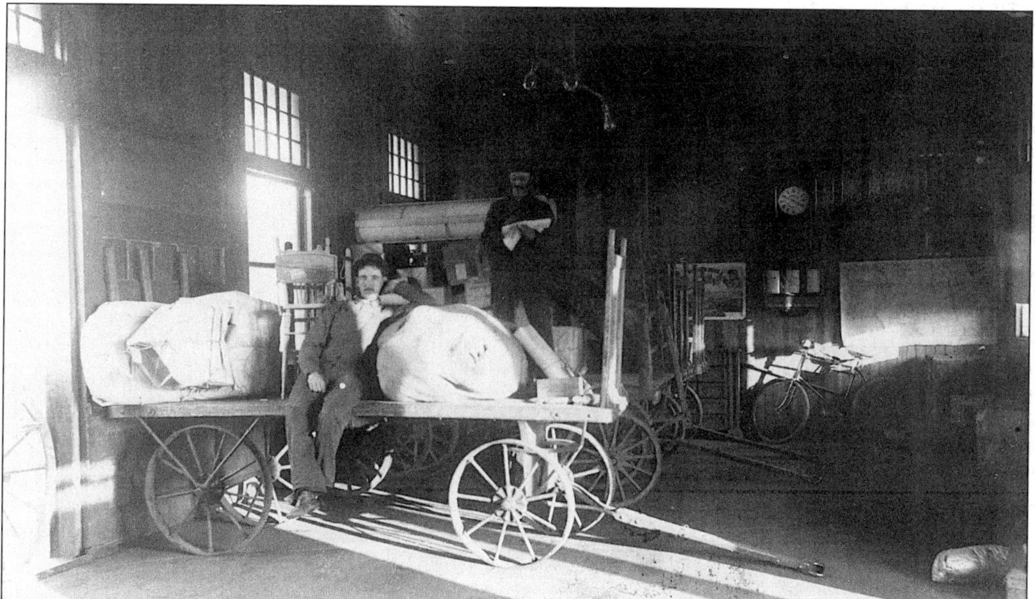

A baggage handler rests in the baggage building just northwest of the railroad station, *c.* 1900. A covered walkway connected the station with the baggage area.

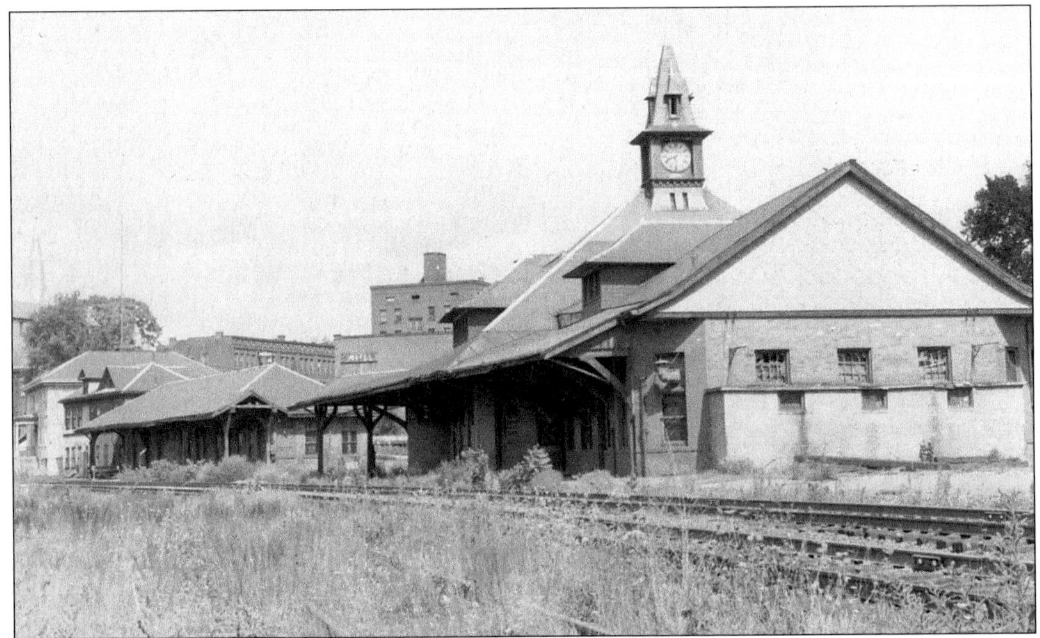

The railroad station complex was torn down in April 1966. Just before this photograph was taken *c.* 1965, there was a minor fire at the station. Note that the covered walkway between the baggage room and station has been removed.

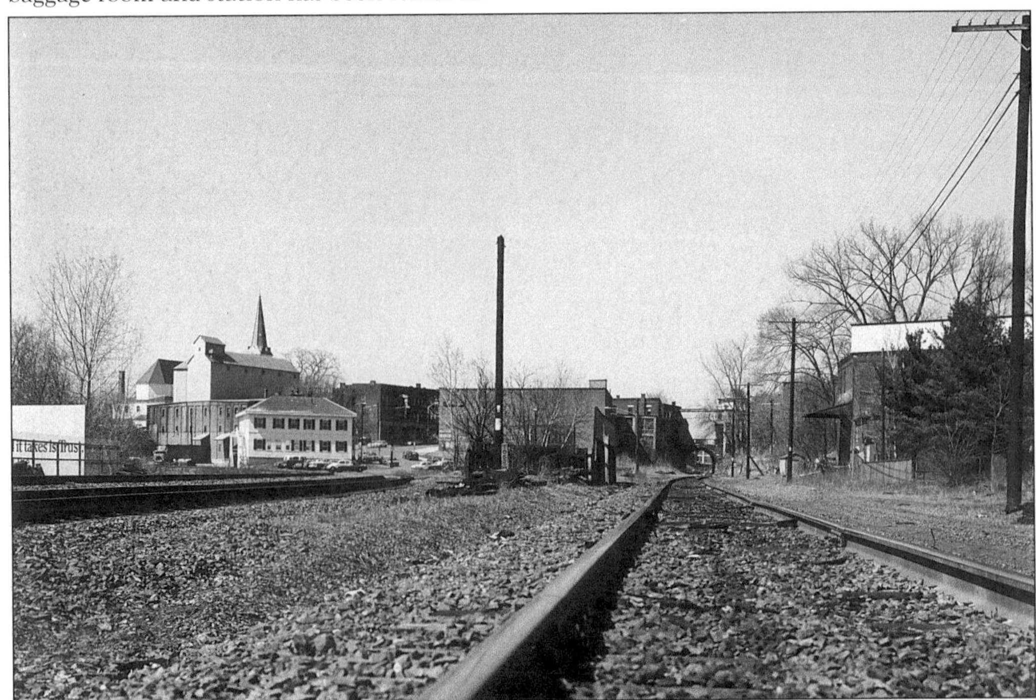

This 1981 photograph was taken looking north at site of the Greenfield Railroad Station. On the right is the old Connecticut River Railroad tracks that were laid through the tunnel under Main Street. On the left is the present Boston & Maine Railroad tracks laid out to the west and the Hoosac Tunnel.

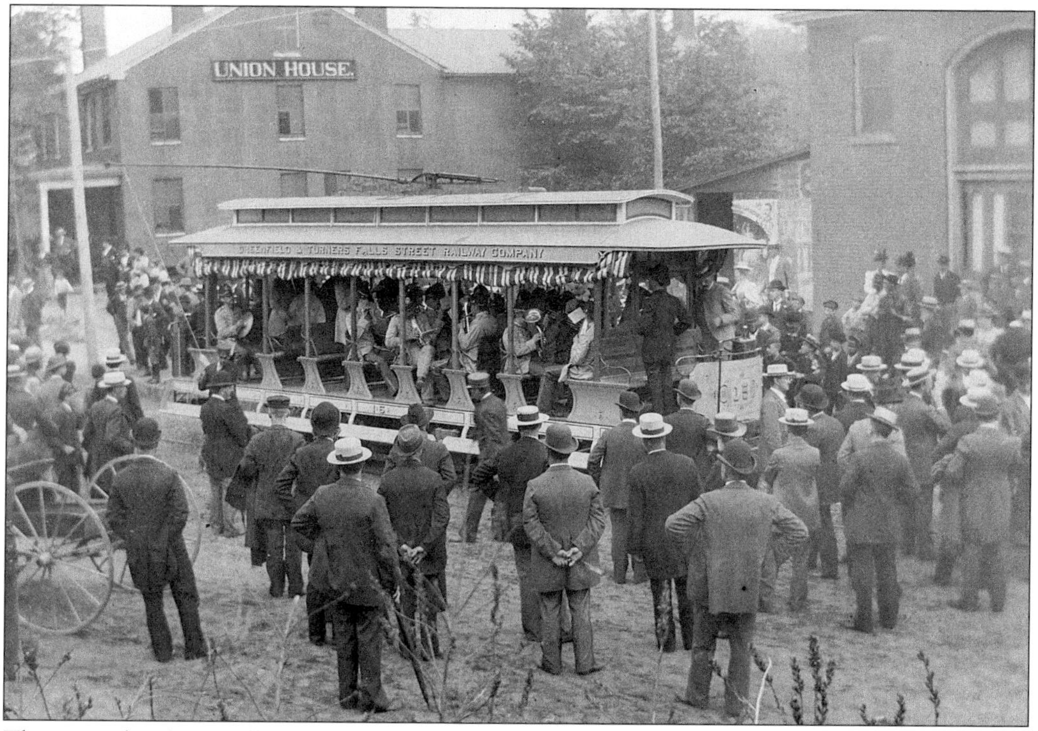

This was the first trolley ride into Greenfield in 1895 on the Greenfield & Turners Falls Railway Company. The Union House, formerly the Jailhouse Tavern, was located on the southern side of the Deerfield Street-Bank Row intersection, near the railroad overpass.

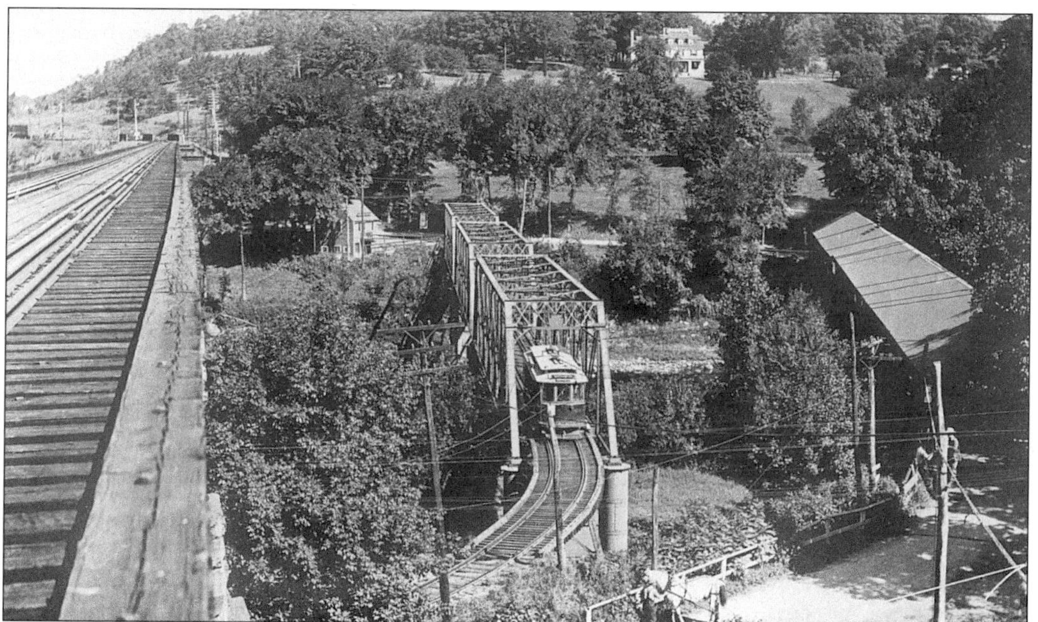

Here are the three bridges of Cheapside, *c.* 1900. This famous Deerfield-Greenfield scene includes the third railroad bridge, the trolley bridge, and the covered bridge. Greenfield is in the background. The Robert Abercrombie House is on the hill.

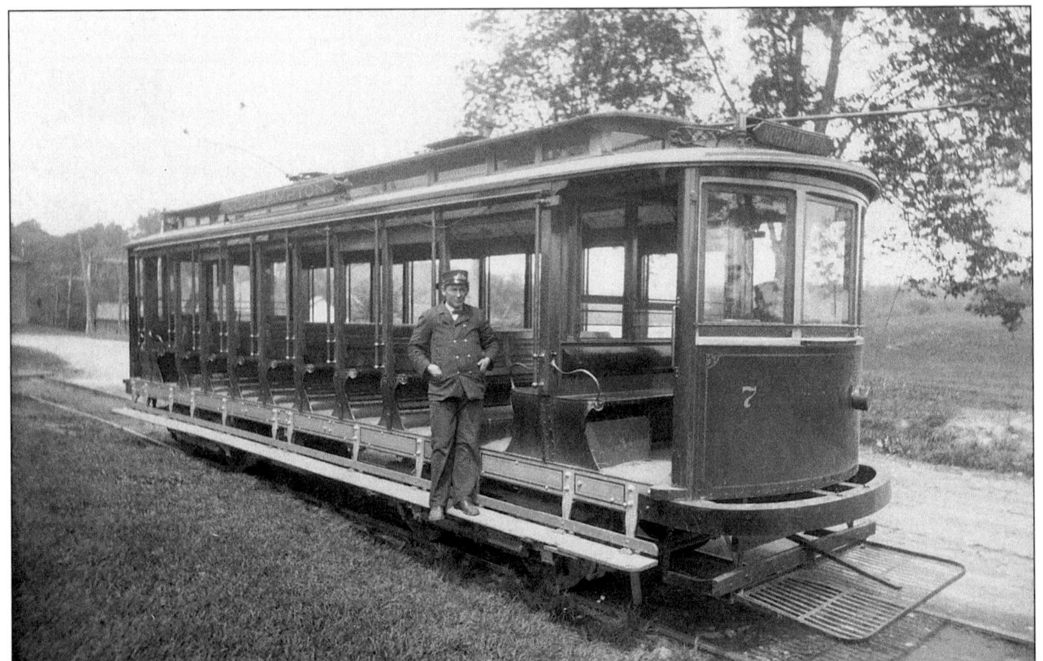

The trolley car Northampton reaches the Conway Street end of the line, *c.* 1905. The Connecticut Valley Street Railway Company named cars for each destination on the line. Northampton is located 20 miles south of Greenfield. Visible at the far left is the North Parish Church.

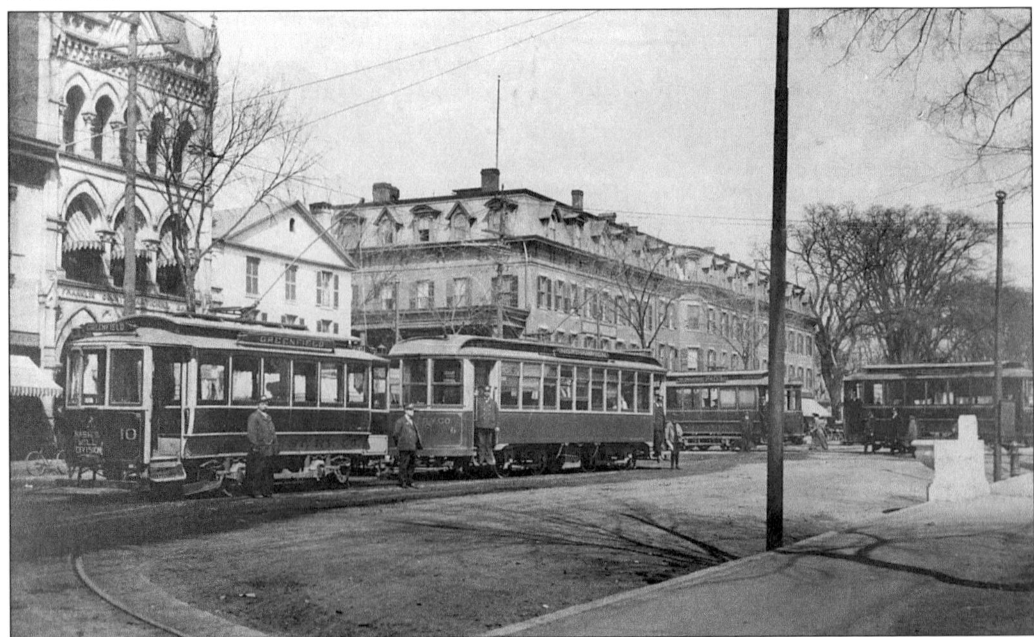

This mid-1920s photograph, looking east toward the intersection of Federal and Main Streets, shows trolleys lined up at the town common. All the buildings in the background are either gone or have been extensively altered. The watering trough at the right is now in Shattuck Park on Federal Street.

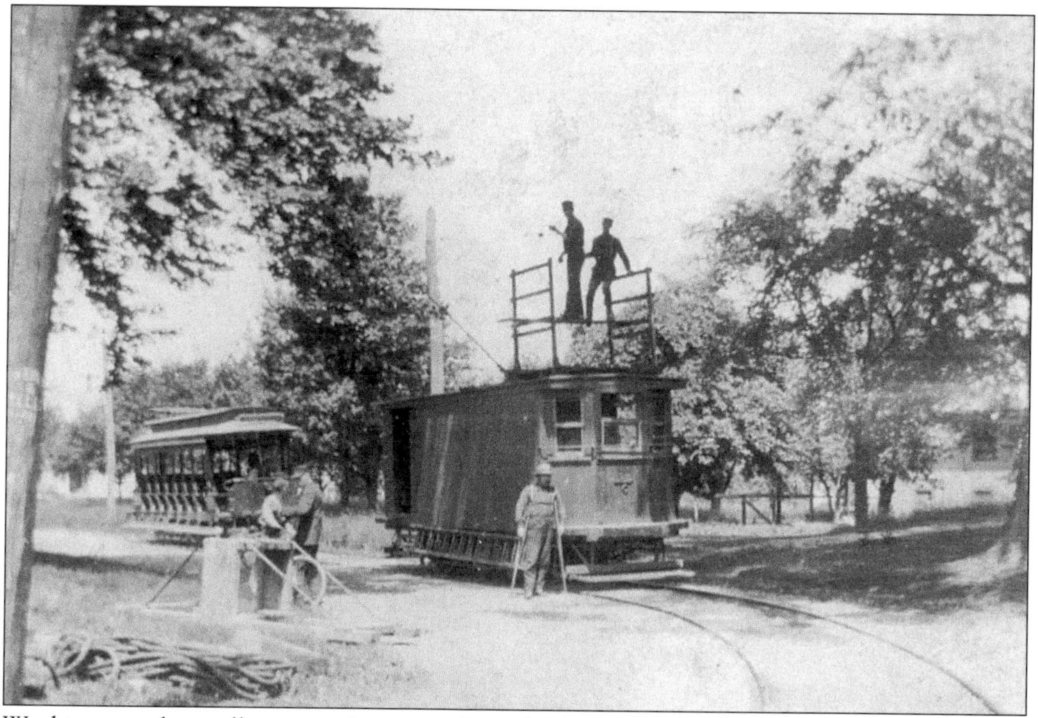

Working on the trolley route between Greenfield and Montague is the repair car for the Greenfield and Turners Falls Street Railway Company. The company operated from 1895 to 1905 and then became part of the Connecticut Valley Street Railway Company. This is one of a series of photographs taken along the entire route of the trolley.

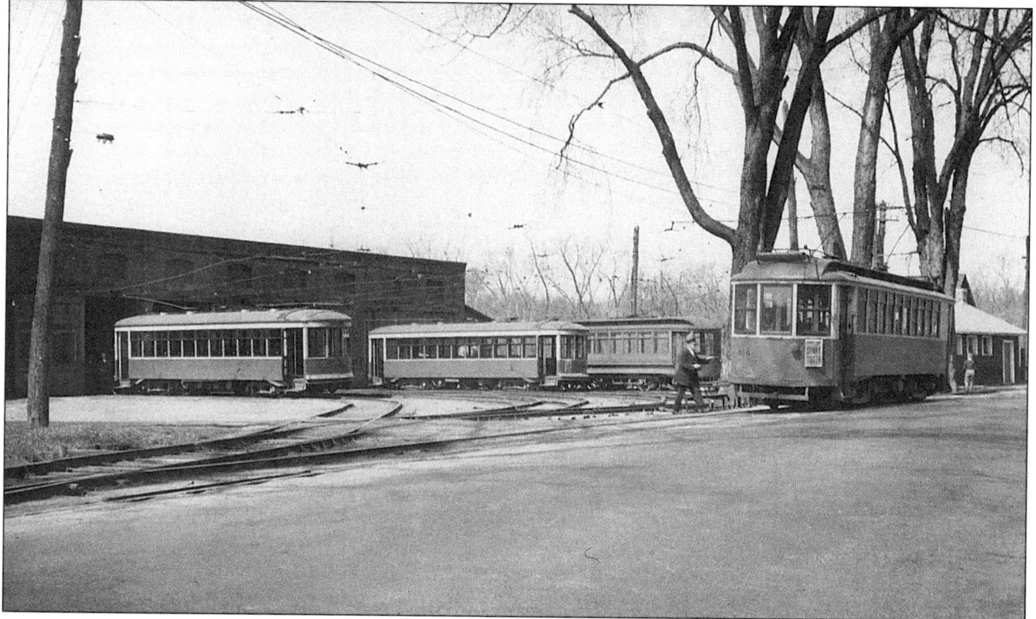

This photograph shows trolleys lined up at the trolley barn on Deerfield Street in 1934. The trolleys are gone, but the building is still used by the Greenfield-Montague Transit Authority for its buses.

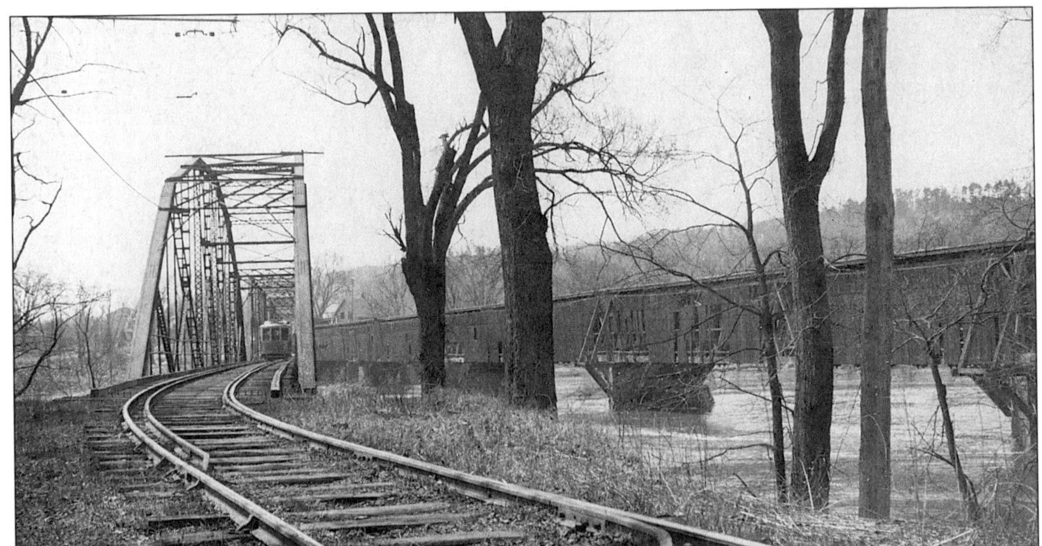

Car No. 106 of the Greenfield and Montague Transportation Company crosses the trolley bridge just south of the old Montague City toll bridge on the Connecticut River. This photograph was taken in 1934. The flood of 1936 took out the covered bridge, which in turn destroyed the trolley bridge.

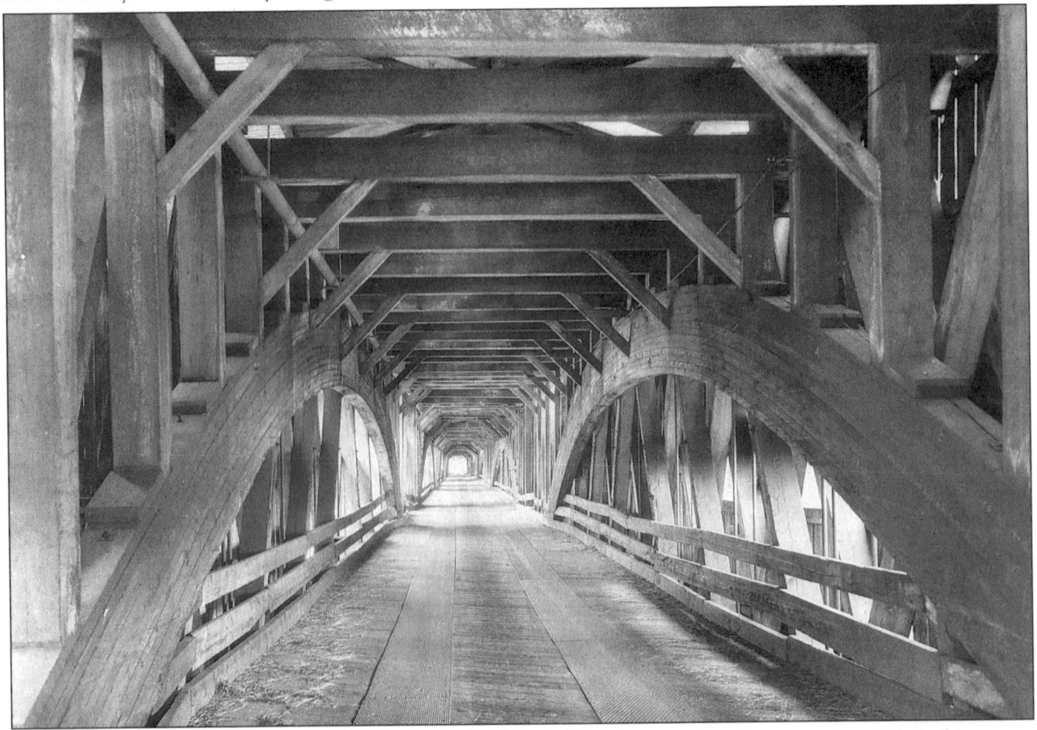

This is the interior of the Montague City Bridge, which spans the Connecticut River between East Greenfield and Montague. The Boston & Maine railroad tracks went over the top of the bridge. According to contemporary accounts, when a train went overhead, it frightened the horses inside and caused them to either run out or drop to the floor. The bridge was destroyed by the 1936 flood and was replaced in 1947 by the General Pierce Bridge.

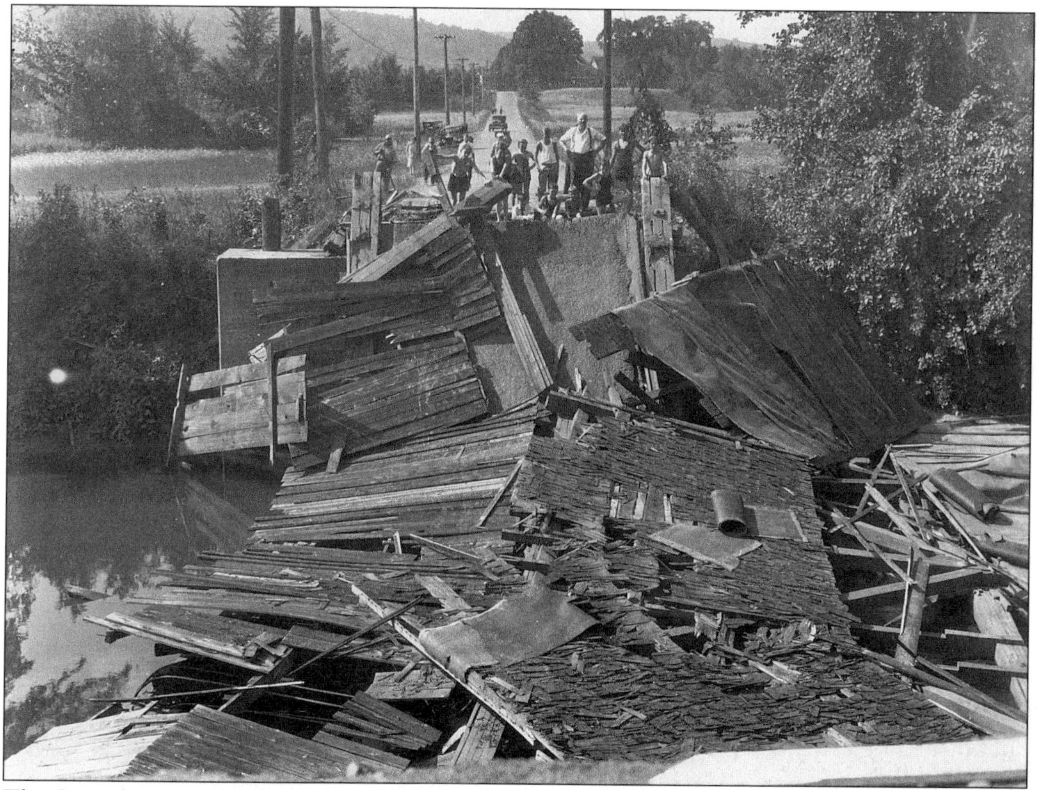

The Smead Covered Bridge on Colrain Road collapsed on August 22, 1932 when a town truck attempted to cross it. At one time, Greenfield had seven covered bridges over the Green River. The field at the left is the current site of the Davenport Trucking Company.

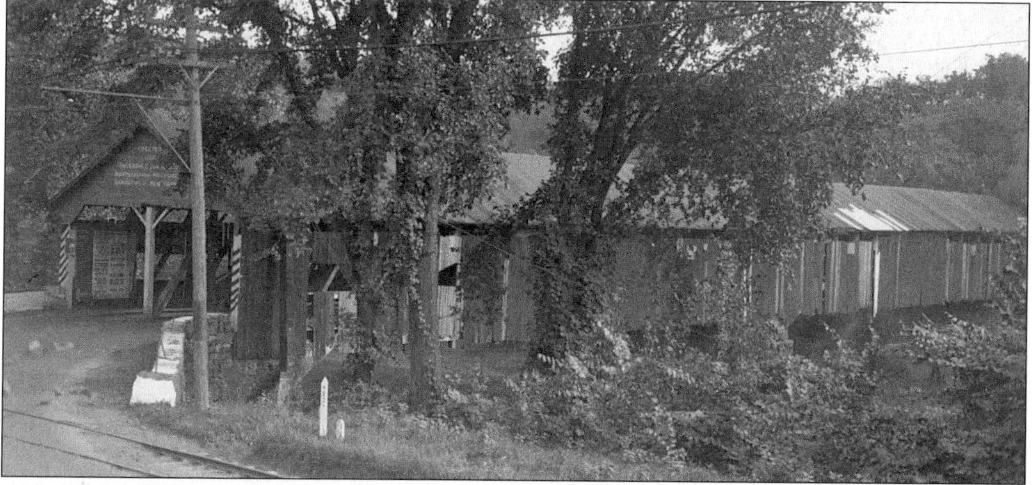

Cheapside was a busy river port at the east end of Greenfield. It saw the arrival of boats, then railroads, automobiles, and trolleys. The double-barreled Cheapside Covered Bridge was built across the Deerfield River in 1806. Deemed obsolete in 1932, it was replaced by an open bridge built to the west of it. Some of the timbers from the Cheapside bridge were used in a house in Shelburne Falls and others were fashioned into three Pilgrim-style chairs, one of which is on display at the historical society.

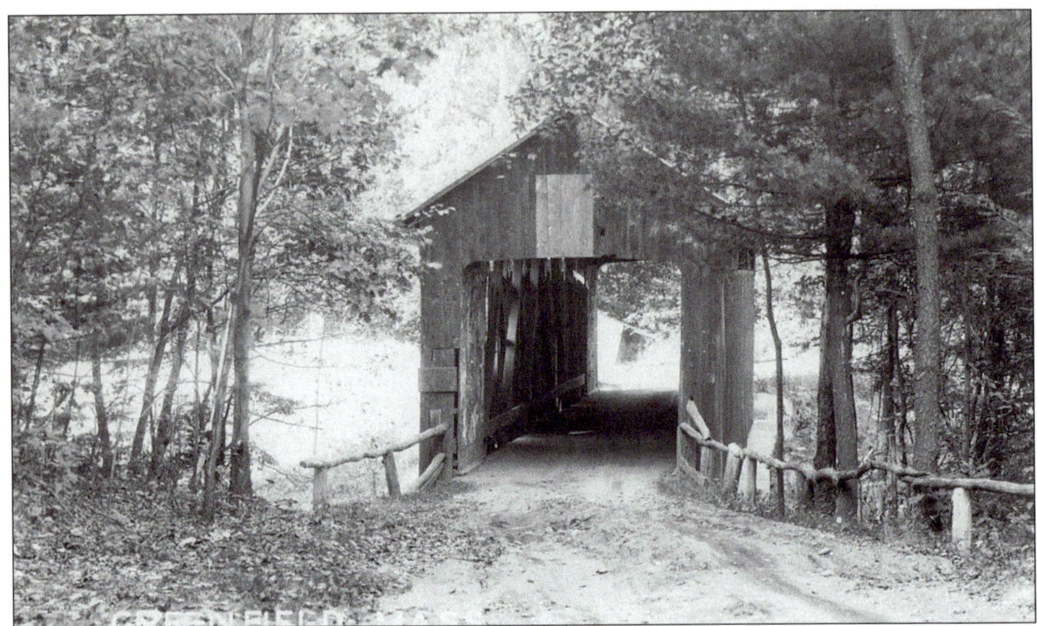

The Country Farms-Pumping Station Covered Bridge on Eunice Williams Drive was built over the Green River in 1870 to replace a bridge a mile downstream that had flooded out once too often. The area was a popular swimming hole and bathers dove off the top of the bridge. On Halloween of 1969, the bridge was set on fire and destroyed. This picture was taken *c.* 1935.

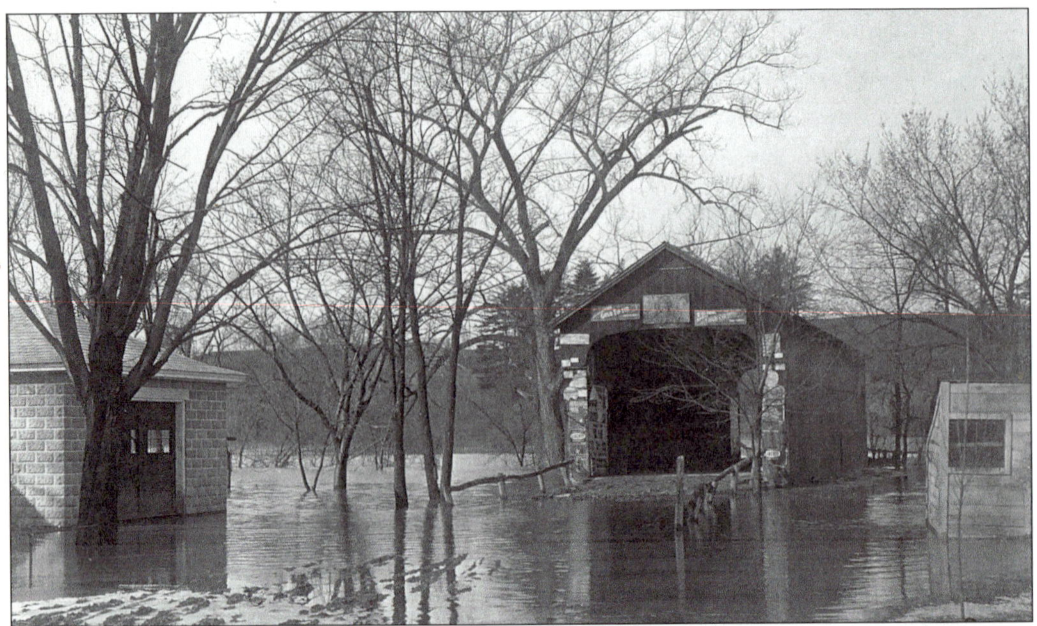

The Petty Plain Covered Bridge crossed the Green River. Note the posters on the end of the bridge; the Green River Park with its old athletic field is located just over the bridge. The bridge was destroyed by the 1936 flood and replaced many years later by a steel footbridge.

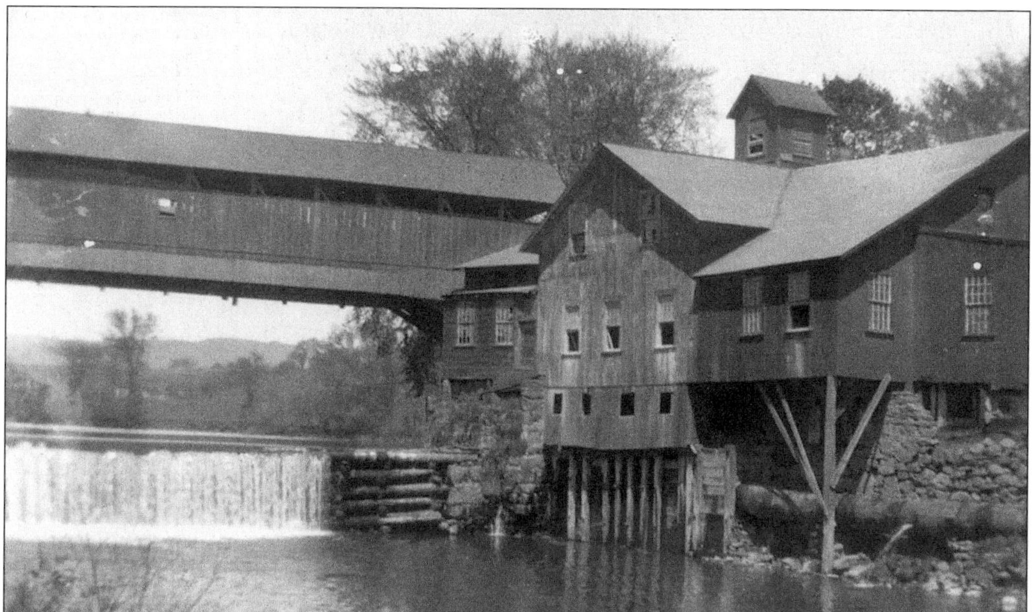

A gristmill operated on this Green River site from 1714 to 1910. This view shows the mill and the covered bridge on Mill Street, *c.* 1900.

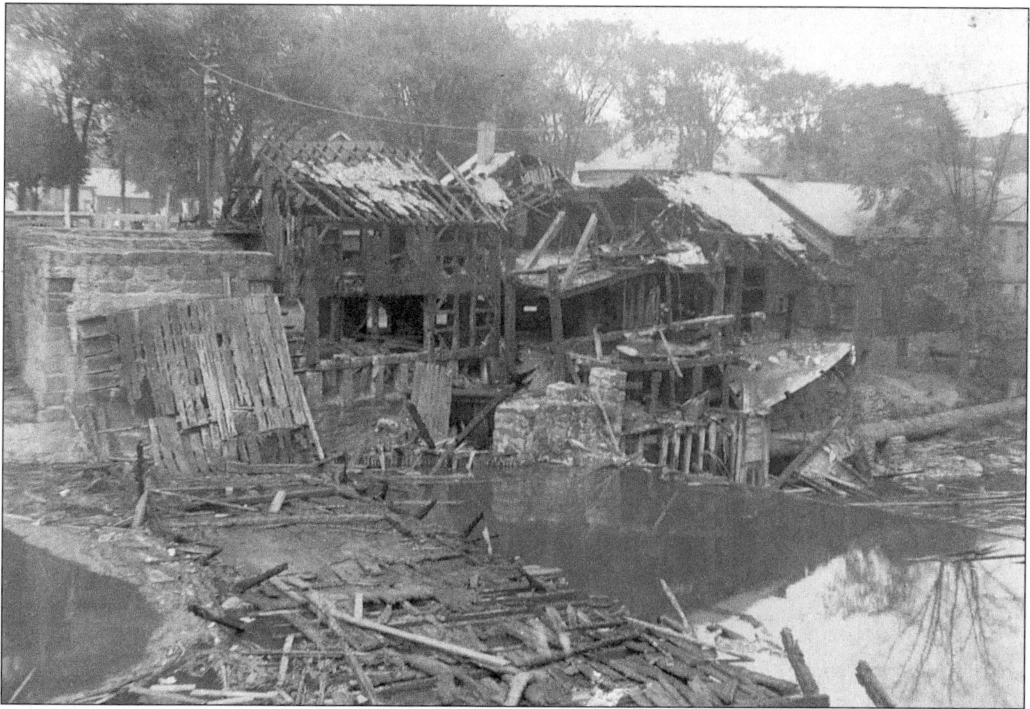

This bridge was destroyed by fire on May 7, 1910, a very windy day. According to reports, a hay wagon going through the bridge caught fire. The wind spread the fire quickly and sent showers of sparks over nearby buildings. A new concrete arched bridge was constructed in place of the covered bridge and then was in turn replaced in the 1980s by a steel and concrete bridge. This photograph was taken *c.* 1900.

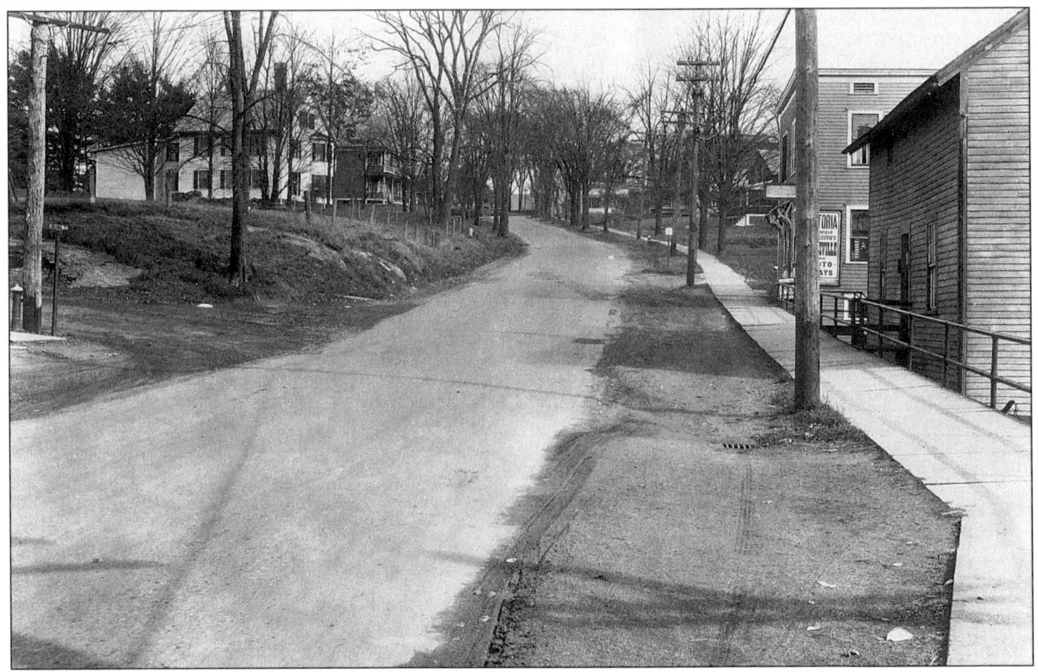

This photograph was taken *c.* 1929, looking east up Shelburne Street at the west end of town. At the top of the hill, to the right, is the present location of Sweeney Ford. Note the partially obscured sign for "photo plays" at the Victoria Theater. The street to the left is Solon Street. The white house on left is the Solon Newton House, now replaced by the D.H. Jones mini mall.

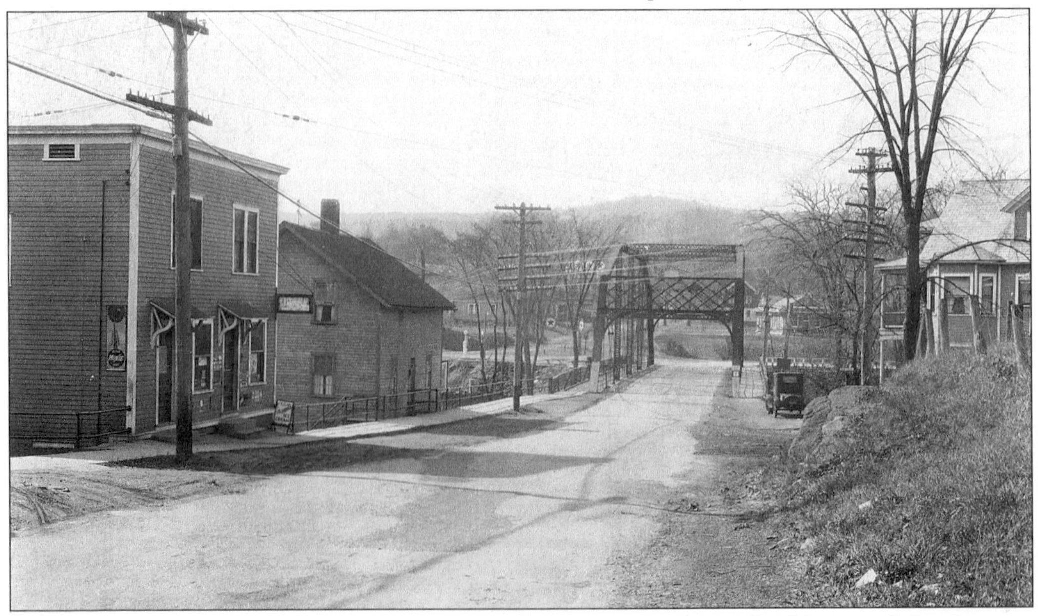

This 1929 photograph, looking west down Shelburne Street, shows the Newton School across the bridge to the right. This area's topography has changed over the years: the road in the foreground is Route 2 (not Route 2A) and at the intersection the Mohawk Trail turns north on the present Shelburne Road. The bridge over the Green River was replaced in the 1950s, and this pastoral scene has been replaced by a commercial strip.

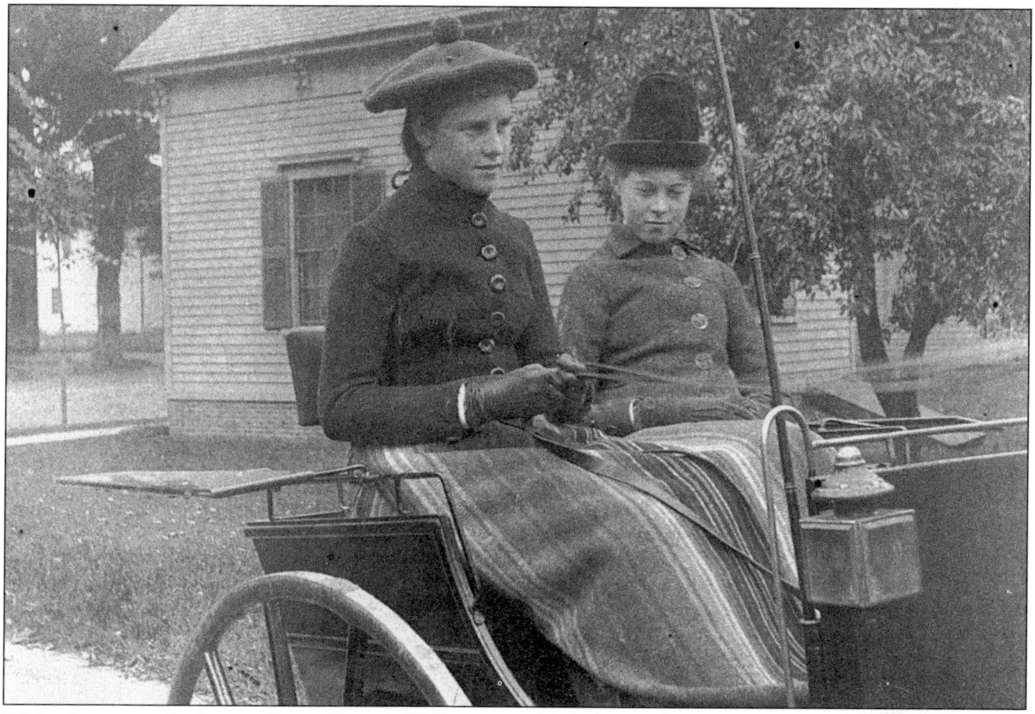

This photograph shows Grace Dean Williams and Edith Finch out for a spin in a buggy.

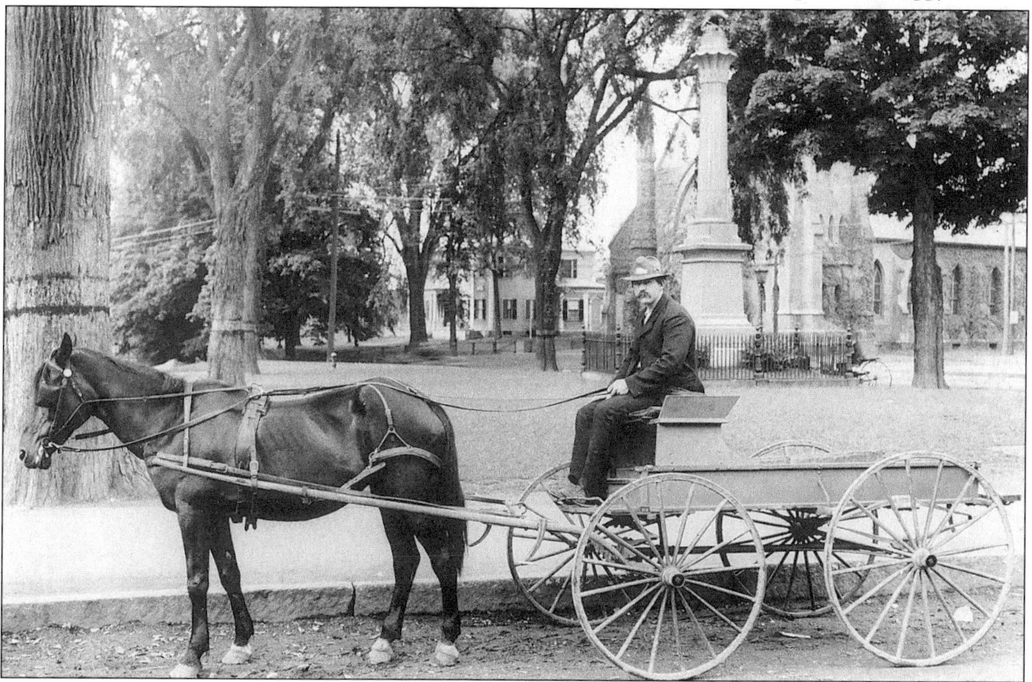

Howard James Wallace and his horse and wagon are shown here in front of the town common. Wallace advertised in the 1910 *Business Directory*, "Express and trucking done of all kinds. Every order will receive prompt attention. Phone 303." Note the bands on trees, put there to discourage caterpillars from climbing.

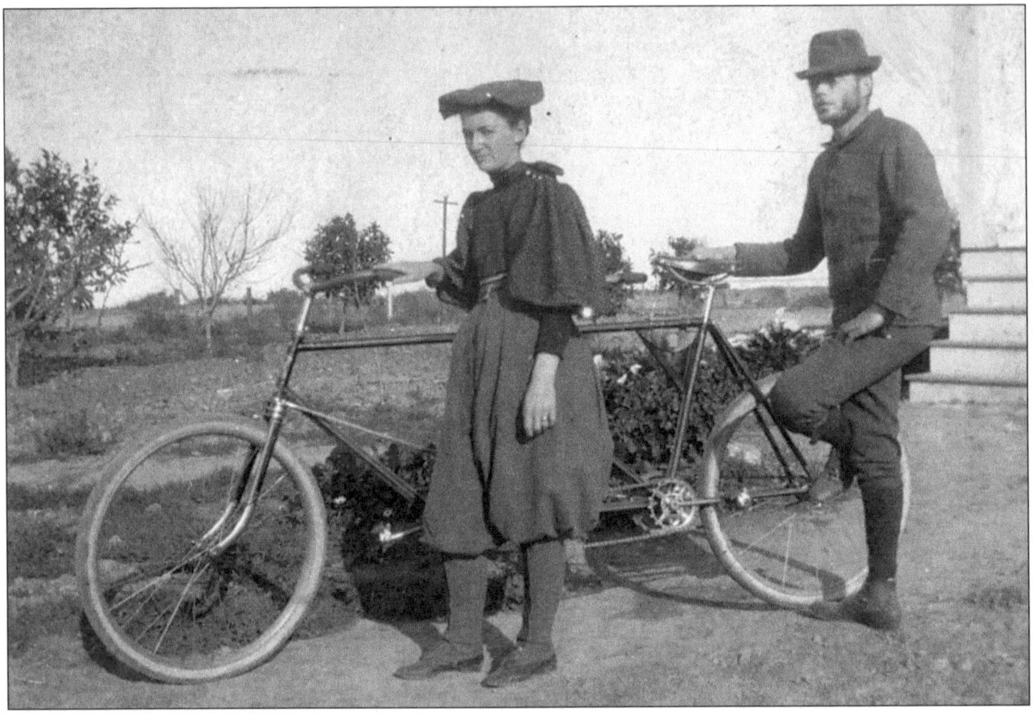

Mr. and Mrs. C.A. Babcock Jr. pose with their tandem bicycle in March 1898. In the late 19th century, bicycling was all the rage across the country.

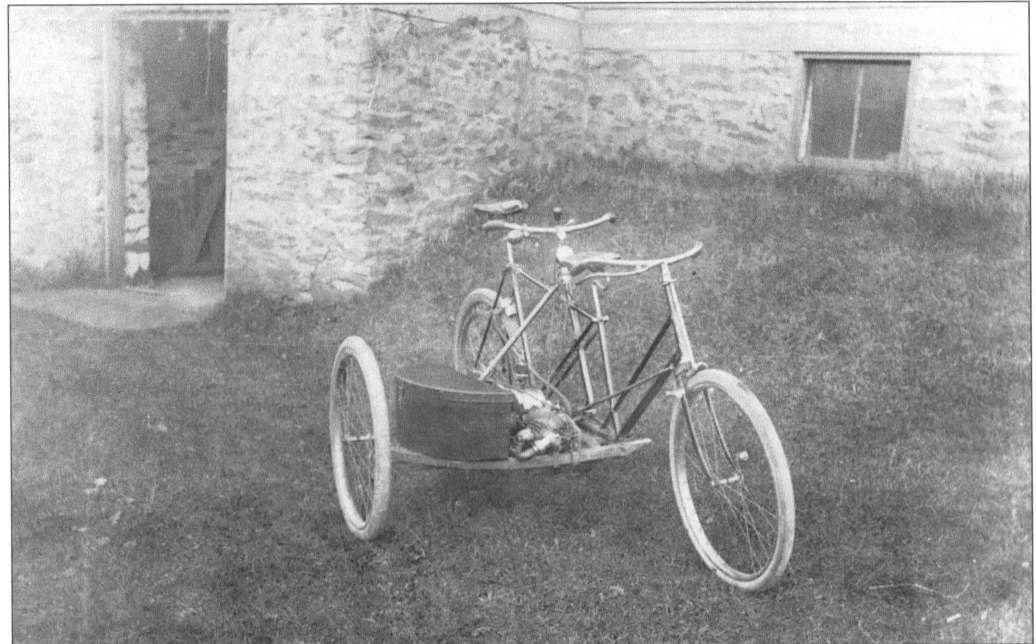

Harry W. Kellogg built this experimental gasoline-powered, two-passenger bicycle in 1902 before building a small passenger car in 1903. Kellogg joined other automobile pioneers in Greenfield, such as Richard N. Oakman and Chauncey Wing, in attempting to create an automobile industry here. None succeeded.

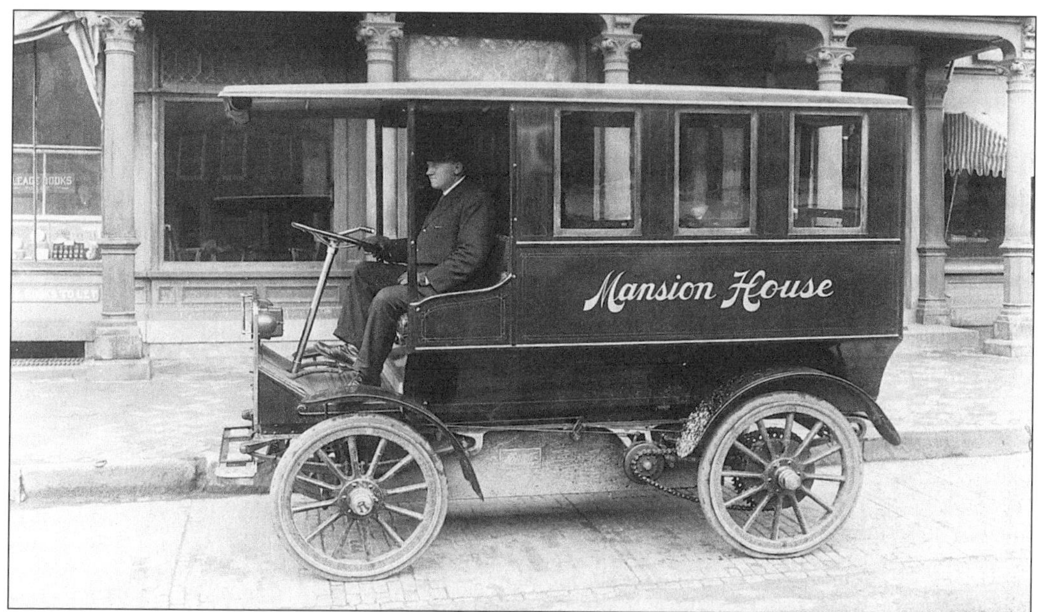

William "Billy" O. Munn is shown here, *c.* 1910, in the Mansion House's electric "station wagon" in front of the Mansion House. Munn carried passengers to and from the train station and the Main Street hotel for many years.

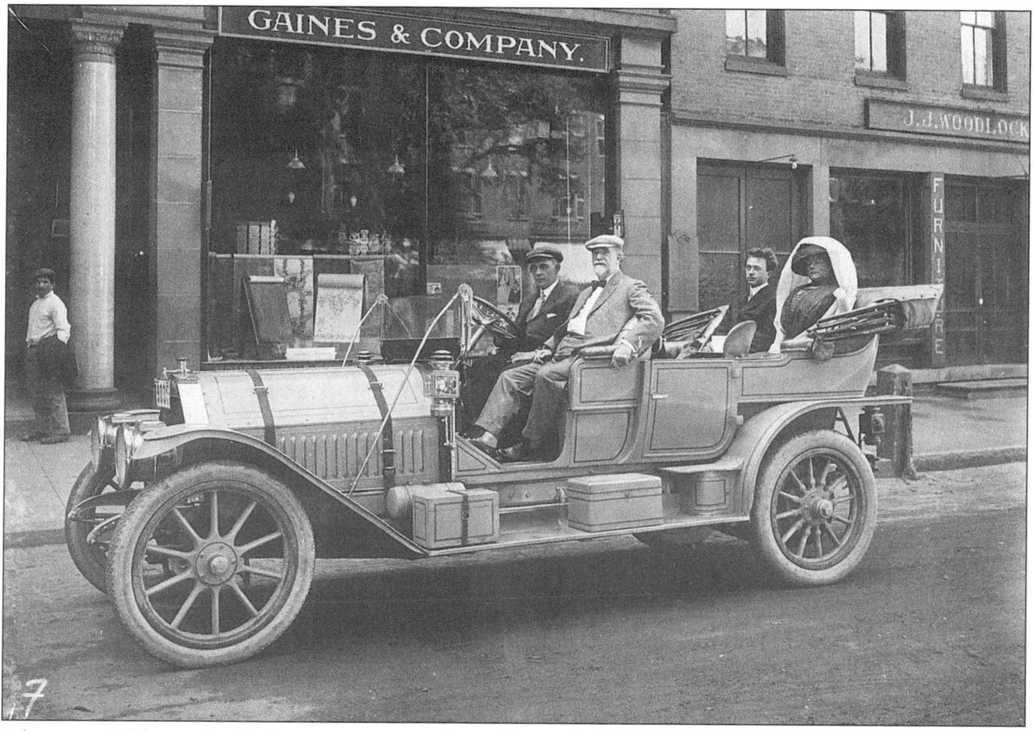

Clarence Eddy, a world-famous organist from Greenfield, poses at the wheel of his automobile in front of the Masonic Block on Main Street, *c.* 1911. Note the formal attire of Mrs. Eddy, complete with a system to keep her hat secure. Gaines & Company sold wallpaper and stationery; the J.J. Woodlock & Company sold furniture and offered undertaking services.

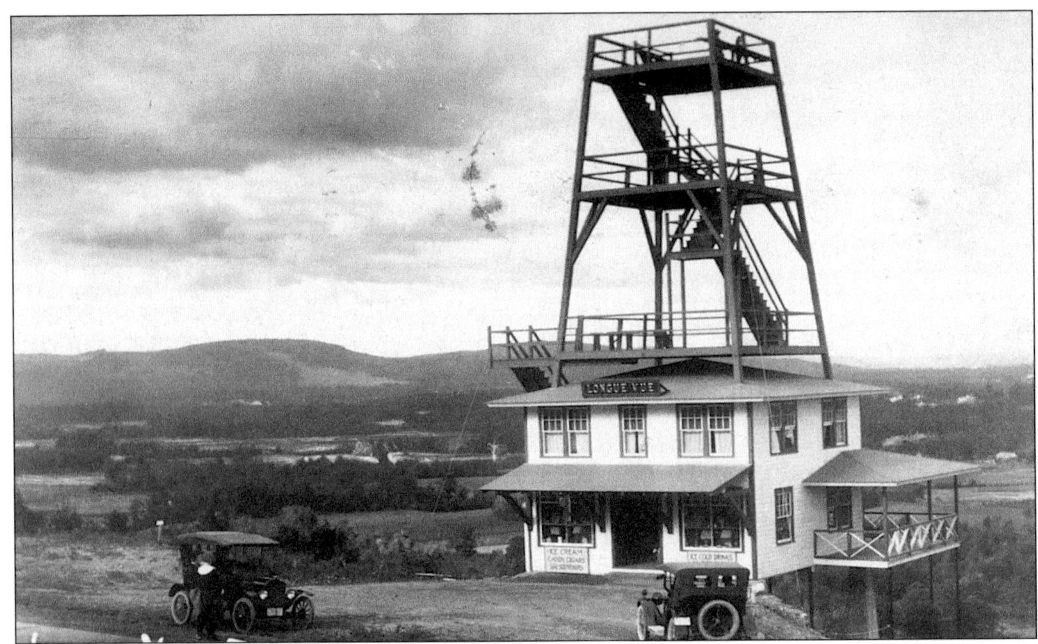

In this 1923 view, the Longue Vue Tower was located on the lower part of Shelburne Mountain on the Mohawk Trail. Later, this tower was replaced by one built just to the north. The tower to the north is still there, entertaining tourists traveling between Greenfield and Williamstown. Postmarked August 28, 1923, the postcard reads, "Dear Mother and Dad: Weather—Great. . .Sunny having the time of his life. Had a wonderful camping place last night. We are in this tower now. Love, Al."

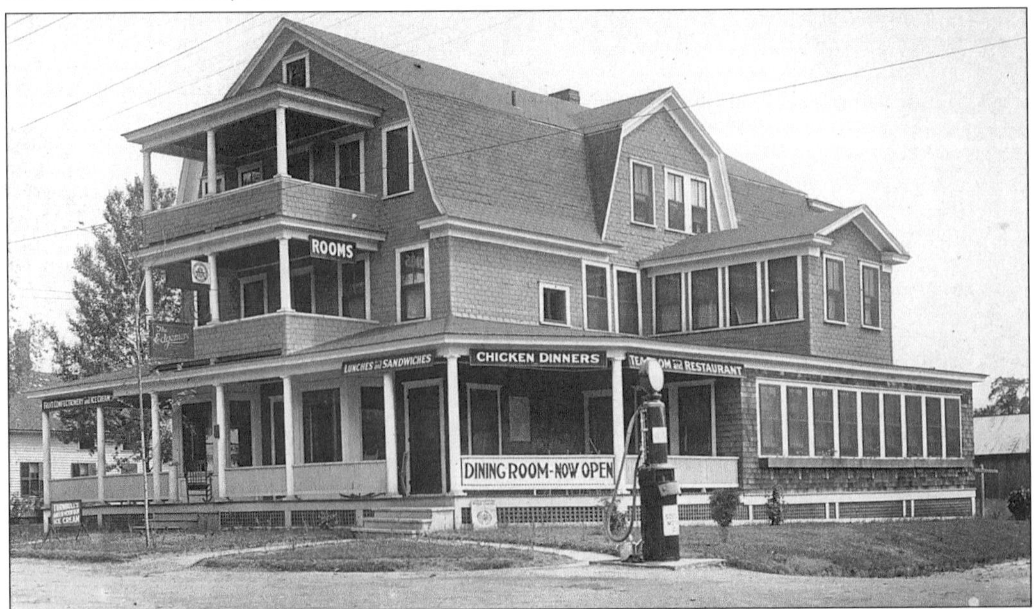

This was the Edgemere Inn, tea room, and restaurant on Shelburne Road, also known as the Mohawk Trail. The Mohawk Trail was one of the first scenic highways in the United States. The photograph taken shortly after the highway opened in 1921. Later, a separate tea room and gas station were built on the property.

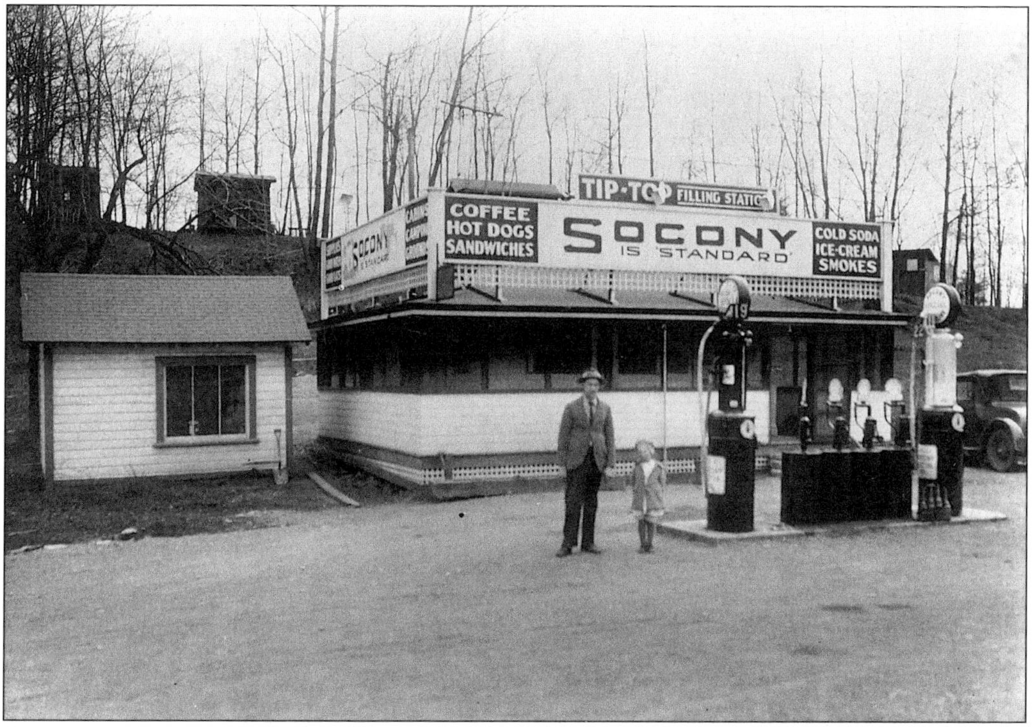

Herbert C. Galbraith and an unidentified child are pictured in front of the Tip-Top Filling Station on the east side of Bernardston Road, just south of the present Jehovah's Witnesses' Kingdom Hall. In back of the station are tourist cabins typical of the early automobile touring days. This photograph was taken *c.* 1922. Gas cost 19¢ a gallon.

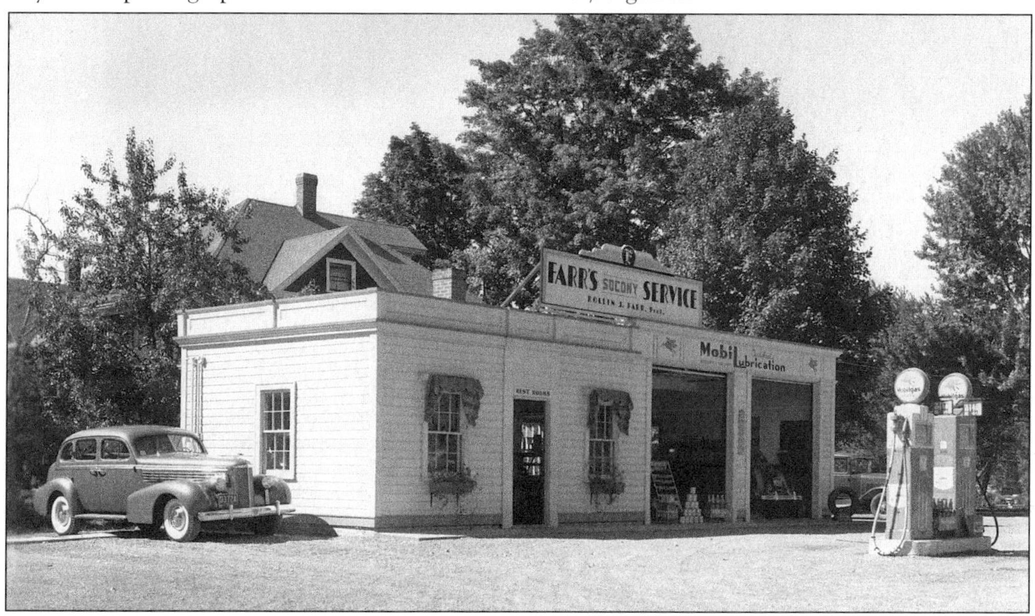

This photograph shows Farr's Socony Garage at Silver and Federal Streets, *c.* 1940. The location is still used for a gas station and mini mart; however, the price of gasoline has risen considerably from the 14¢ per gallon advertised at these pumps.

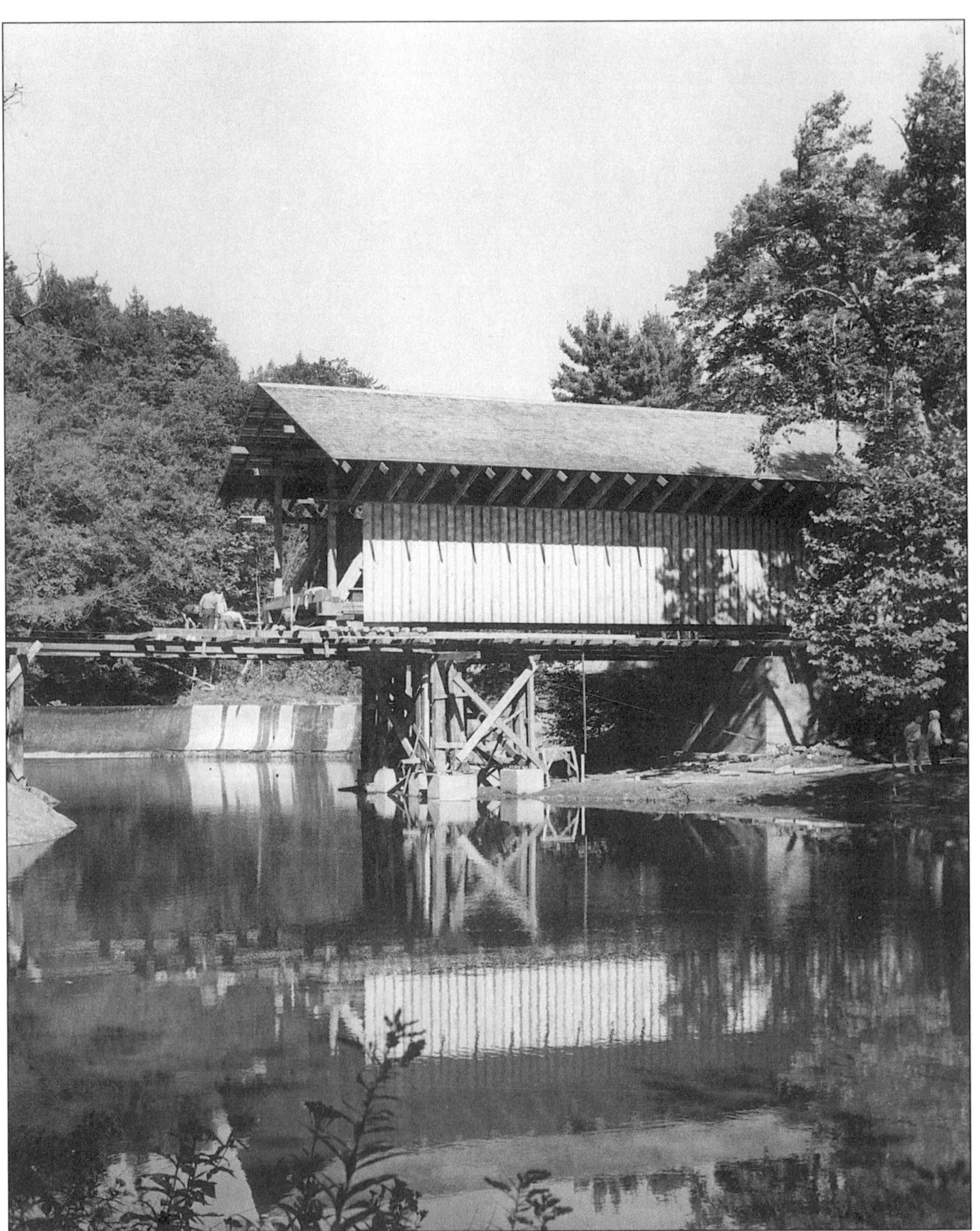

Many Greenfield residents were heartbroken by the burning in 1969 of the Pumping Station Covered Bridge and wished to replace it with a similar wooden bridge. As seen in this photograph, the present bridge was built with donated labor and materials in 1972. Donald Williams of Greenfield designed the bridge. Contractor Clayton Davenport used a crane to pull the completed bridge across the river. The town, because of liability concerns, closed the area to swimming in the 1980s because too many swimmers were jumping off the roof of the bridge.

Five
GOING TO WORK

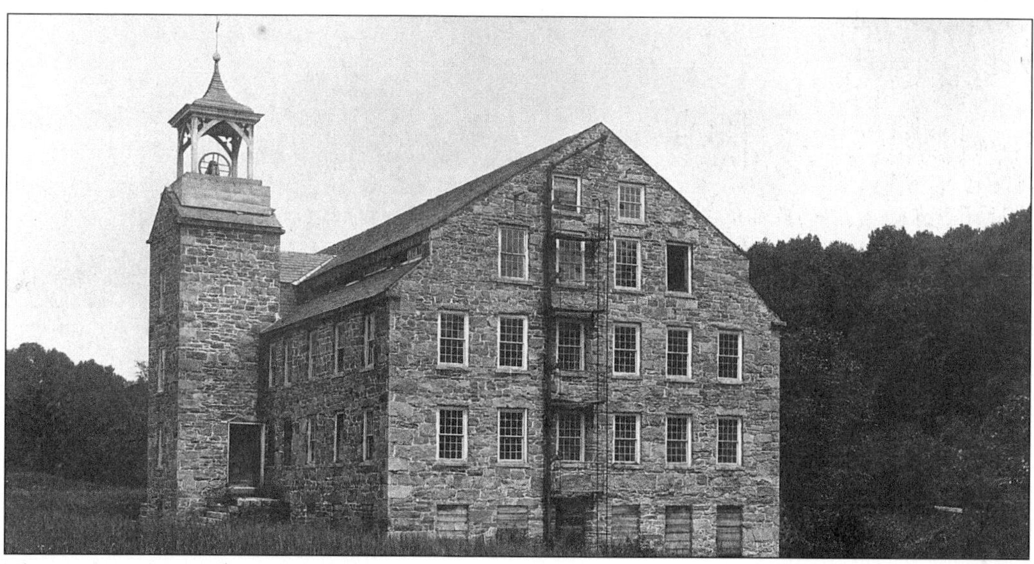

This early industrial site is called Factory Hollow. The stone textile mill was built by Nathaniel E. Russell and Company in 1830. The 100- by 140-foot granite mill, built on the site of an earlier wooden mill that burned in 1828, thrived until 1869, when the firm declared bankruptcy. The machinery was sold in 1872. The same year, water rights were sold to International Paper Company of Turners Falls. Vandals burned the building on July 4, 1933. The stones were reused in the construction of the Girl Scouts' building off Barton Road. The bell tower is the only remaining evidence of the entire factory complex. The bell, which originally hung in the county's first courthouse, was melted down for scrap metal during World War I.

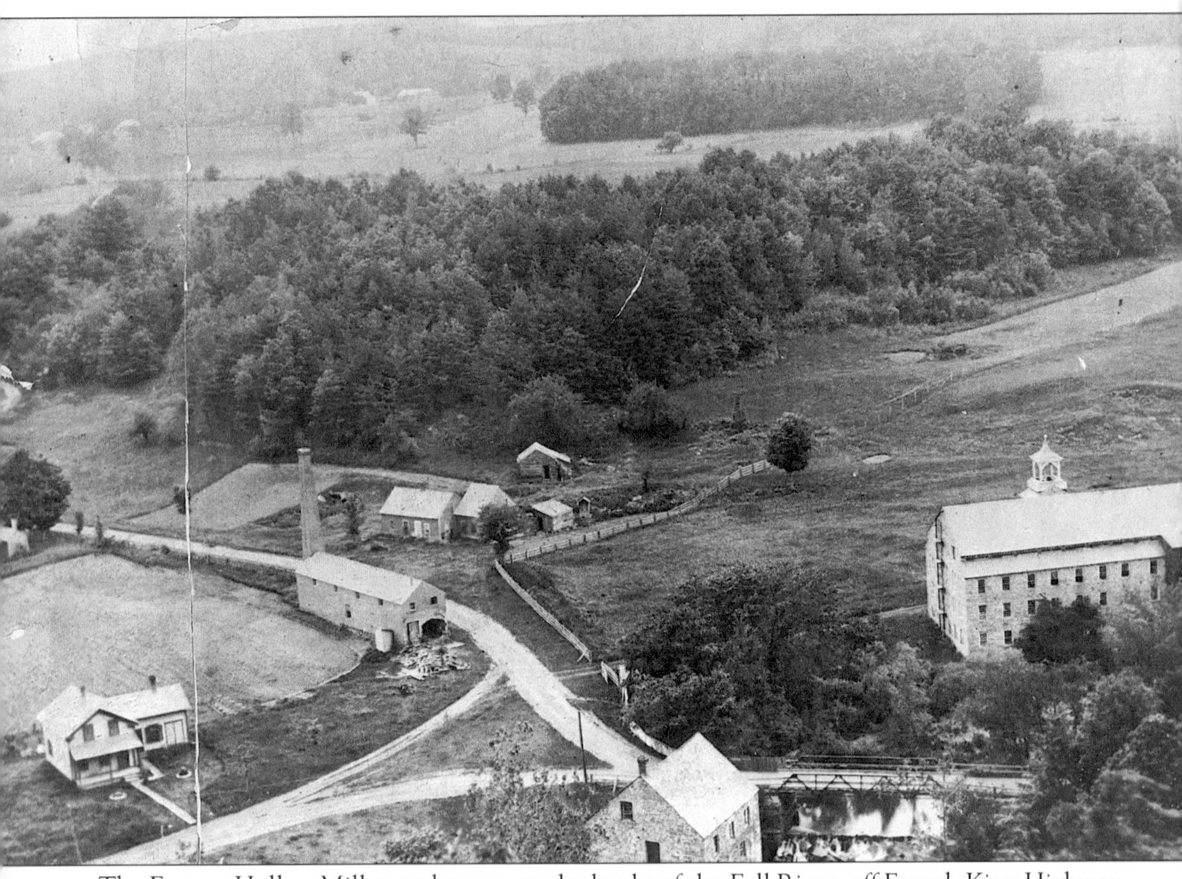

The Factory Hollow Mill complex was on the banks of the Fall River, off French King Highway east of Adams Road. The factory made broadcloth for Civil War uniforms. The upper mill was the main factory and the lower building the drying house. This photograph was taken *c.* 1890. All that remains today of this once bustling hamlet are the three houses and part of the factory tower. The road was once the main highway from Greenfield to Gill, but the bridge over the Fall River was discontinued *c.* 1958. The road to lower left went to Riverside Hill. The area to the upper left is now the I-91 Industrial Park.

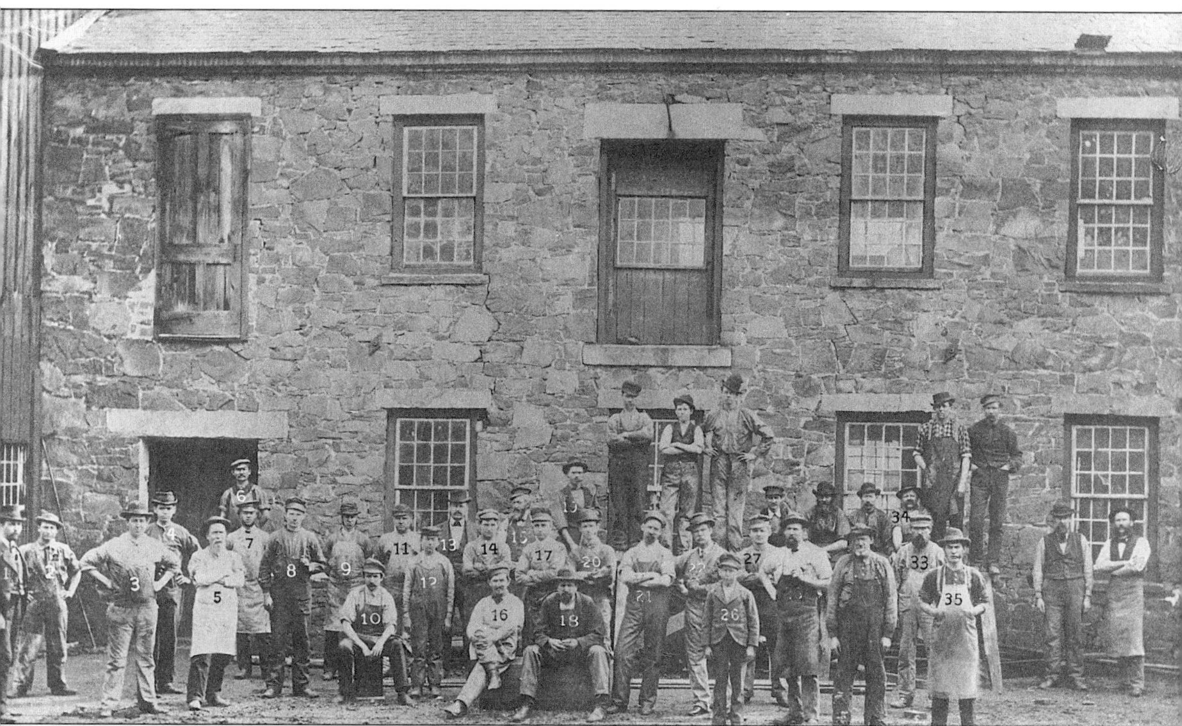

This stone building is featured in the only known remaining photograph of the original Russell Cutlery plant on the Green River. The building was later incorporated into the Russell-Wiley plant. Note the numbers added for a caption to this 1874 photograph of Russell-Wiley workers. (Photograph courtesy of Greenfield Industries.)

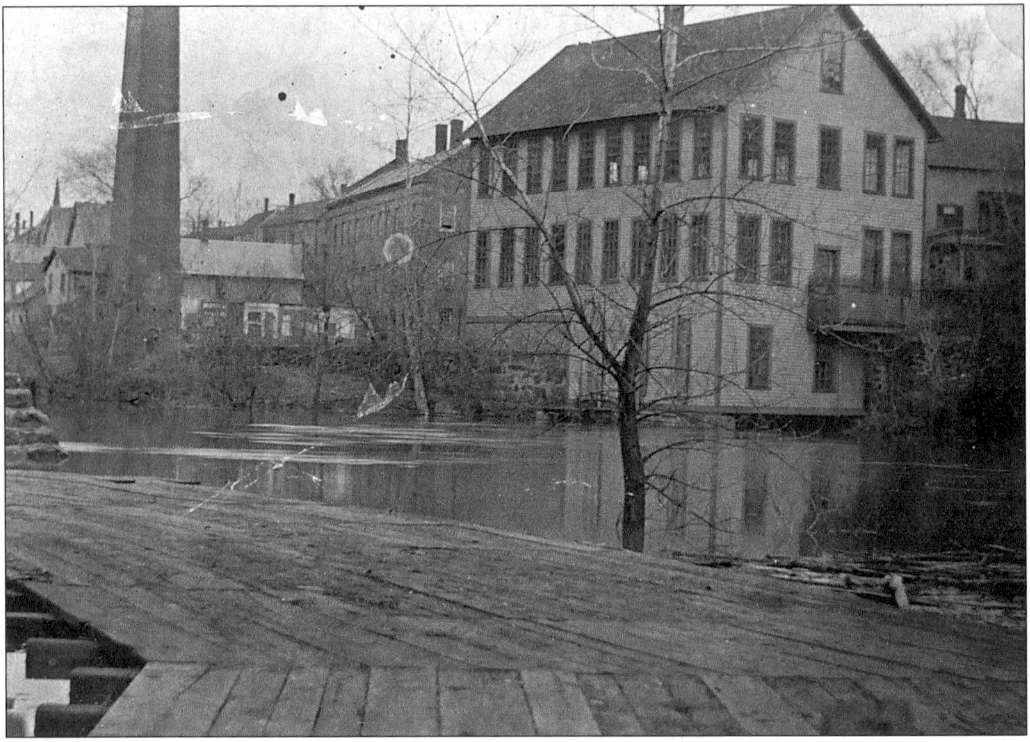

These factory buildings stood along the Green River on the Deerfield Street side. One of the buildings was occupied by Chauncey Wing before the Wing mailer company moved to Pierce Street. (Photograph courtesy of Greenfield Industries.)

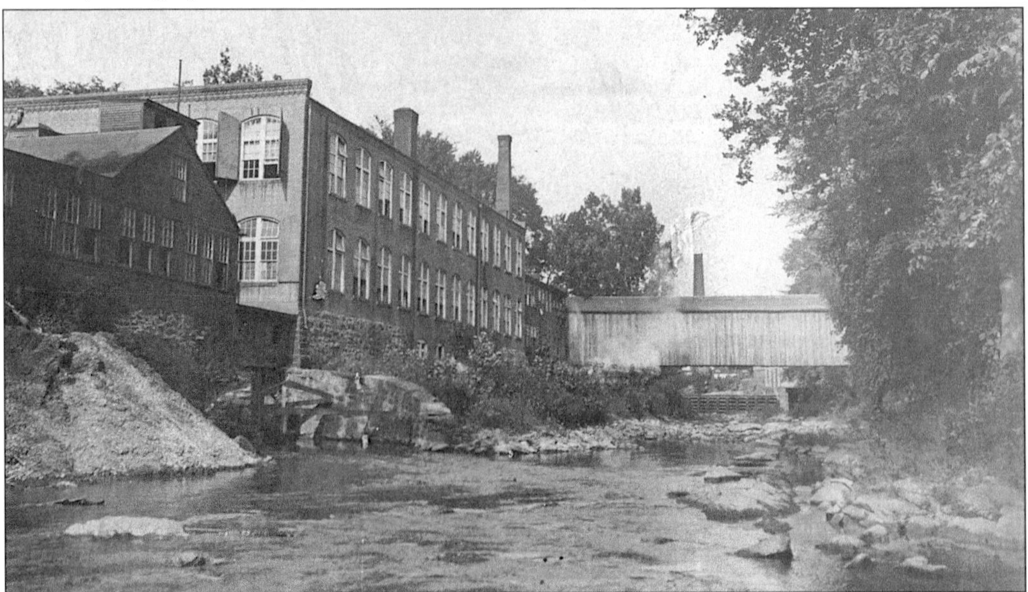

Looking north, this photograph of the Wiley & Russell Manufacturing Company factory on banks of Green River was taken *c.* 1890. In the background is a dam. Wiley & Russell manufactured taps and dies. The factory eventually became part of the Greenfield Tap & Die Plant No. 1. (Photograph courtesy of Greenfield Industries.)

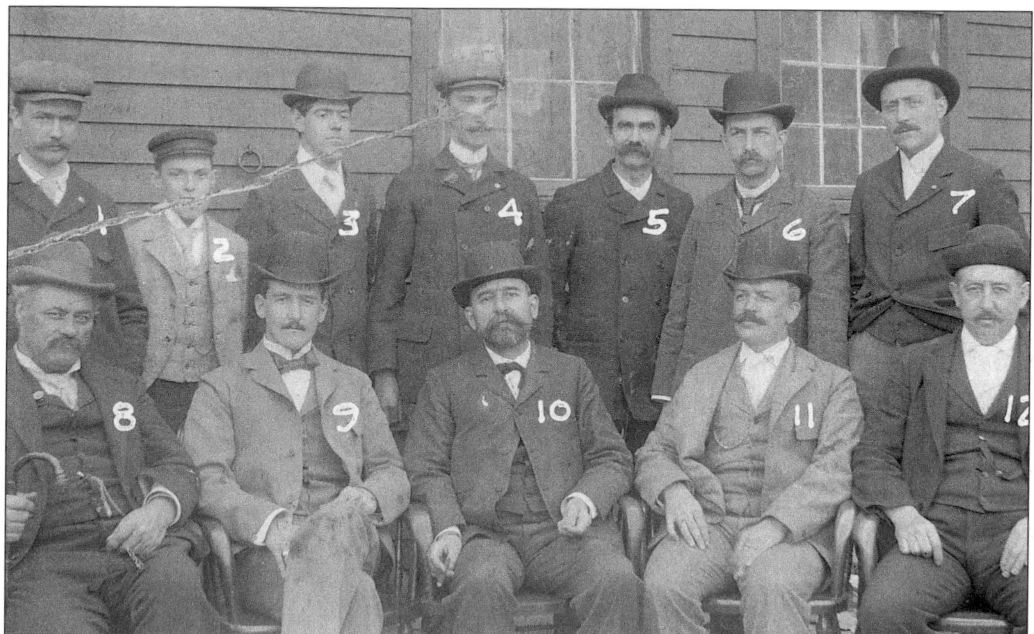

This *c.* 1890 photograph shows the office work force of the Wiley & Russell Manufacturing Company on Meridian Street. Pictured, from left to right, are the following: (front row) ? Pierce, Charles C. Russell, Charles P. Russell, Frederick Hawks, and Albert J. Smart; (back row) Frank Maxwell, Duffie Stetson, Whitman Russell, Frederick Strecker, ? Hamilton, and Frederick Ulrich. Charles P. Russell was the Russell of Wiley & Russell. In 1912, this company merged with the Wells Brothers Company and others to form Greenfield Tap & Die. (Photograph courtesy of Greenfield Industries.)

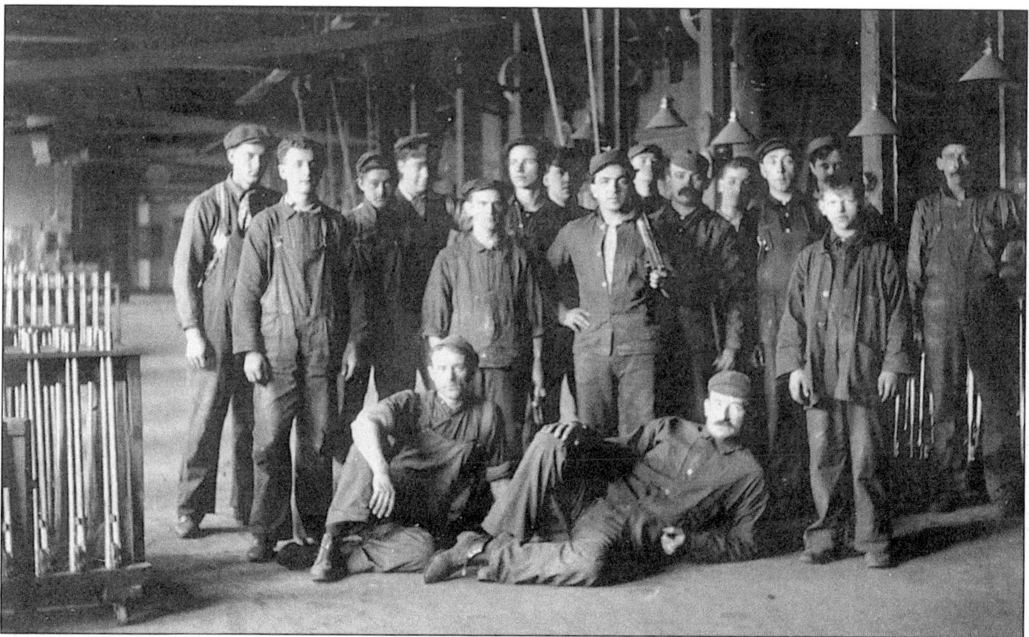

Wiley & Russell shop floor workers pose for a photograph, *c.* 1905. Herbert C. Galbraith is at far left. (Photograph courtesy of Greenfield Industries.)

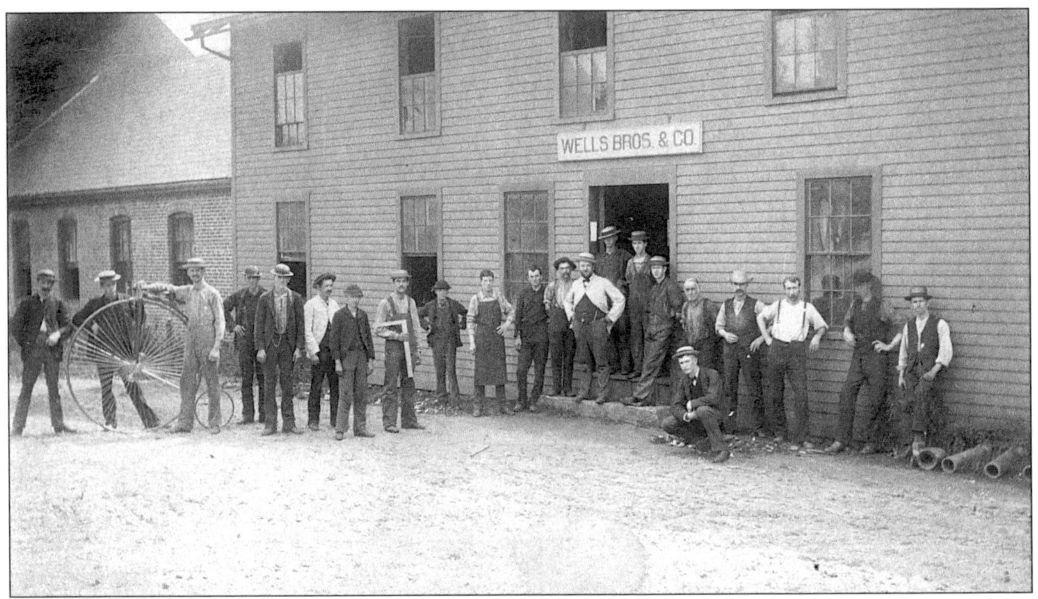

Workers pause in front of the Wells Brothers Company building on Mill Street by the Green River, *c.* 1890. (Photograph courtesy of Greenfield Industries.)

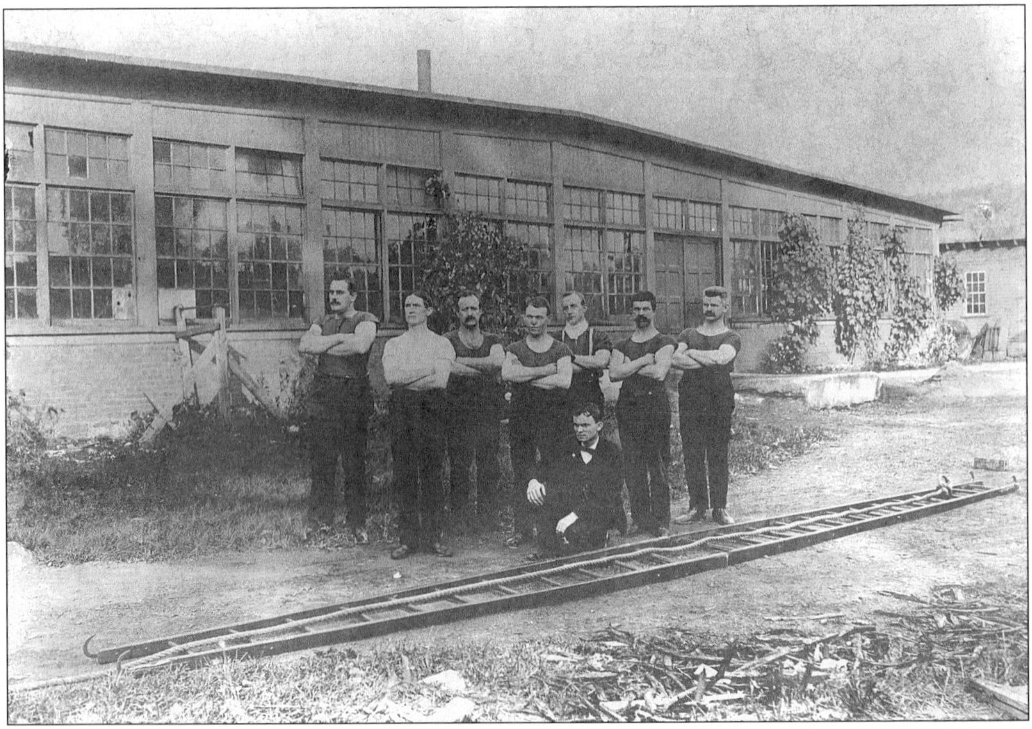

These Wells Brothers workers were on the company's tug-of-war team. Their photograph was taken in front of the company's original plant on North Street, *c.* 1900. (Photograph courtesy of Greenfield Industries.)

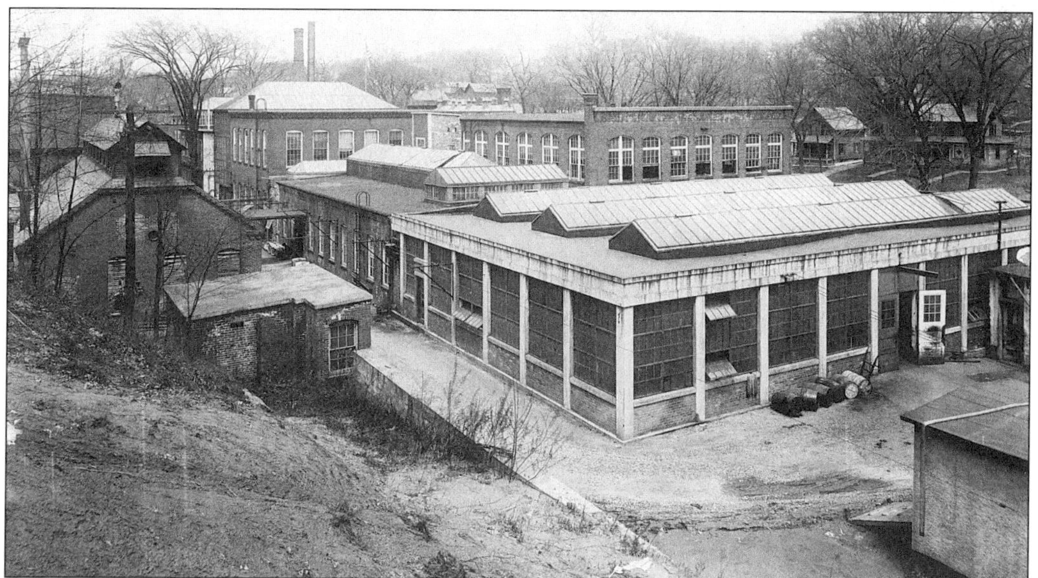

This photograph of the rear of the Wiley & Russell tap and die factory on Meridian Street was taken looking north. The houses on the right are located on Deerfield Street. Wiley & Russell took over the John Russell Cutlery building in 1872. Russell Cutlery had moved to Turners Falls in 1870. (Photograph courtesy of Greenfield Industries.)

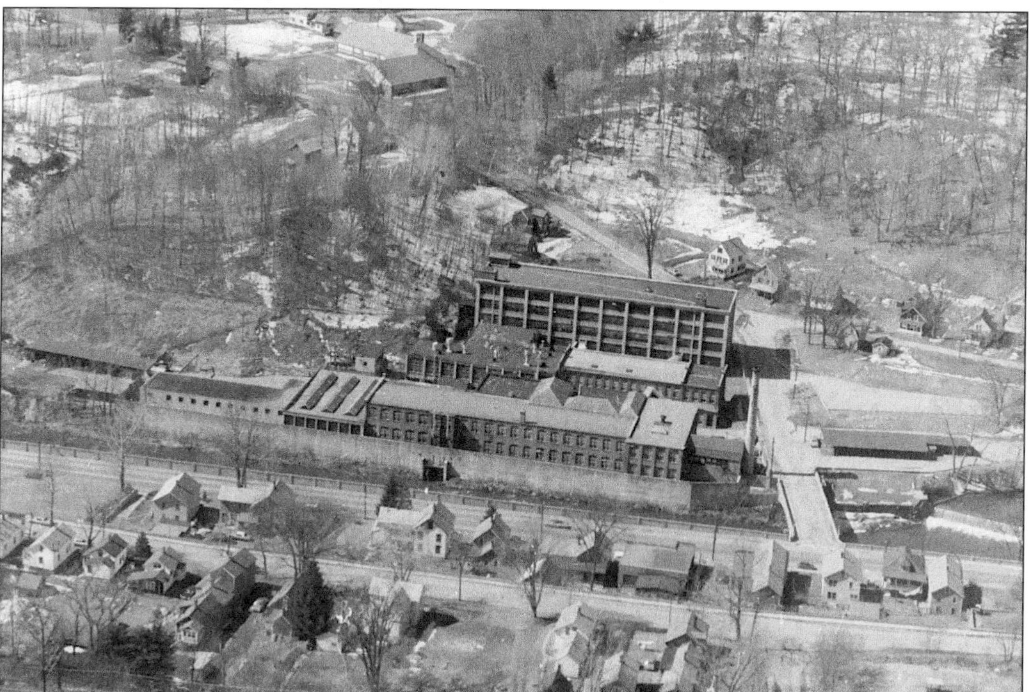

This aerial view of the Greenfield Tap & Die Plant No. 1 on Meridian Street was taken in the late 1950s, at the height of the company's activity. The flood wall by Deerfield Street was built following the floods of 1936 and 1938 and was removed in 1999. After the plant was abandoned in the 1980s, the town of Greenfield took it over for taxes with plans to redevelop it. (Photograph courtesy of Greenfield Industries.)

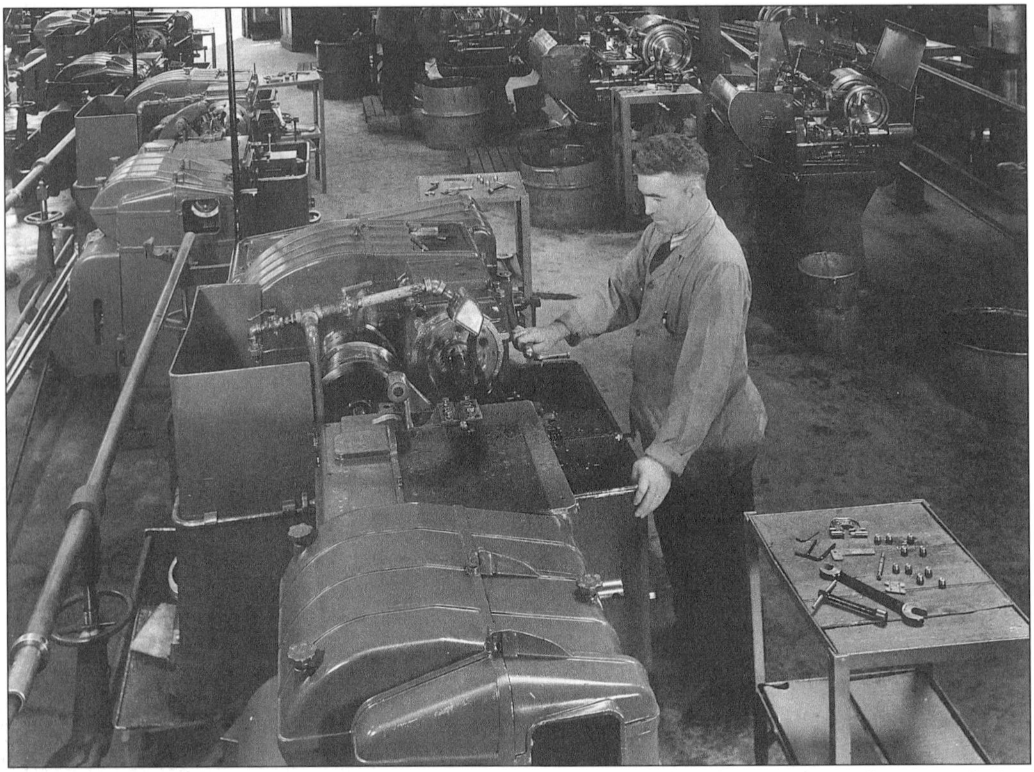

A worker inside one of the Greenfield Tap & Die factories blanks out acorn dies on a lathe. (Photograph courtesy of Greenfield Industries.)

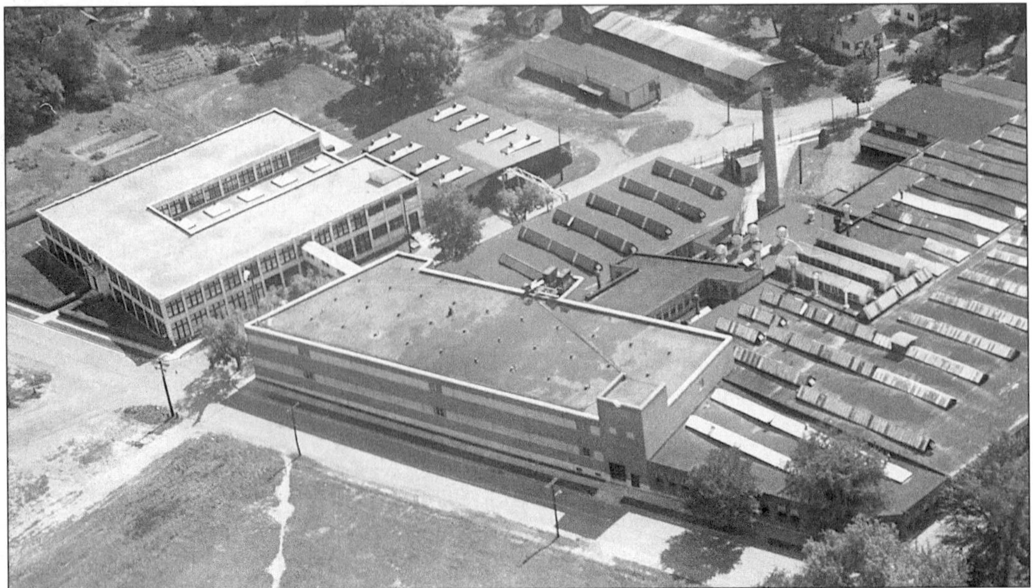

This photograph shows the Greenfield Tap & Die plant No. 2 in 1949. The nearest large building is the last remaining portion of the plant in operation. A division of a large international corporation, the plant now operates under the name of Greenfield Industries. (Photograph courtesy of Greenfield Industries.)

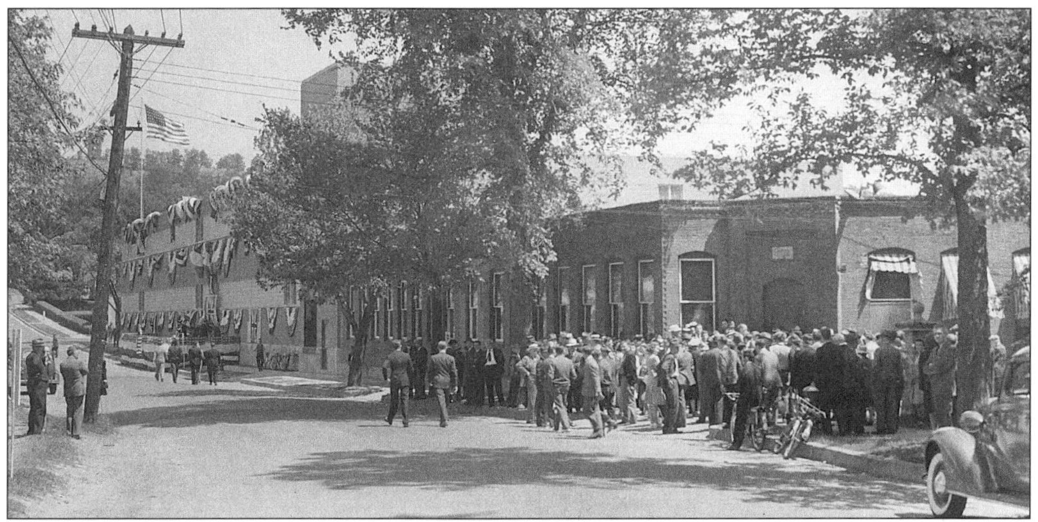

The Greenfield Tap & Die Plant No. 2, at the corner of Sanderson and North Streets, was dedicated during World War II. The government financed the new facility, which ran full blast during the war, supplying vital machine tools for the war effort. (Photograph courtesy of Greenfield Industries.)

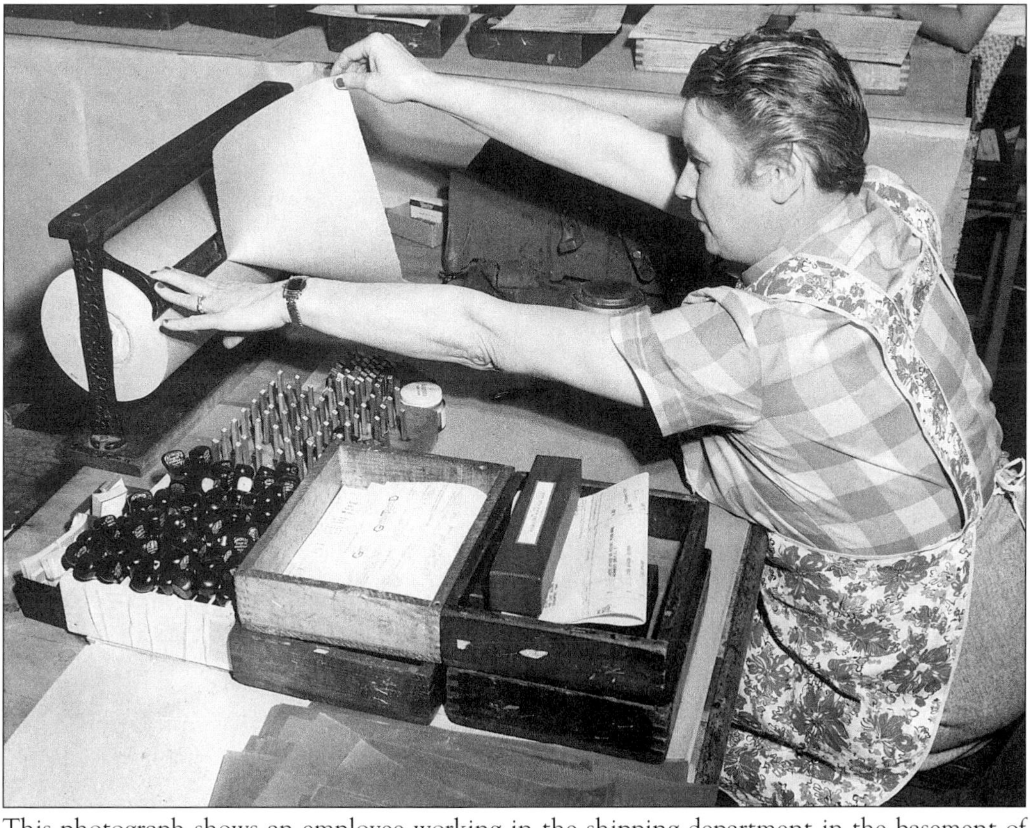

This photograph shows an employee working in the shipping department in the basement of Greenfield Tap & Die's old administration building on North Street. (Photograph courtesy of Greenfield Industries.)

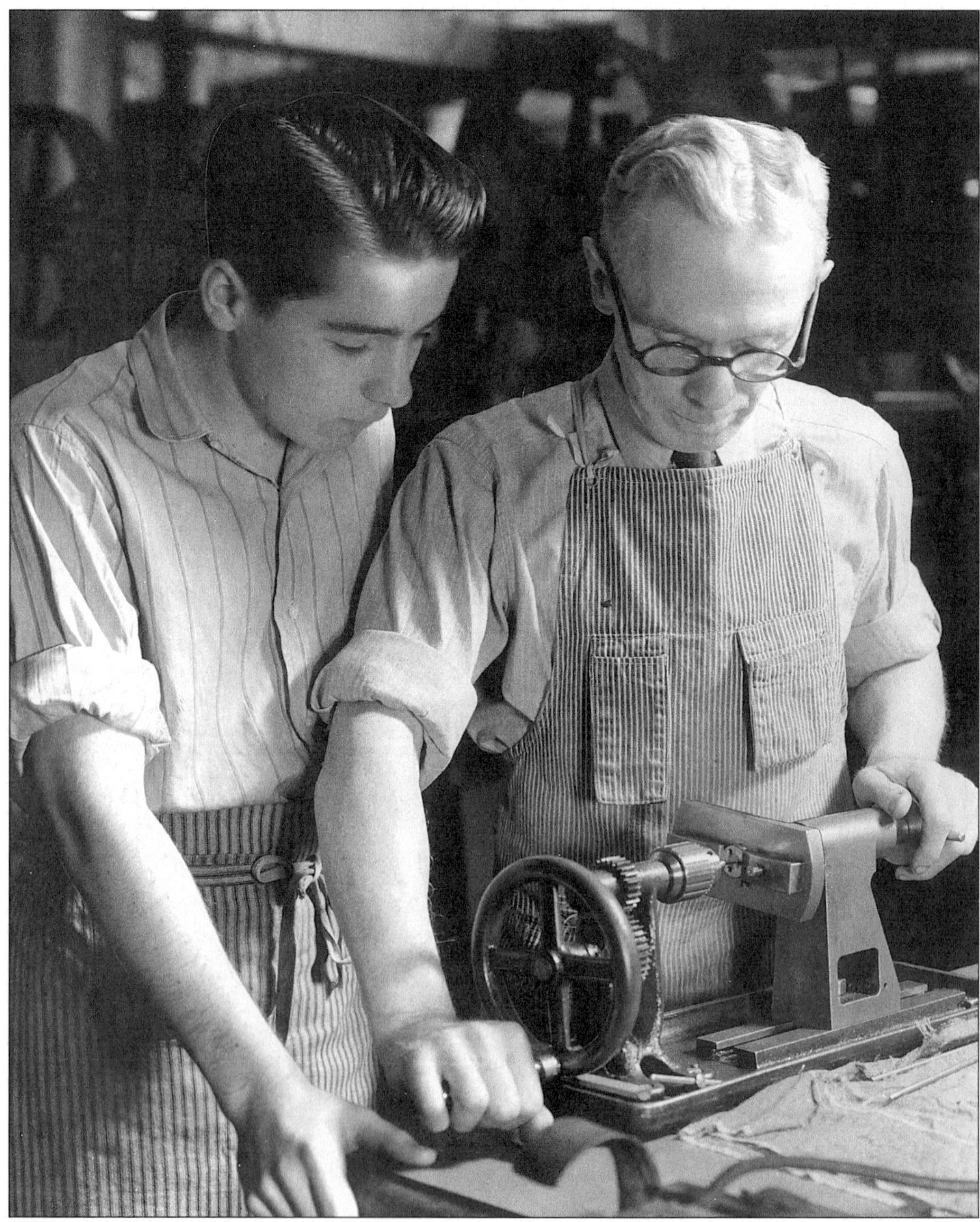

This *c*. 1920s photograph shows an apprentice at Greenfield Tap & Die learning the intricacies of machining. (Photograph courtesy of Greenfield Industries.)

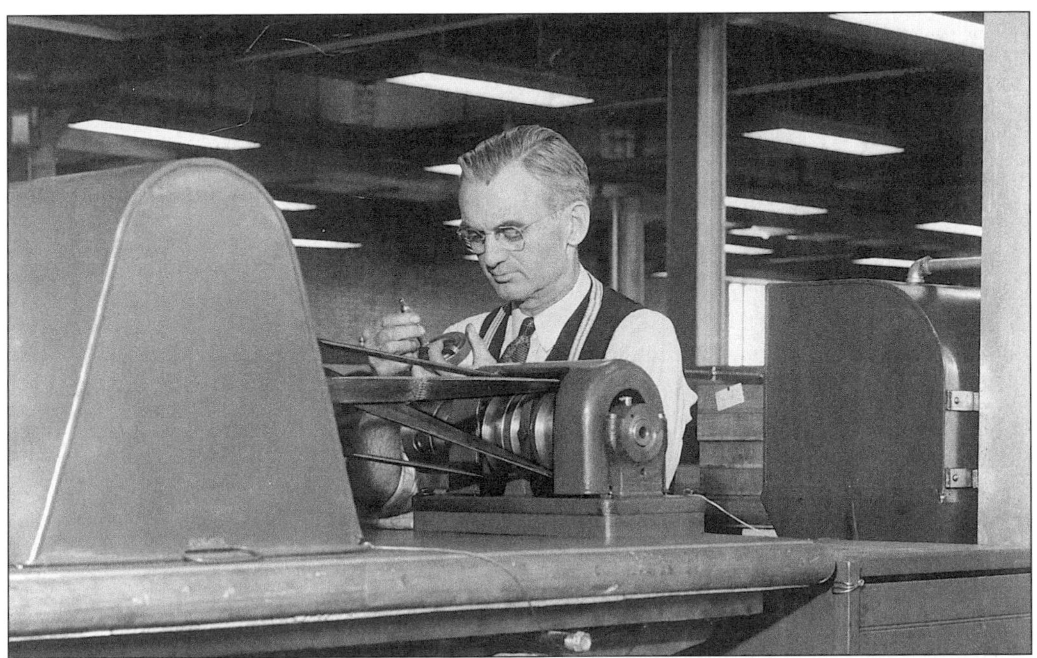

A machinist at Greenfield Tap & Die checks the accuracy of his work with a gauge. (Photograph courtesy of Greenfield Industries.)

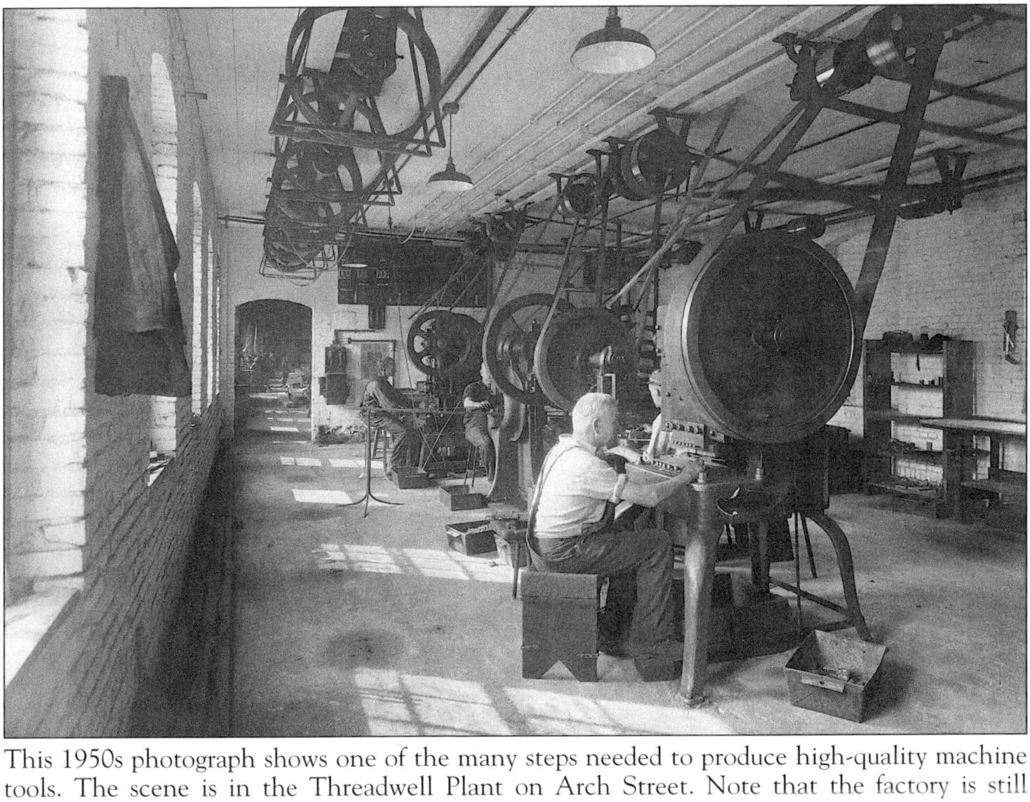

This 1950s photograph shows one of the many steps needed to produce high-quality machine tools. The scene is in the Threadwell Plant on Arch Street. Note that the factory is still equipped with belts driven by a central power source rather than individual electric motors.

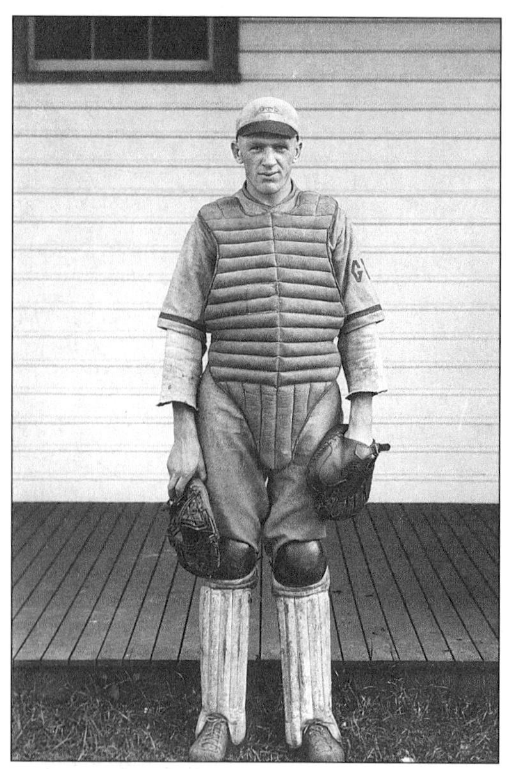

Two baseball players from Greenfield Tap & Die-sponsored teams pose for these *c.* 1920s photographs. (Photograph courtesy of Greenfield Industries.)

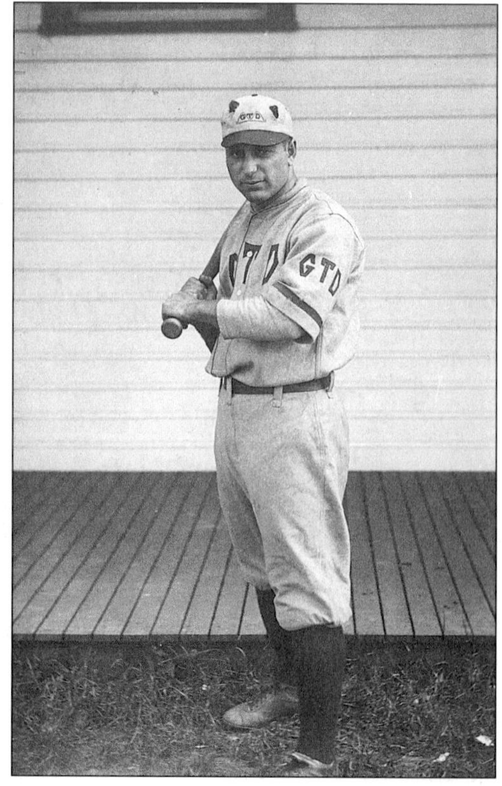

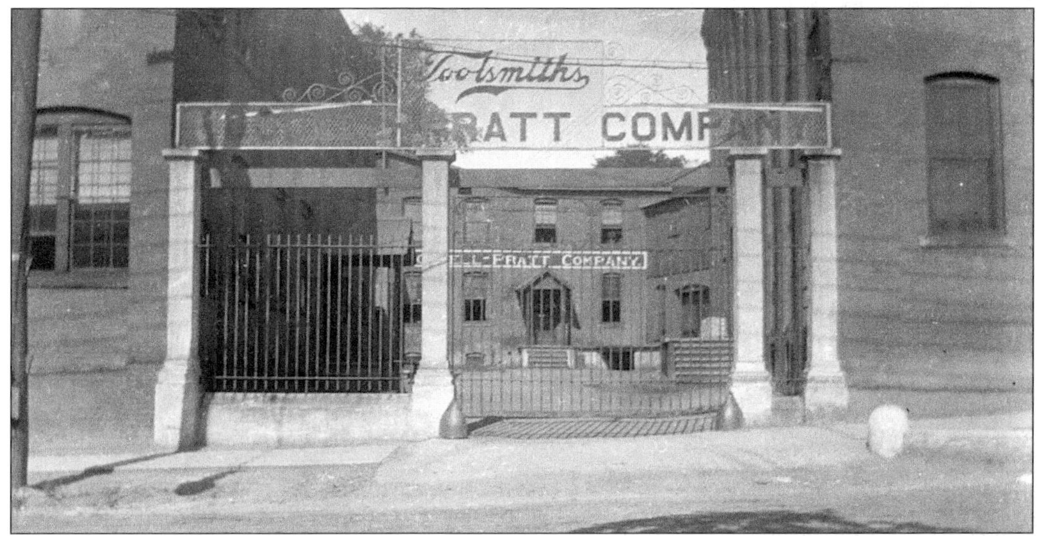

Here is the main entrance to the Goodell-Pratt Company on Wells Street, *c.* 1930. This company evolved into the Millers Falls Tool Company. The Massachusetts Tool Company is on the left, and the Goodell-Pratt office building is on the right. Other earlier tool companies in town included the Greenfield Tool Company, which primarily made wooden planes, and the Stratton Brothers Level Company. Both were eventually bought out by Goodell-Pratt.

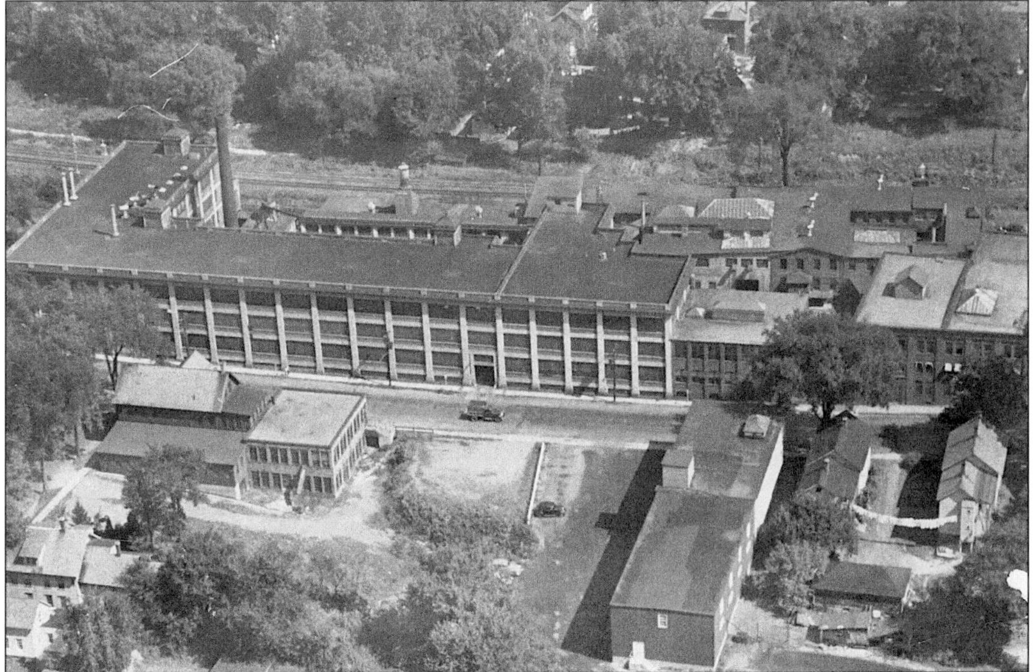

This aerial view of the Millers Falls Tool Company complex on Wells Street was taken in 1949. Directly to the rear of the complex is the Boston & Maine railroad tracks. By 1977, owner Ingersoll Rand had abandoned the site. The town of Greenfield took over the complex, and all but one of the buildings were removed. The large U-shaped building was converted into apartments.

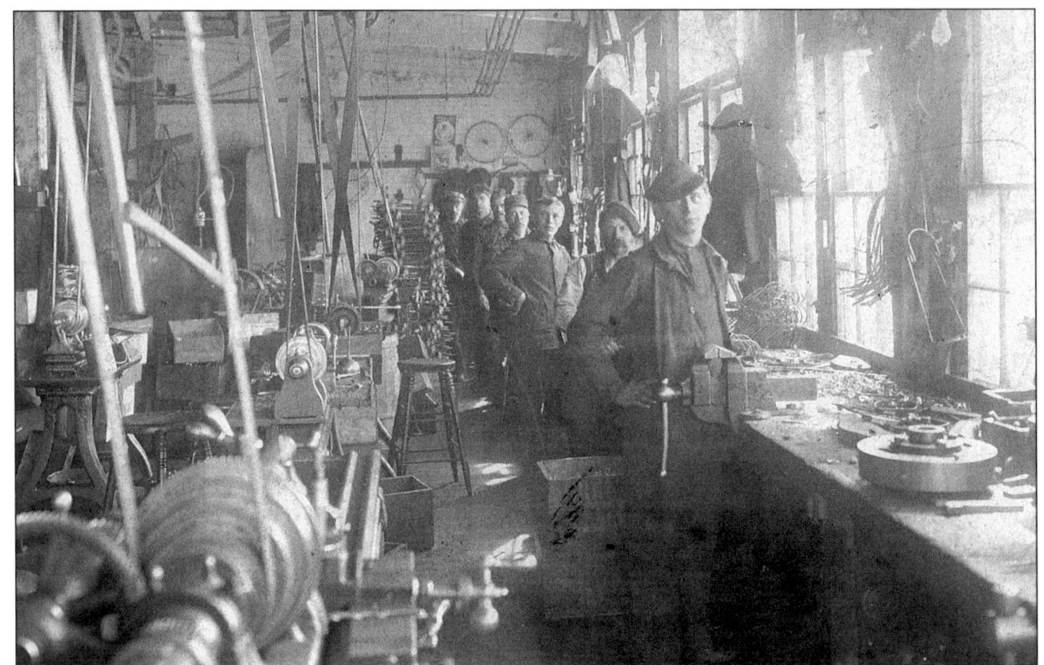

This workroom was in a knife factory in this northern part of Greenfield, the Warner Manufacturing Shop in Nash's Mills. Jacob Schuhle is third from the front in this pre-1912 photograph.

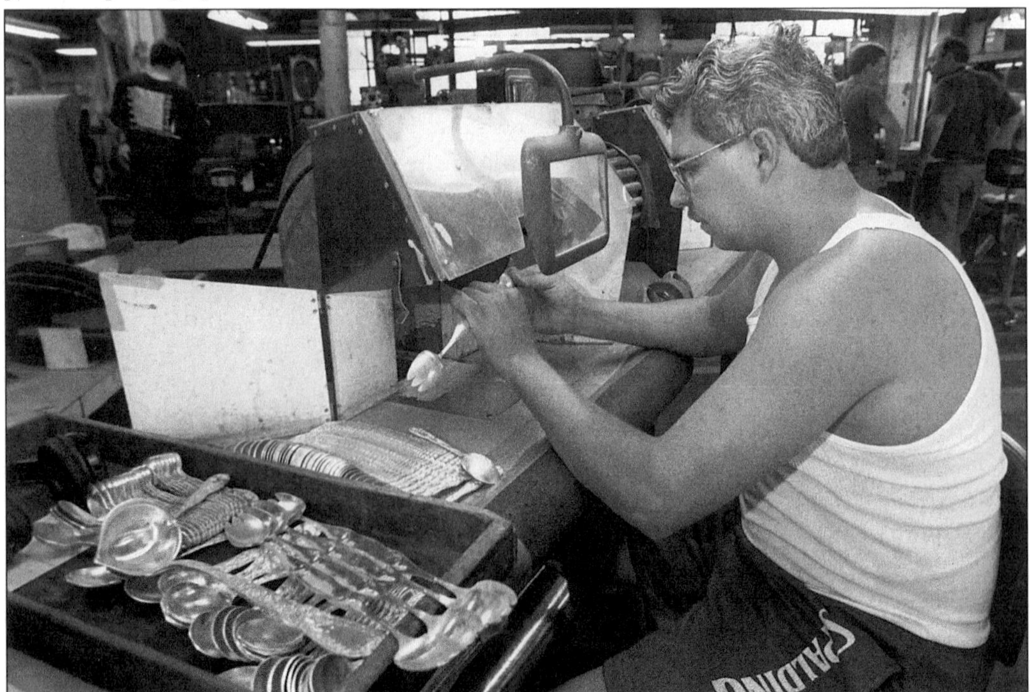

A worker at Lunt Silversmiths polishes flatware. The venerable company changed its approach radically in 1996 and opened a Lunt retail store and restaurant. (Photograph courtesy of *The Recorder*.)

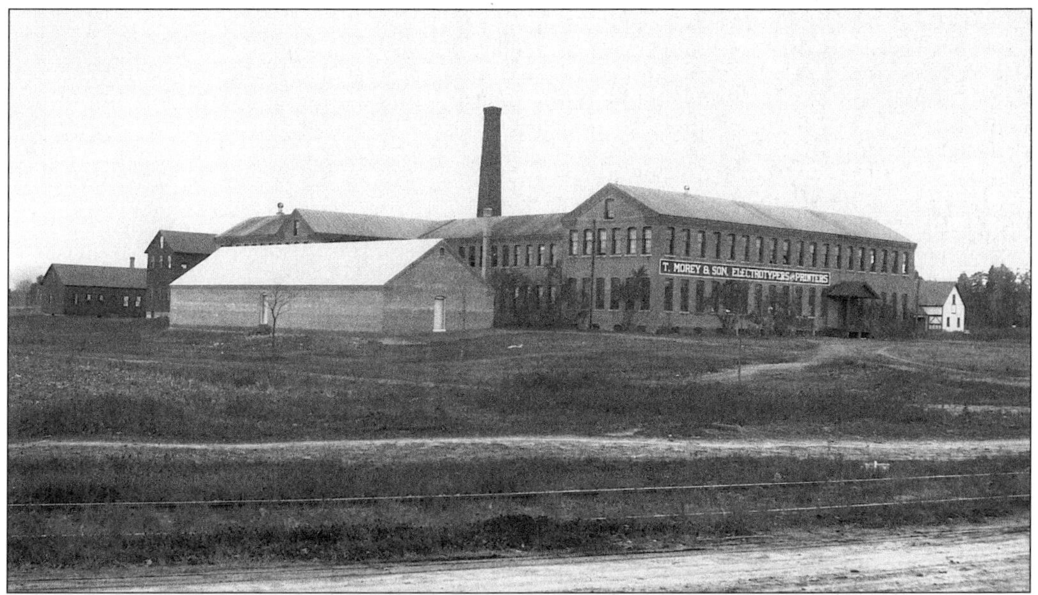

This *c.* 1900 photograph shows the former A.F. Towle & Son building on Federal Street. In 1897, the wooden structures were used to make Oakman automobiles, designed by Max Hertel. R.N. Oakman, president of the silverware company, tried to diversify by making bicycle pedals and automobiles. He eventually ran out of money and had to sell out to Rogers, Lunt, and Bowlen. Part of the complex was used by T. Morey & Son until 1911. The buildings are now part of Lunt Silversmiths.

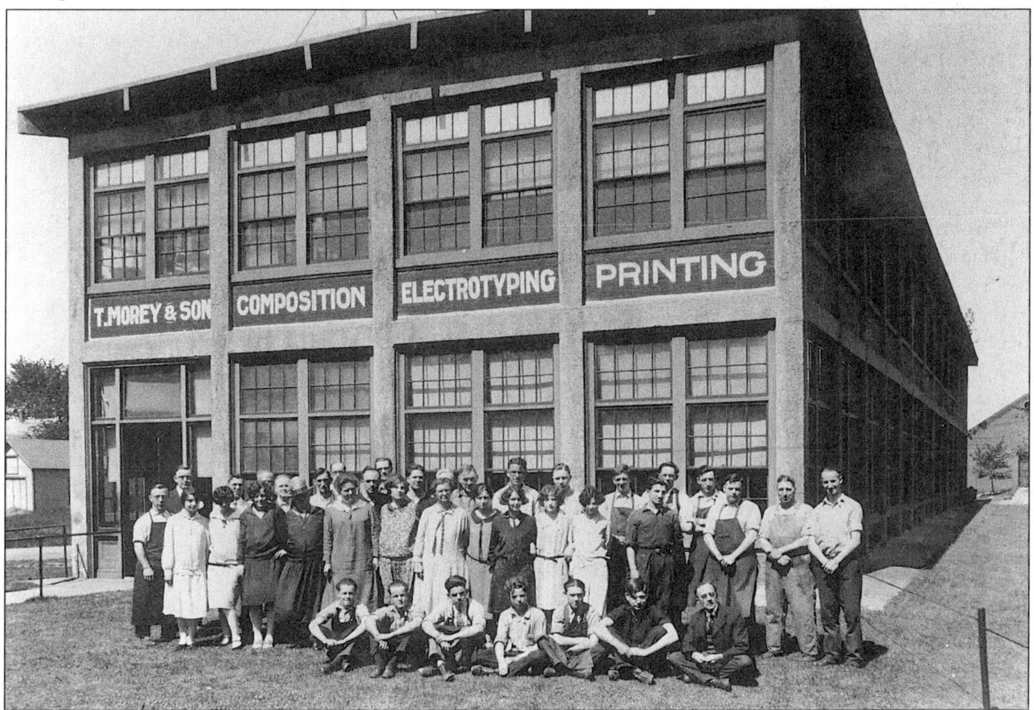

Employees of T. Morey & Son gather for a group photograph, *c.* 1925. The building is located at the corner of Federal and Kenwood Streets and is now used by Lunt Silversmiths.

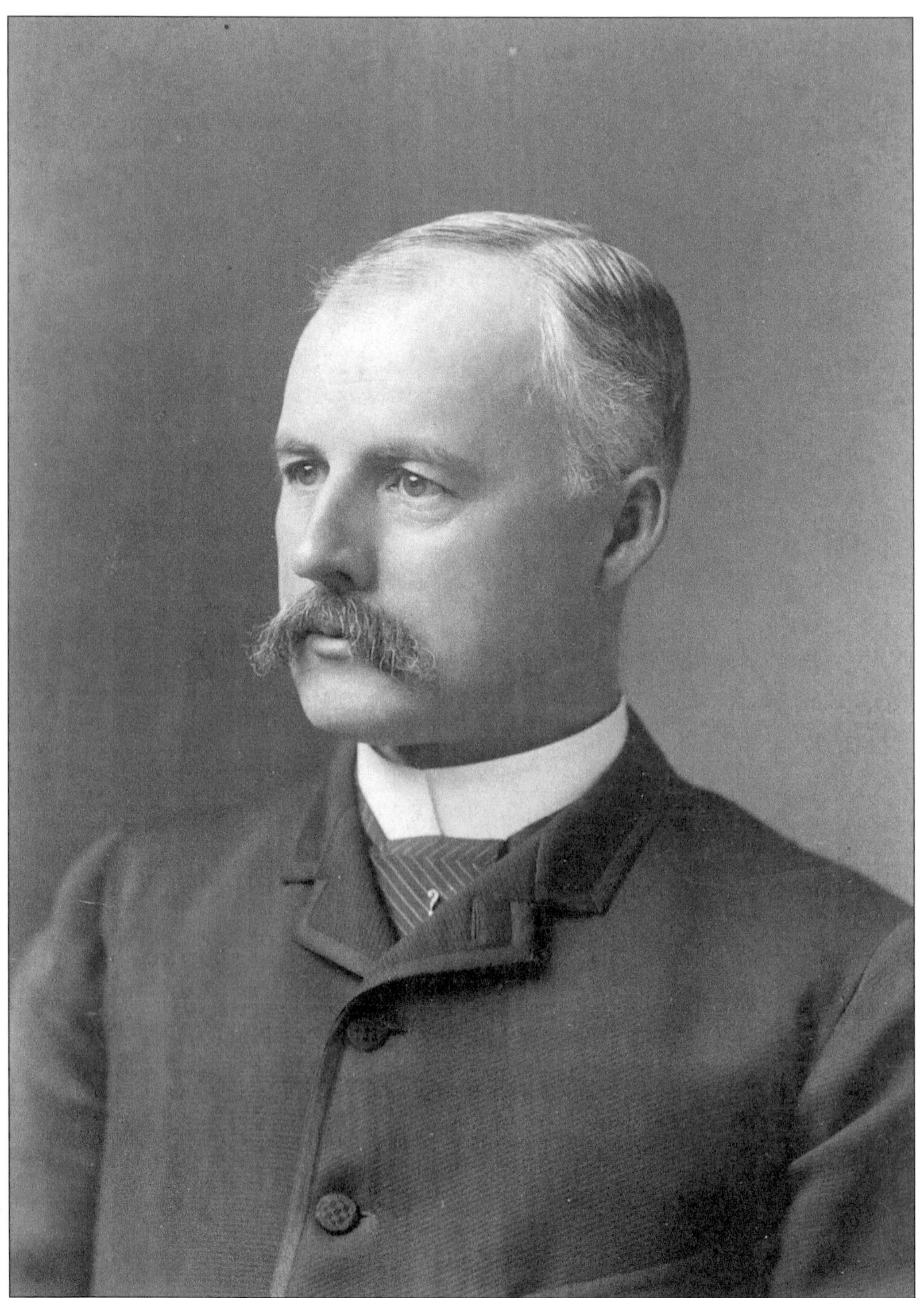

Richard N. Oakman competed with the earliest builders of automobiles in this country. Duryea, the Grout brothers, and Oakman were all building cars in the Greenfield area in the 1890s. None of them succeeded.

Six
AND A FEW MORE

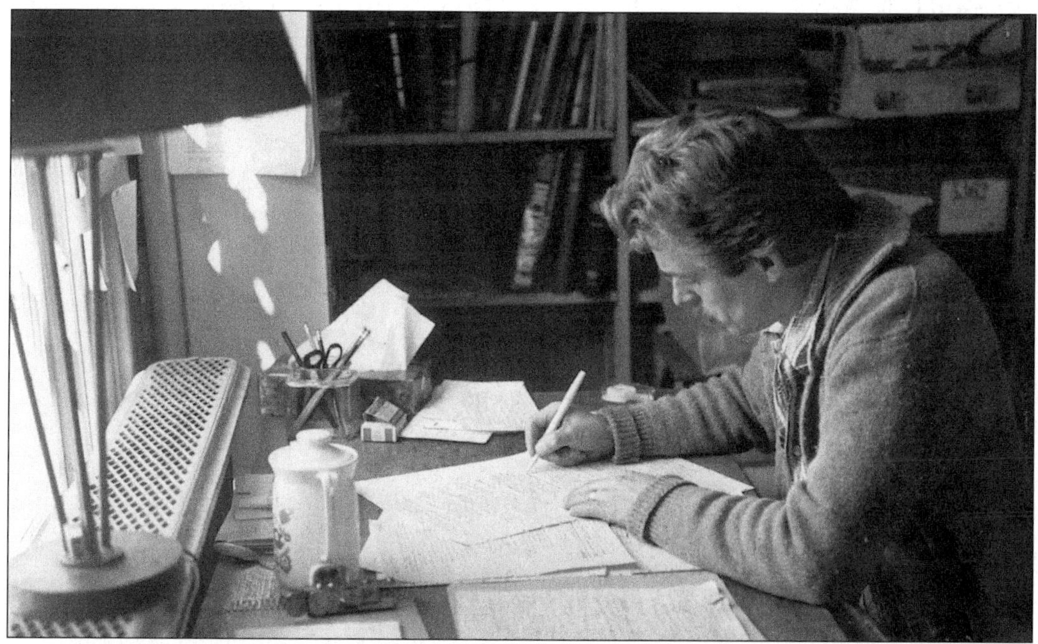

This 1979 photograph shows Paul Jenkins writing *The Conservative Rebel* in the Greenfield Public Library. Jenkins's was the fourth of the sequential histories commissioned by the town. The first history of the town's existence up to 1900 was in two volumes written by Judge Francis Nims Thompson. The second history was by Lucy Cutler Kellogg in 1931. The third was by Charles Sidney Severance for the town's bicentennial in 1953. Jenkins's book was a social history rather than a chronological one. (Courtesy Peter Miller.)

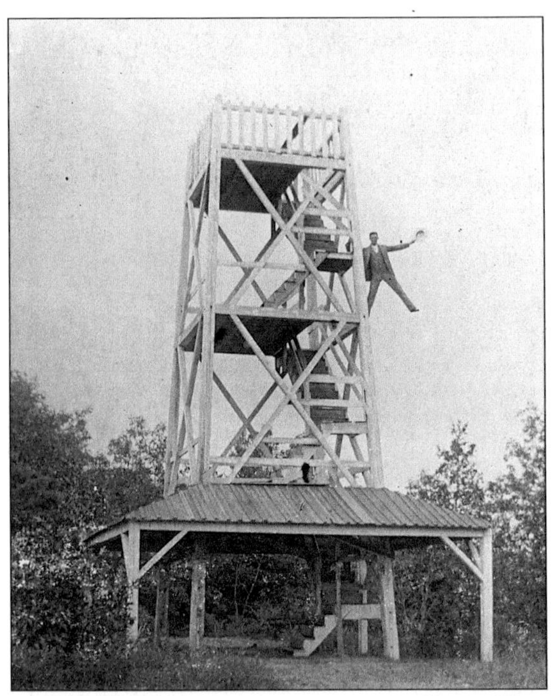

This is the original Poet's Seat Tower atop Rocky Mountain. It was built in the late 1870s. After it fell into disrepair, it was set afire and destroyed in 1908. The wooden tower was constructed by the Greenfield Rural Club. Contrary to popular belief, the name predates the era of poet Frederick Goddard Tuckerman, who is commemorated with a plaque on the current stone tower.

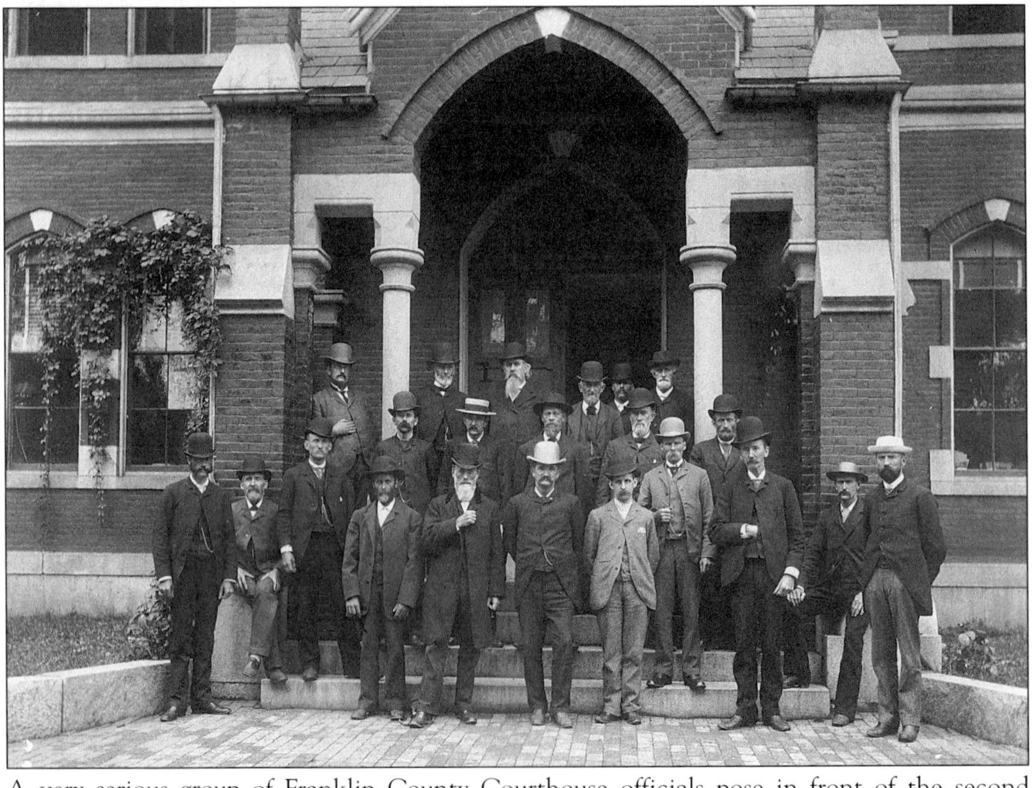

A very serious group of Franklin County Courthouse officials pose in front of the second county courthouse in 1877. The man in the back row with the longest white beard is District Attorney Bond.

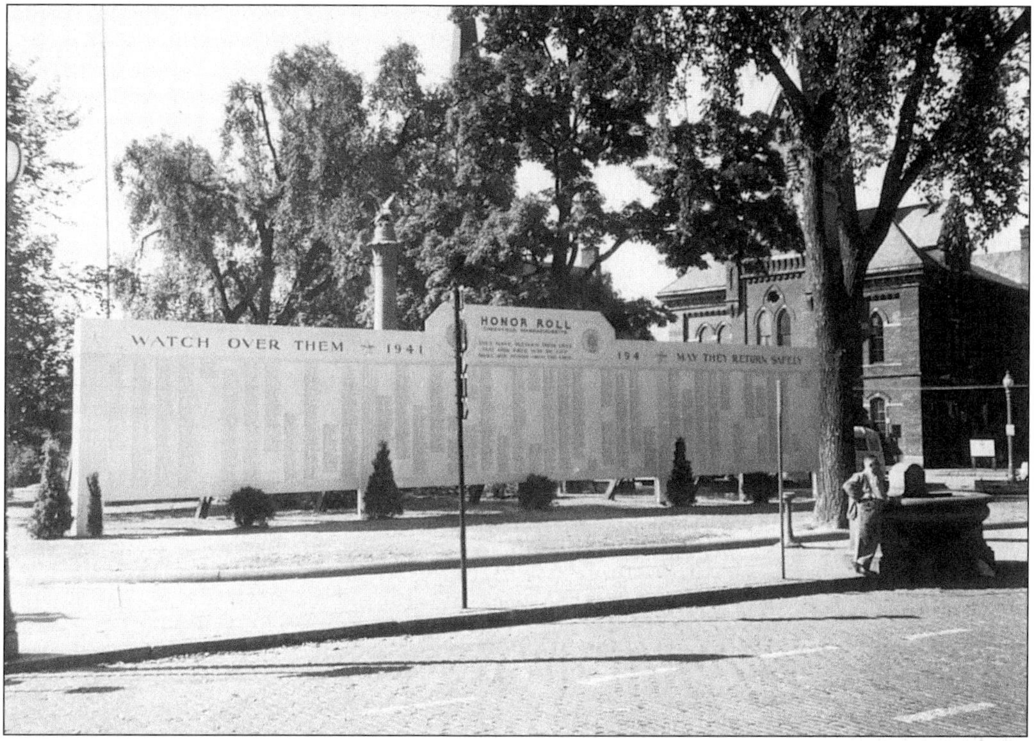

This World War II-era photograph shows the honor roll of men and women serving in the armed forces. The honor roll was located along the north edge of the town common. Note that the ending date of the war is not filled in, and there are these hopeful words: "May they safely return." Greenfield provided not only soldiers, marines, and sailors who fought but also factory workers who produced many items critical to the war effort.

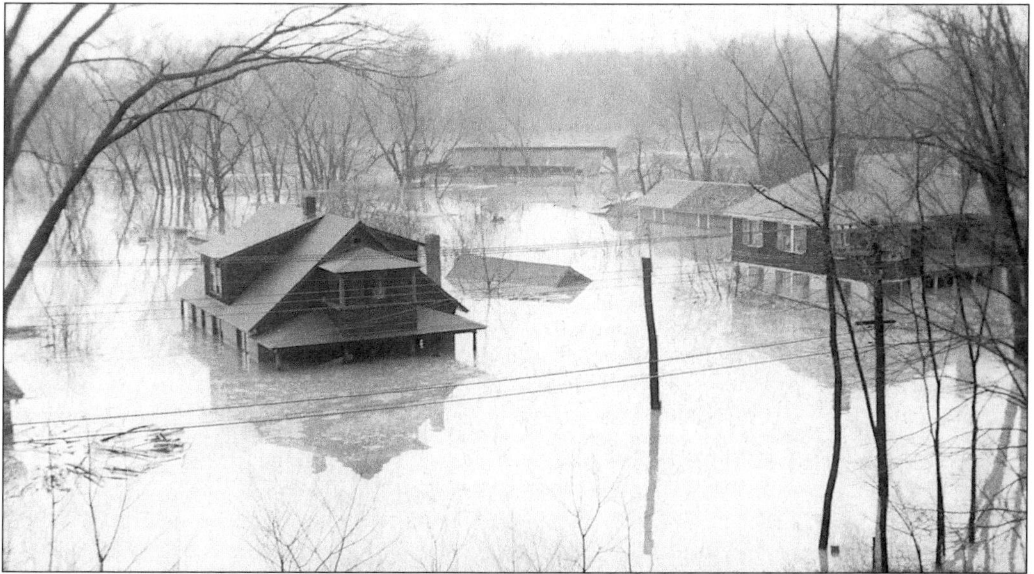

This photograph, taken during the 1936 flood, shows the covered bridge from Petty Plain floating downstream near Deerfield Street.

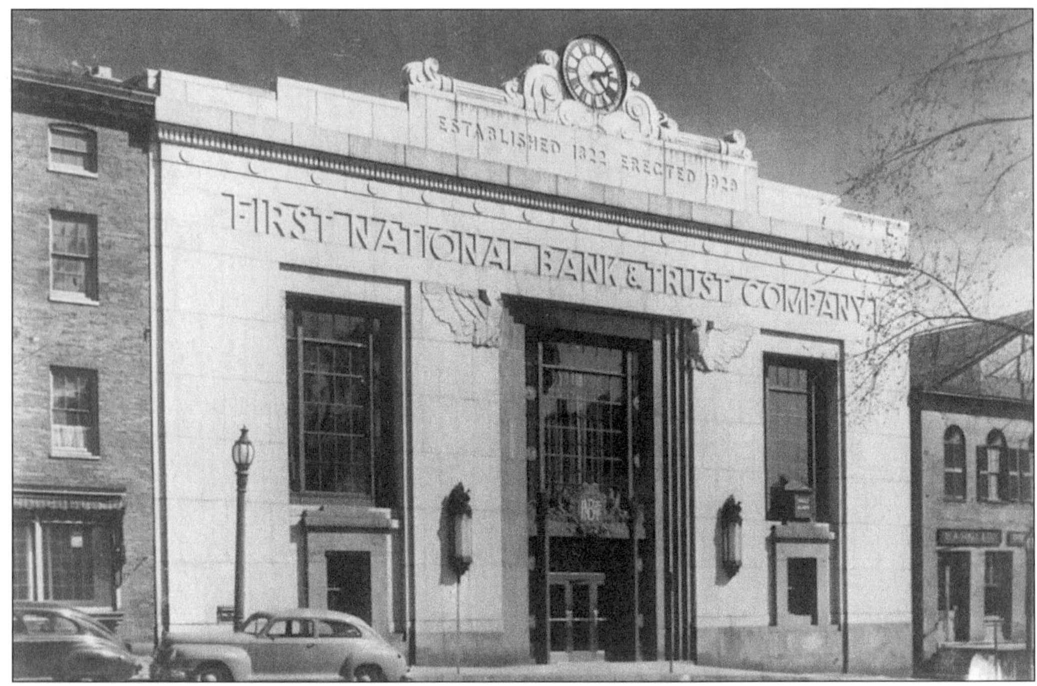

Here is the First National Bank and Trust, erected in 1929 on Bank Row.

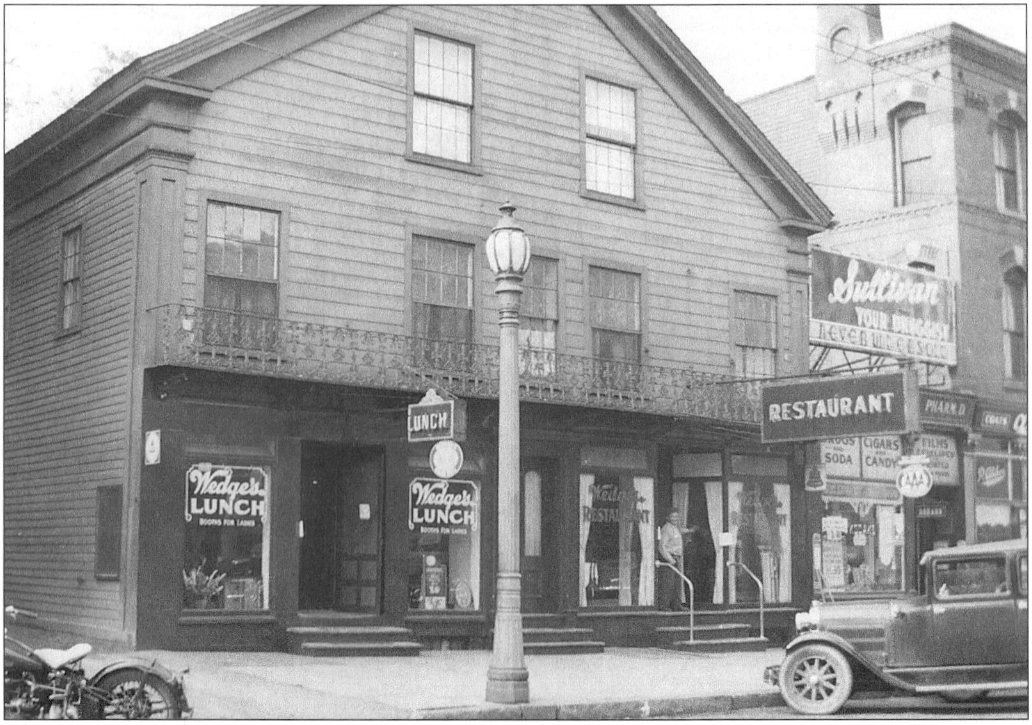

Wedge's, a popular eatery on the south side of Main Street, is shown here *c.* 1925. This building was torn down in the 1940s to make room for the Borosky Block.

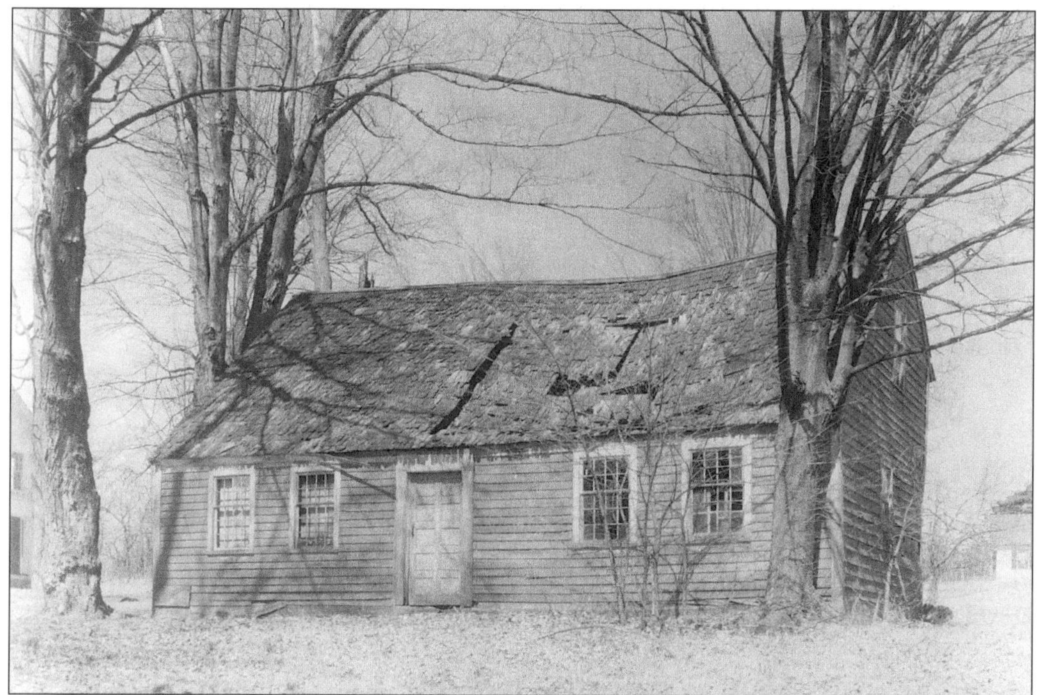

The McHard House, *c.* 1740, is one of the two oldest standing houses in Greenfield. This 1934 photograph by Arthur E. Haskell shows it at its present Newell Pond site in almost ruined condition. Shortly afterward, it was renovated and turned into a tea room. Over the years, the house has been moved twice. At one time, it was the office of the Channing L. Bete Company, which later went moved to larger quarters.

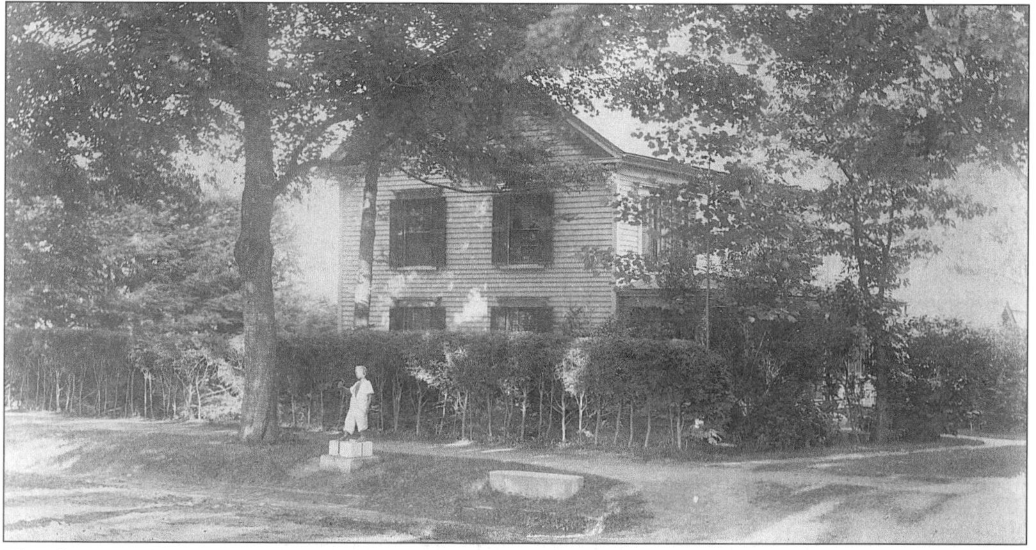

The home of Anna Pierce Judah on Federal Street was later moved to make way for the construction of the high school (now the middle school). The hitching post—a favorite landmark for generations of children who passed it on their way to school—was later relocated to the Pierce House property on Abbott Street. Because it is both a town icon and a reminder of a less racially sensitive era, the post is now in the historical society's museum.

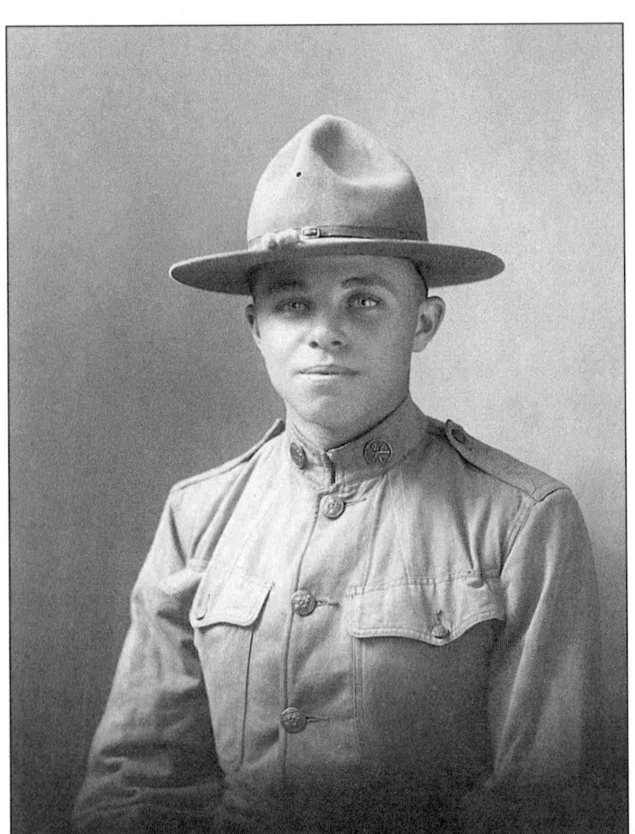

Hubert P. Putnam served overseas in Greenfield's Company L, 104th Infantry, U.S. Army during World War I.

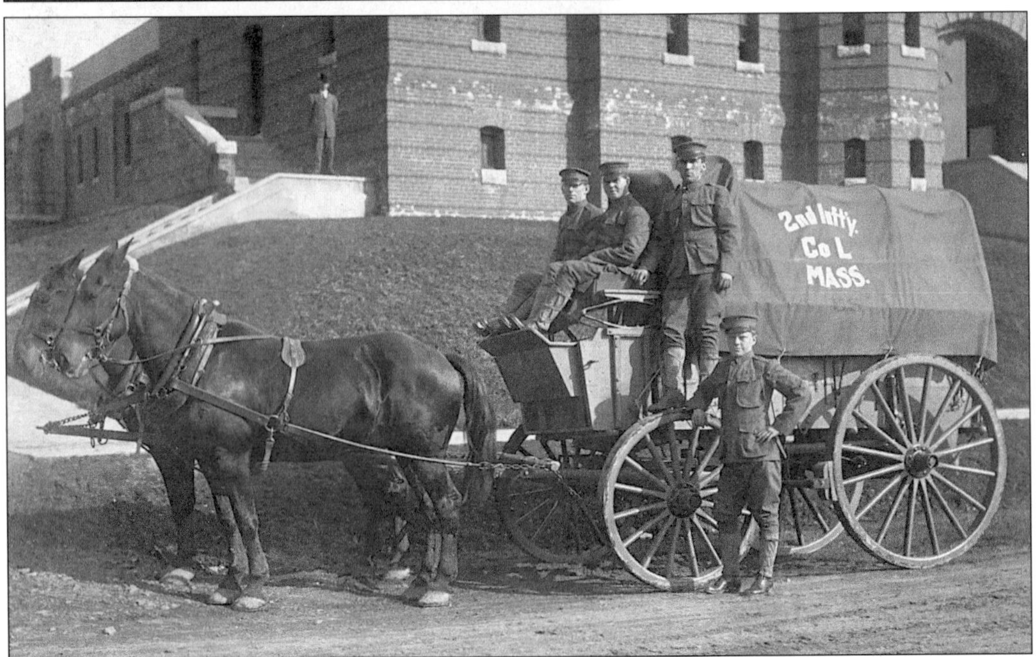

Soldiers of Company L, 2nd Massachusetts, pose with a horse-drawn wagon in front of the armory on Hope Street, *c.* 1910.

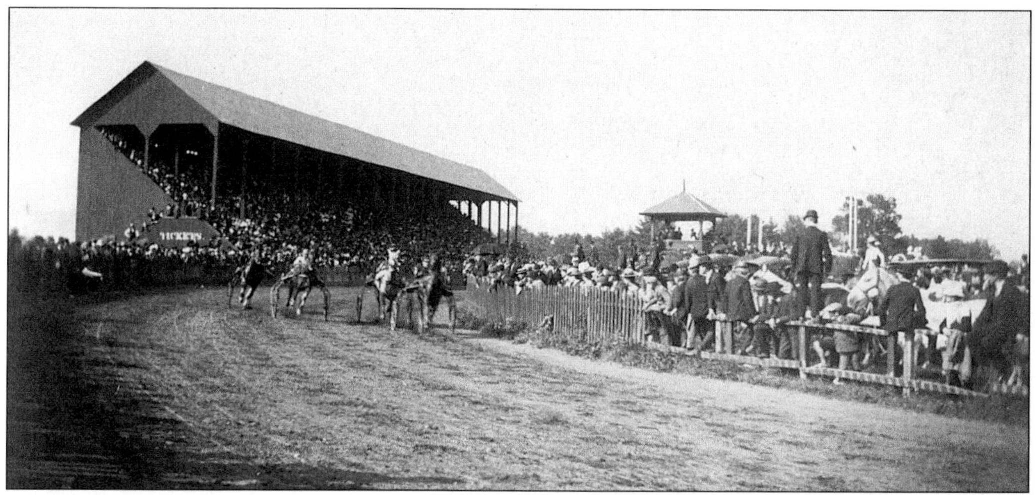

For many years, sulky races were held at the Franklin County Fairgrounds. For more than 100 years, the grandstand, built in 1876 and shown here *c.* 1900, was a landmark at the fair. It was torn down in 1985.

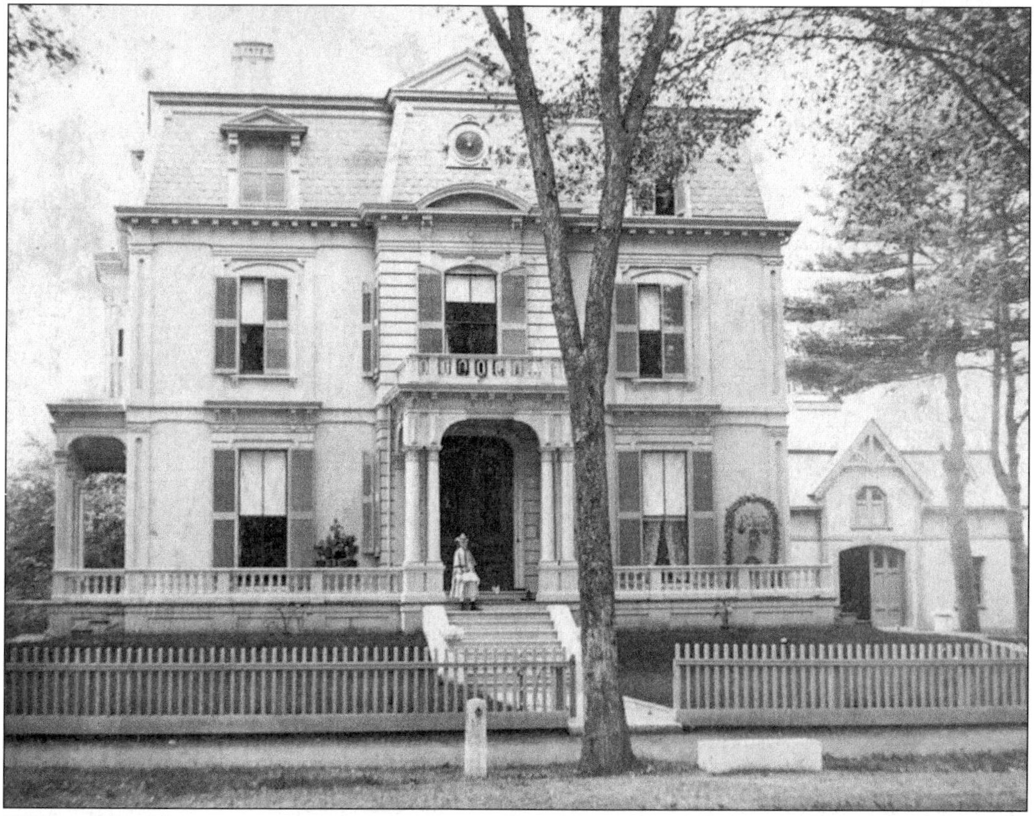

William Washburn was a prominent citizen of Greenfield, involved in banking and railroads. He served in the U.S. Congress and as governor of Massachusetts. As seen in this *c.* 1869 photograph, his grand house and carriage barn on east Main Street reflected his wealth. After the Washburn family gave the property to the YMCA, the house and barn were used for offices and exercise facilities. The old buildings gradually gave way to a modern complex.

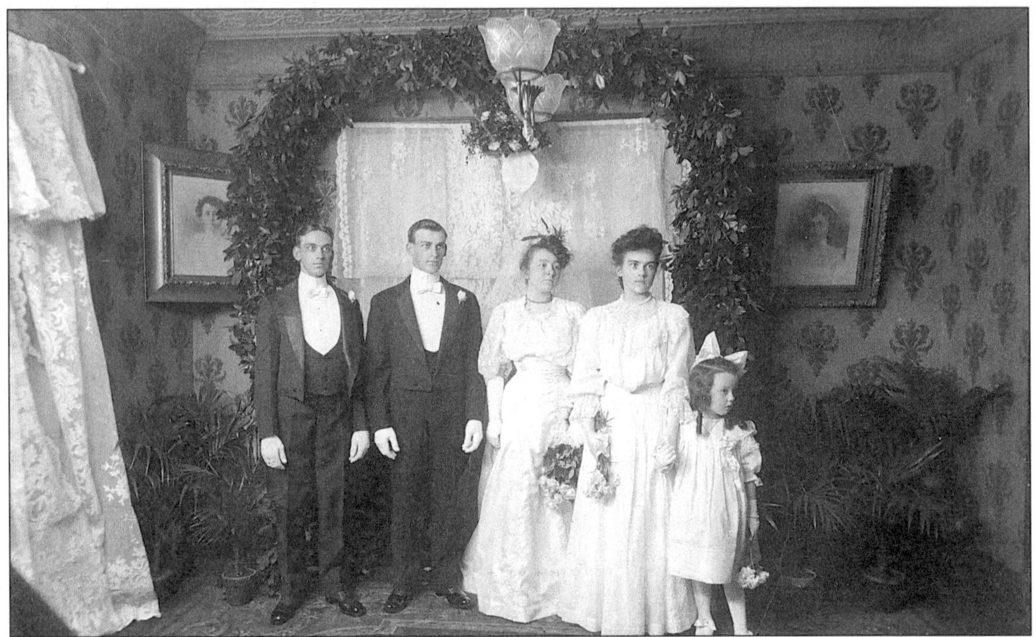

This photograph was taken at the wedding of Winifred B. Allis and Walter Barker on October 9, 1905. The couple is standing in the front room of the house at 236 Chapman Street, accompanied by the groom's parents, Haughton and Susan Barker. On the left is Walter Barker's brother Cleon H. Barker, and to the right is their sister Rose Barker Grant and her daughter Ruth.

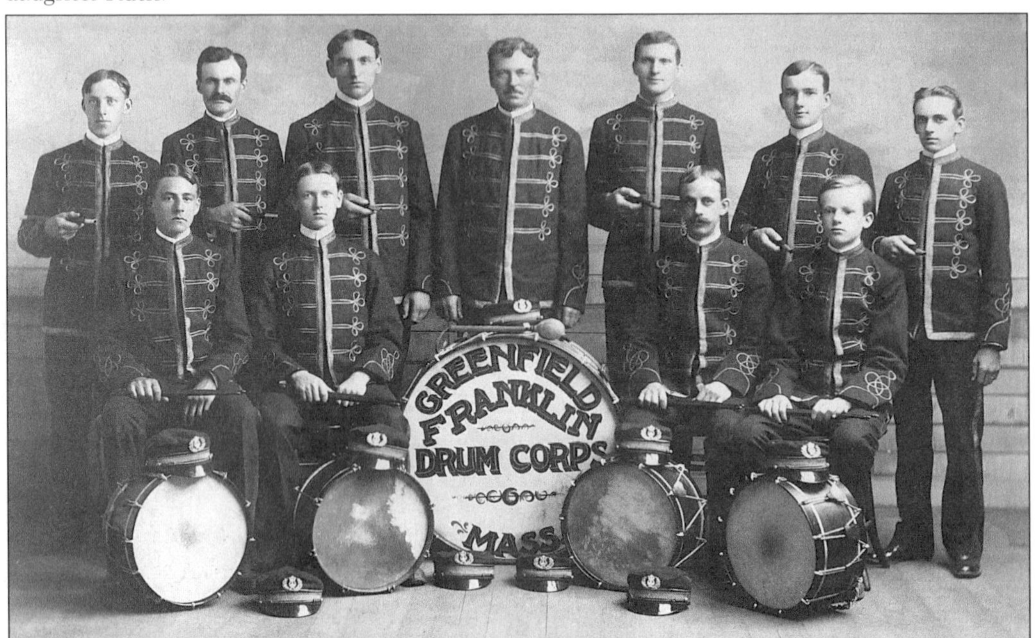

In October 1902, a group of young men from North Parish formed the Science Hill Drum Corps. They changed their name to the Franklin Drum Corps (spending $2.50 to have the name painted on the bass drum) just before having their portrait taken at the Enterprise Studio on Federal Street on June 23, 1904. Cleon H. Barker is standing at the far right.